T0217124

Lecture Notes in Computer Science 922

Edited by G. Goos, J. Hartmanis and J. van Leeuwen

Advisory Board: W. Brauer   D. Gries   J. Stoer

Springer

Berlin
Heidelberg
New York
Barcelona
Budapest
Hong Kong
London
Milan
Paris
Tokyo

Heiko Dörr

Efficient Graph Rewriting
and Its Implementation

 Springer

Series Editors

Gerhard Goos
Universität Karlsruhe
Vincenz-Priessnitz-Straße 3, D-76128 Karlsruhe, Germany

Juris Hartmanis
Department of Computer Science, Cornell University
4130 Upson Hall, Ithaca, NY 14853, USA

Jan van Leeuwen
Department of Computer Science, Utrecht University
Padualaan 14, 3584 CH Utrecht, The Netherlands

Author

Heiko Dörr
Institut für Informatik, Freie Universität Berlin
Takustrasse 9, D-14195 Berlin, Germany

Library of Congress Cataloging-in-Publication Data. Dörr, Heiko, 1962– Efficient
graph rewriting and its implementation / Heiko Dörr. p.cm. – (Lecture notes in computer science; 922) Includes bibliographical references and index. ISBN 3-540-60055-8
(alk. paper). – ISBN 0-387-60055-8 (U.S.: alk. paper). 1. Rewriting systems (Computer science) I. Title. II. Series.
QA267. D67 1995

005. 13' 1–dc20   95-30326 CIP

CR Subject Classification (1991): F.4.2, D.3.2, D.3.4, D.2.1

ISBN 3-60055-8 Springer-Verlag Berlin Heidelberg New York

CIP data applied for

© Springer-Verlag Berlin Heidelberg 1995
Printed in Germany

Typesetting: Camera-ready by author
SPIN: 10485935   06/3142-543210 - Printed on acid-free paper

Preface

Graph rewriting systems have come of age. In autumn 1994, the 25th anniversary of the first publication in this area was celebrated at the 5th Workshop on Graph Grammars and their Applications to Computer Science. In the interim, the subject has evolved. The current situation can be described by a three-stage model. At the very low level there is a common idea of graph rewriting as the basic mechanism, where a graph is transformed by the application of a rewriting rule.

In the second stage, this mechanism is expressed in several ways. Usually, two so-called approaches are distinguished: the algorithmic (or set-theoretic) and the algebraic approach. Both provide a formalisation of graph rewriting. They give a precise semantics to the idea of graph transformation and, hence, allow for a formal treatment. In that sense, they are similar to the semantics of programming languages.

The upper stage is partitioned into several branches. At one extreme, theoretical studies on the generational power, on semantic constructs, or on restricted formalisms are undertaken. At the other extreme, specifications of real-world systems, or implementations of rewriting environments are developed. Because the individual problems to solve are complicated enough, the branches are not very aware of each other.

The monograph builds bridges between various areas of interest: 1) it studies a class of graph rewriting systems which is very suitable for an efficient execution; 2) it presents a compilation approach to the implementation of an environment for graph rewriting; 3) it develops an implementation of a functional programming language to show that and how the presented ideas apply to real-world problems.

This publication is my dissertation which I submitted to the *Fachbereich Mathematik und Informatik* at the *Freie Universität Berlin*. It was finished in December 1994, and presents the results of the research carried out at the *Institut für Informatik*. In that respect I would like to thank several people who accompanied my work. Prof. Elfriede Fehr provided an excellent environment for my studies and gave me any support I requested; Prof. Gregor Engels introduced me to graph rewriting and encouraged my progress with valuable comments; the GraGra-AG, in particular Prof. Hartmut Ehrig and Gabi Taenzer, provided a refuge from the graph rewriting Diaspora; Prof. Raúl Rojas posed the very question initiating the whole theoretical consideration; Albert Zündorf and Andreas Schürr provided me with the newest versions of PROGRES and the additional information which was not included in the documentation; my colleagues at work provided an important social background; Elke Kasimir implemented most parts of the environment and was a very valuable critic;

Peter Hofmann developed a compiler for functional languages based on the ideas presented in Chapter 6; Gaye Rochow and John Kelly helped me by proof-reading the manuscript to eliminate the mistakes made by a non-native speaker: Thanks to you all.

Berlin, April 1995   Heiko Dörr

Contents

1 Introduction

1.1 Graph Rewriting Everywhere? — The Purpose of Graph Rewriting Systems

Many problems in everyday life can be stated in terms of graphs. For instance, when we need to know the best route connecting two different points in a town, we look on the town's road map and solve the shortest path problem for graphs. The road map is well-suited to illustrate three different views of graphs. First of all, a graph is a mathematical object. Hence it provides an unambiguous treatment of problems such as finding the shortest path. The road map in mathematical terms consists mainly of two sets; one containing the crossings and the other containing the street segments between crossings. Both sets make a simple graph. Second, graphs are important data structures in many areas of computer science. Examples are data dependency graphs in compiler construction or class hierarchies in object-oriented programming. Based on the data structure graph, algorithms are designed and implemented. They solve graph theoretical problems, such as the best route, but also maintain information represented as a graph data structure. Finally, and most important from an application point of view, graphs have a natural visualization. Thus they often serve as a common base for the communication and explanation of complicated issues. This feature has led to a widespread use of graphs in everyday life as well as in computer science. These three views of graphs can be summarized as:

Graphs are precise, programmable and pictorial.

In applications a graph appears either in a static or a dynamic manner. If, for example, we determine a best route, we assume that the road map is fixed. Most graph theoretic problems are stated for a static graph, i.e. the graph must not be altered during the run of the algorithm. In the area of data structures, graphs are dynamic. A particular data structure is mainly specified by a set of operations which may be applied to objects conforming to the structure. In case the data object is a graph, any execution of an operation performs a graph transformation. Consequently a data structure is not only a single graph but a whole class of graphs.

Apparently, we need a means to decide which graphs belong to a certain class and which do not. Otherwise, the notion of a class of graphs would be superfluous. Mostly graph classes are defined in a declarative way, i.e. as a set of graphs with a distinct

property. Take, for example, sorted lists. Usually they are drawn as a linked list; and
each element holds a data and a pointer component.

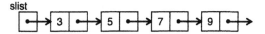

Specified in a declarative style, any graph is a sorted list if

(i)   it is a linear list and

(ii)   the data component of each element is smaller than the data component of
       the succeeding element.

Graphically denoted, it must hold for any sublist

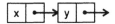

that $x < y$. The graph specification language GRAL developped by Ebert and Franzke
has chosen the declarative approach to graph classification [EbFr94].

Besides the declarative style, there is also an operational way to characterize the
elements of a graph class. In the declarative approach, a list of constraints identifies the
members of a class. An operational specification, to the contrary, provides a number
of operations which transform class elements into each other. Given an initial class
member, the successive application of operations generates the elements of a class. For
the sorted list, we have operations like "insert" or "remove". Any operation may
consist of a number of individual transformations. So to insert an element into a sorted
list we may first put it in front of the list and then propagate it to the appropriate
position. Figure 1 shows the steps which are performed to insert the element 6.

The propagation can be specified in terms of graphical pre- and post-conditions. For
example, whenever the following sublist with $x > y$ appears in a graph

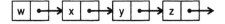

then the propagation must transform the sublist to

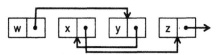

Hence the operation swaps the two inner elements and redirects the pointers to the rest
of the list. This example also shows how elegantly the operation on graphs can be

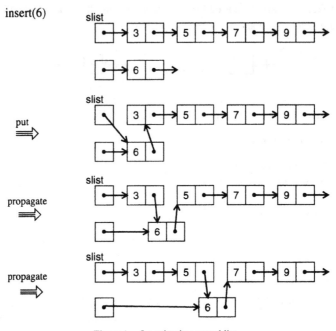

Figure 1   Insertion in a sorted list

denoted. The graphical representation is definitely easier to read than any program fragment juggling with pointers.

Formally the operational characterization of graph classes is obtained by a graph grammar. Like ordinary string grammars they define a graph language. It is the set of graphs which can be derived from an initial graph by rules of the grammar. Simple graph grammars provide only basic rules like "put" or "propagate". More advanced formalisms also allow the combination of basic rules to complex operations like "insert". Hence the class of sorted lists can also be precisely defined as the language of graphs generated by an appropriate grammar.

In the application of graph grammars the emphasis is often not placed upon the mere generative aspect. The major interest moreover is to use graph grammars for the operational specification of complex systems. This approach is especially suited for systems whose state can be modelled as a graph. Any state transition, then, is a graph transformation. It is denoted as a complex graph grammar operation. The sorted list requires just a small set of rules. Thus it is a quite tiny system, but there are also specifications of larger systems like

- software development environments [EnSch89],
- graphical editors [Göt88],

- code optimization [Nag81],
- transaction modelling in data bases [EhKr80],
- semantics of parallel programming languages [FeSch90],
- feature recognition in CIM projects [KBL91] or
- computer architecture [Alb87].

In these applications, the main interest lies in the specification of valid operations. The generative aspect of graph grammars is of minor importance. Schürr explicitly distinguishes the different intentions of graph grammar by use of the additional notion of graph rewriting systems [Sch91]. We adopt the distinction between graph grammars and graph rewriting systems. In the former sense we concentrate on the generative aspect, whereas for the use of graph rewriting systems, the operational features are important.

The main feature of graph rewriting systems with respect to operational performance is the concept of a rewriting step. In our example we specified a graph transformation by graphical pre- and post-conditions. Graph rewriting systems interpret the conditions as a rewriting rule and define a rewriting step. The implementation of a rewriting system now performs the actual transformation as stated by the pair of conditions. After the rewriting step, the transformed graph is available.

1.2 The Major Flaw of Graph Rewriting - Its Complexity

The choice of graph rewriting systems for operational specification instantaneously brings forth the wish to execute a specification. When the description of a system already consists of a number of operations, why should it be impossible to execute them? At this point the complexity of the specified system returns to our focus. A graph rewriting system may be very suited to specify the behaviour of a complex system; but the specification also reflects the system's complexity. A graph may directly express a complex system's state; but we must also notice that the computation on and with graphs exhibits difficult problems.

A significant property of graph rewriting systems in general is the computational complexity of an individual graph rewriting step. For each application of a rewriting rule to a host graph, a subgraph isomorphic to the rule's left-hand side must be determined. This problem in general is NP-complete [GaJo79]. Thus the execution of graph rewriting systems presents a severe drawback. Any of the current implementations suffer from this deficiency. They either leave the difficult problem open to the user, or accept it as being unavoidable. Consequently applications of graph rewriting systems are very rare.

The lack of an efficient execution component is a major reason for the limited use of graph rewriting systems. Graph editors like GraphEd by Himsolt or Edge by

Paulisch [Him89, Pau93] are a first step towards a tool-based specification with graph rewriting systems. The state of the art is realized in the PROGRES environment. It provides an integrated tool set consisting of editor, data base, browser and execution component [Sch94]. Even here, however, the aspect of an efficient execution of graph rewriting is not the main interest. Hence any user of the environment is confronted with long run times. Thus up to now there is no sufficient realization of the basic tool for the analysis of graph rewriting systems: *a fast execution component.*

This severe drawback limits the dissemination of graph rewriting systems. Most applications mentioned before remain mostly on the conceptual level. The correctness of the specification and the behaviour of the specified systems must be studied manually. The big advantage of graph rewriting specifications, their operational aspect, is almost never exploited because the efficient execution component is missing.

The wish to execute graph rewriting specifications efficiently, however, is quite modest. In fact, if an efficient execution of graph rewriting can be provided, it not only enables the execution of specifications, but also yields an efficient graphical programming language. Programming in terms of graphs will be realized with acceptable run times. Several other improvements will be required also, but the efficient execution of the application test breaks the ice and provides *graphical programming with rewriting systems.*

1.3 The Plan of Attack - Finding the Gap

This thesis develops a condition under which the subgraph isomorphism problem can be solved efficiently. Furthermore it specifies an implementation which supports the optimized execution of graph rewriting systems.

The initial point of our work is a specific algorithm which checks whether a rewriting rule is applicable to a given host graph. The algorithm performs a breadth-first search and determines all subgraphs isomorphic to the rule's left-hand side. If there is no isomorphic subgraph at all then the rule is not applicable. Otherwise a rewriting step can be performed. The algorithm follows a search strategy, which is derived from the left-hand side of a rule. In combination with the search strategy the algorithm realizes an individual abstract machine for each left-hand side. It inputs a given host graph and computes the set of subgraphs isomorphic to the left-hand side. In general the search strategy could be determined in each rewriting step; but since we are interested in a fast implementation, we cannot afford this large overhead at run time. Moreover we must determine a search strategy for each left-hand side which performs best for all host graphs.

Based on the abstract machine implementing the subgraph isomorphism problem. we approach efficient graph rewriting on a theoretical level. In general the subgraph isomorphism problem is NP-complete. We might, however, determine a class of graph rewriting systems for which the complexity is definitely smaller. In many areas of computer science, the identification of subclasses has led to efficient solutions for a subset of difficult problems. Take, for example, parsing of string languages. For any context-free language, a recursive descent parser solves the word problem, though its performance is poor due to backtracking. When the string grammar is known to be LL(1), parsing is deterministic and performs in constant time.

The theoretical part of our study adopts this policy. We will identify a class of graph rewriting systems which perform the application test in constant time. Thus the main obstacle for efficient graph rewriting will be removed. The characterization of the class is based on the abstract machine for the subgraph isomorphism problem. We develop a *sufficient condition* for which the abstract machine performs in *constant time* for any host graph. To satisfy the condition there must be an appropriate search strategy for all rules. If that strategy exists for all rules, then the rewriting system belongs to the class of so-called UBS graph rewriting systems.

This thesis furthermore develops a procedure which checks whether a graph rewriting system is UBS (stands for *U*nique vertex label and *B*ypassing *S*trong V-structures). The procedure must find an appropriate search strategy for each rewriting rule. Since a rule may be applied to any host graph, the procedure must know some properties of the graph language. In our approach, two characteristics of a graph language are sufficient: the sets of unique vertex labels and strong V-structures. With respect to both sets, the procedure checks whether the application test for a rewriting rule takes at most constant time. It therefore tries to find a search strategy initiating in a uniquely labelled vertex and bypassing all strong V-structures. If such strategy exists for all rewriting rule of a system it is UBS. The information on the graph language required by the procedure is gathered by *abstract interpretation*.

The theoretical treatment deals only with simple graph rewriting systems. For real applications, however, single rewriting rules cannot sufficiently represent complex operations. This is already exhibited in the small example of inserting in a sorted list. Thus we follow the common approach and extend simple graph rewriting by attributes and control structures. Opposite to other authors we give a denotational semantics of the control structures. Thus we can, for instance, prove the equality of graph rewriting programs. The results for UBS rewriting systems also apply to the extended formalism of *attributed programmed graph rewriting systems*.

The extensions to simple graph rewriting systems introduce several areas of further improvement. We study one specific optimization for programmed graph rewriting systems where one control structure forms a set of rewriting rules. Whenever the set is applied, one of the applicable elements is chosen for the rewriting step. In a naive implementation the applicability of the elements of a rule set is checked individually. Our optimization, to the contrary, checks the applicability of the rules in parallel: first it tries to find an optimal overlap of all left-hand sides; then the intermediate results of the application test can be reused. We support the overlapping application test in the *abstract machine for graph rewriting*. This machine not only performs the application test but implements the complete definition of programmed attributed graph rewriting systems. As suggested by advanced compiler construction, we use the abstract machine as an explicit interface between compilation and execution. Thus both components of the execution component for attributed programmed graph rewriting systems can be developed and improved separately.

To show that the UBS property really applies, we implement a functional programming language as a UBS graph rewriting system. We give translation schemes for functional expressions and definitions and extend them step by step. The final translation generates a graph rewriting system which implements a functional programming language. Besides the mere implementation, the example serves also as a comprehensive case study for programming with graph rewriting systems. The given example exploits both improvements, UBS-rewriting and overlapping application test for rule sets. Hence we indeed implemented rather than specified a functional language.

1.4 Outline

In the following chapter, we introduce the basic notions of graphs and graph rewriting systems. Furthermore we give the abstract machine for the subgraph isomorphism problem and analyse its run time.

Chapter 3 defines sets of unique labels, label triples, and strong V-structures which appear in a graph language. The main effort is to give algorithms which compute approximations of the sets. Based on these approximations, a sufficient condition for UBS rewriting systems is given.

In chapter 4, simple graph rewriting systems are extended by attribution and control structures. The semantics of the latter are given in a denotational framework.

A fast implementation of attributed programmed graph rewriting systems is presented in chapter 5. We especially develop an optimization for the application of rule sets and specify an abstract machine tailored to the optimization. We give the instruction set and list the rules for the compilation of an optimized graph rewriting system to the instructions. Furthermore we demonstrate the improvement of the optimization on a real implementation.

Chapter 6 develops the translation of functional programs to UBS graph rewriting systems. The rewriting system is able to evaluate a functional expression based on the rewriting rules which have been generated from the function definitions by the translation.

The last chapter draws the main conclusions and sketches unsolved problems.

Appendix A lists the figures and tables. In Appendix B, we present a graph rewriting system which implements the evaluation of a functional program. It may be generated by the translation of a functional program. A list of references and an index finishes the presentation.

2 Graph Rewriting Systems — The Basic Concepts

In the introduction we sketched how graph transformations can be described in terms of graphical pre- and post-conditions. The presentation, however, can be made more precise. Graph transformation is not accessible for an analysis or even for implementation. In the current chapter, we provide a sound and precise notation for graph transformations. The notation will be rule-based, i.e. any graph transformation is performed by the application of a graph rewriting rule. Before we define graph rewriting rules, we must first of all know on which graphs a rewriting rule may operate. Based on these two concepts, graph transformations can be explicitly defined by a graph rewriting step. Such a step performs the actual graph transformation which is expressed by a rewriting rule.

There are several frameworks for the rule-based definition of graph transformation, for example: algebraic graph transformation [EKL91]; hyperedge replacement [DrKr91]; node label controlled rewriting [ER91]; or algorithmic graph rewriting [Nag86a]. The frameworks differ first in the underlying mathematical notation and second in the capabilities of the rewriting rules.

The mathematical notation is either of categorical or set-theoretic type. The categorical notation has the advantage that several properties of graph rewriting systems can be elegantly derived in this framework. These properties are mainly concerned with independence and serializability of rewriting rules. In the algorithmic framework, a graph transformation is expressed in terms of set operation. This notation has two significant advantages. First, the set-theoretic notation provides a definition much closer to the intuitive understanding of graph rewriting. Given a subgraph satisfying the precondition, it is replaced by a graph corresponding to the post-condition. The replacement of subgraphs can be very naturally expressed in terms of set operations. Second, the set-theoretic notation provides an easy access for the analysis of rewriting systems. The effect of a graph rewriting step will be derived from the applied rewriting rules. If the rules are denoted in set-theoretic terms, the effect again is expressed by set arithmetic. It is thus directly accessible for analysis.

The power of individual rewriting rules differs also in the various frameworks. In node label controlled and hyperedge replacement systems, only single entities, a node or an edge respectively, can be replaced. This limitation is too strong for general application requirements. In the introductory example, for instance, we replaced a graph consisting of four nodes. In the algebraic and the algorithmic frameworks, no limitations are imposed on the pre- and post-conditions of a graph rewriting rule. Hence they provide sufficient means to characterize pre- and post-conditions.

The considerations on the different mathematical notation and the capabilities of the rewriting rules now indicate that the algorithmic framework should be chosen for the precise and formal treatment of graph rewriting systems.

In this chapter we introduce the basic formalism of graph rewriting systems which will be subject to our theoretic studies. First, however, we review some well-known notions of graph theory. The components of graph rewriting systems are defined in the succeeding section. Lastly we present an abstract machine, which computes the subgraph isomorphism problem. The machine is central to our implementation of graph rewriting systems. A summary and a discussion of related work close the chapter.

2.1   Vertices, Edges, and Labels make a Graph — Preliminary Definitions

This section recalls well-known graph theoretic concepts and define some specific concepts used in the following. The mathematics used in the sequel is based on [Epp90]. For graph theory we refer to the textbooks of Harary and Gould [Har71], [Gou88].

Traditional graph theory deals with either directed or undirected graphs. If we consider the sorted list example, it becomes apparent that directed graphs are a preferable representation of a list. The direction of the edges can naturally express the order of the elements. Directed graphs, though, are not sufficient. Take, for example, the operation "insert" which we want to state as a graph rewriting rule. The operation requires the insertion of an element exactly between the list pointer and the list's first element. In the application this position is indicated by the types of the data objects. Any new element must be inserted between the list pointer and the first element. If we want to map this distinction to the formally defined graph, we must extend its definition. Usually the information on the type of the represented data object is represented as a label assigned to the corresponding vertex. Similarly, edges carry labels to denote distinct relations between vertices. In this chapter we abstract from the data component of an element. Thus we just deal with ordinary linked lists. Such a list has the graphical representation shown in figure 2.

The label "list" indicates the list pointer whereas "elem" denotes elements of the list. The first element is referred by an "f"-edge with source vertex "list". All elements point to their successor by an "n"-edge, where the label "n" stands for next. We give the corresponding textual notation after the definition.

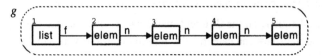

Figure 2   Graph g representing a linked list

Definition 2.1.1   DIRECTED LABELLED GRAPH, EMPTY GRAPH, UNDERLYING GRAPH

Let Σ_V, Σ_E be finite alphabets, V a finite set, and $E \subseteq V \times \Sigma_E \times V$. The set of *vertices* is V, the set of *edges* is E, and Σ_V and Σ_E are the sets of *vertex* and *edge labels* respectively. Let $l: V \rightarrow \Sigma_V$ be a total function, the *vertex labelling function*. The triple

$$g = (V, E, l)$$

is a *directed labelled graph* over Σ_V, Σ_E, or just *graph*. The graph $g_\varnothing = (\varnothing, \varnothing, \bot)$ is the *empty graph* where $\bot$ is the undefined function.   ∎

The textual definition of the graph shown in figure 2 is the triple

({1, 2, 3, 4, 5},
 { (1, f, 2), (2, n, 3), (3, n, 4), (4, n, 5) },
 { 1 → list, 2 → elem, 3 → elem, 4 → elem, 5 → elem})

Note that vertices could be any objects, but usually they are natural numbers. In general, we do not operate on the label alphabets. Thus we assume Σ_V, Σ_E to be arbitrary but fixed in the sequel unless otherwise stated. We will not explicitly mention the label sets in our further definitions. We introduce the following notational convention: the components of a structure are indexed or designated according to the index or designator of the structure, i.e. $g' = (V', E', l')$, or $g_i = (V_i, E_i, l_i)$. The vertex set of a graph g_r is thus denoted by V_r.

The next definitions recall standard graph theory.

Definition 2.1.2 $\subseteq$, SUBGRAPH, INCIDENT EDGES

Let g, g_1, g_2 be graphs, $W \subseteq V$ be non-empty subset of V.

a) The graph g_1 is a *subgraph* of g_2, in symbols $g_1 \subseteq g_2$ iff

$$V_1 \subseteq V_2, E_1 \subseteq E_2, \text{ and } l_1 = l_2|_{V_1}.$$

b) The set of edges of g *incident* to $v \in V$ is $inc_g(v) = \{(s, el, t) \in E \mid s = v \text{ or } t = v\}$. Accordingly, $inc_g(W) = \bigcup_{v \in W} inc_g(v)$ is the set of edges incident to a vertex of W.   ∎

A specification of a graph transformation in terms of graphical pre- and post-conditions requires the following: if the graph to be transformed satisfies the pre-condition, then the transformation may take place. According to our intuition, the pre-condition holds when there is a subgraph which looks like the graphical pre-condition.

Take, for instance, the informal specification for the insertion of an element to a list. If the graph

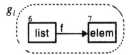

appears in the graph, it must be replaced by

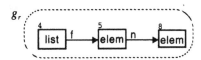

to put a further element in front of a list.

The notion "looks like" is precisely defined as a graph monomorphism. The graph monomorphism is induced by an injective vertex map which must respect the connectivity and labels of the vertices. Additionally, adjacent vertices must be mapped to adjacent ones, and the label of the connecting edge in the image must be equal to that of the original edge. An example of a graph monomorphism follows the definition.

Definition 2.1.3   GRAPH MORPHISMS

Let g be a graph. Let V' be a set and $h_V: V \rightarrow V'$ be a total injective vertex map. The edge map induced by h_V is $h_E((s, el, t)) = (h_V(s), el, h_V(t))$ for $(s, el, t) \in E$.

The *graph monomorphism* $\hat{h}$ based on h_V is defined as $\hat{h}(g) = (h_V(V), h_E(E), l \circ h_V^{-1})$. where $h_V(V) = \{h_V(v)| v \in V\}$ and $h_E(E) = \{h_E(e)| e \in E\}$.

If h is a bijection, then $\hat{h}$ is a *graph isomorphism*, and g and $\hat{h}(g)$ are isomorphic, in symbols $\hat{h}(g) \cong g$.   ∎

We denote h_V or h_E simply by h when the intended meaning is obvious from the context. The graph monomorphism $\hat{h}$ of figure 3 is induced by the injective vertex map $h = \{6 \rightarrow 1, 7 \rightarrow 2\}$.

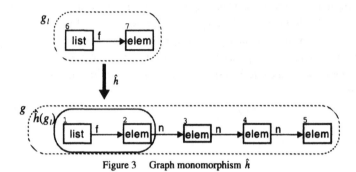

Figure 3   Graph monomorphism $\hat{h}$

2.2 Algorithmic Graph Rewriting Systems — The Basic Formalism

This section defines the execution of a graph rewriting step which, for example, performs the insertion of an element into a list. To put the static specification of the graph transformation into operation, a graph rewriting step is executed as follows. At first, the pre-condition must be evaluated with respect to the graph to be transformed. Intuitively, the graph must provide a subgraph which corresponds to the pre-condition. The intuition is formally reflected by a graph monomorphism. The graph satisfies the pre-condition if there exists a monomorphism from the graphical condition into the graph. The morphism then also determines the subgraph on which the rest of the rewriting step is performed. No other part of the graph must be affected by the transformation.

When the application area is fixed, the correspondent subgraph is simply removed. We obtain the rest graph together with so-called dangling edges. They will be used to connect the inserted subgraph with the rest. The removal of the isomorphic subgraph from the graph given in figure 2 leads to the following structure shown in figure 4. The rest graph is spanned by vertices 3, 4 and 5. There is one dangling edge which only sticks to its target vertex 3. The source vertex is undefined.

After the deletion of the isomorphic subgraph, the post-condition graph is inserted. Note that no vertex may occur twice in a graph. Thus eventually not the original graph but an isomorphic image is actually inserted. In our case, we map vertices 4 and 5 to the new vertices 10 and 11.

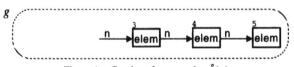

Figure 4   Graph g after removing $\hat{h}(g_i)$

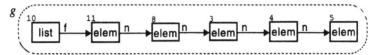

Figure 5   Graph g after replacing $\hat{h}(g_i)$ by a graph isomorphic to g_r

Finally the rewriting step embeds the inserted graph into the rest graph. Therefore it evaluates so-called embedding descriptions. In our example, the connection of both components should be established by the dangling "n"-edge. Thus the graph rewriting step replaces the dangling edge by the edge

$$(8, n, 3)$$

The resulting graph given in figure 5 consists now of both components connected by the edge mentioned above.

The outline of a rewriting step reveals nicely why the chosen framework is called algorithmic graph rewriting. The execution of a rewriting step can be stated as the following algorithm:

1.   find an isomorphic subgraph,

2.   remove that subgraph and keep the dangling edges,

3.   insert a new subgraph, and

4.   connect it to the rest graph with respect to the dangling edges.

A precisely defined graph rewriting rule must explicitly denote how dangling edges connect the inserted graph to the rest graph. For that purpose, the concept of an embedding description does not only encompass the identical replacement of dangling edges, but also provides means to delete or duplicate, as well as to change the orientation and label of an edge.

The embedding of an inserted graph, again, is performed by combined cut and paste operations. An individual embedding operation is specified by a pair of so-called cut- and paste-descriptions. Any dangling edge which may serve for an embedding must be denoted by a cut-description. The actual embedding edges are then provided by the evaluation of the corresponding paste-description.

The cut- and paste-descriptions must be stated independently from an actual graph transformation. They shall denote the embedding determined for the application of a rewriting rule to an arbitrary graph. Hence an embedding description can be defined only in terms of the corresponding rule and must provide an abstract characterization of dangling and embedding edges. This characterization is realized by the declaration of labels and orientation of an edge and the incident vertices.

The cut-description which fits to the dangling edge in our example is

$$(7, \text{n}, \text{elem}, \text{out}).$$

It fits to any edge with label "n" which has the image of vertex 7 as its source. The target vertex must be in the rest graph and labelled by "elem". The set of dangling edges which fits to a cut-description will be determined in each rewriting step.

The corresponding paste-description controls the embedding of the inserted graph. It takes the embedding vertices determined by the cut-description and connects them to a distinct vertex in the image of the inserted graph. The properties of the embedding edges are given by the paste-description. In our example, the evaluation of the paste-description

$$(8, \text{n}, \text{out})$$

provides the edge which connects vertices 8 and 3. Again, the direction of the embedding edge is given by the third component. The "out" states that an image of vertex 8 will be the source of an embedding edge.

Graphically the embedding description given in the example is denoted by the shaded extensions to both parts of the transformation specification. (see figure 6). Note that the vertex 10 actually denotes a set of vertices, namely those vertices determined by the cut-description. If the set of vertices obtained is empty in a rewriting step, then the embedding description has no effect. No edges are removed, hence none are inserted.

The notion of an embedding description and its evaluation is defined separately from the main definitions of a graph rewriting rule and graph rewriting step. Thus the evaluation of a description must anticipate the vertex map h applied in a rewriting step, as well as the set of vertices and the labelling function l of the transformed graph.

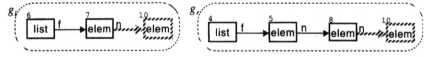

Figure 6   Graphs g_l and g_r with embedding descriptions

Definition 2.2.1   EMBEDDING DESCRIPTION, EVALUATION OF AN EMBEDDING
DESCRIPTION

Let V, W be vertex sets, Σ_V and Σ_E sets of labels. Let h be a bijection from V to a vertex set V' and l be a labelling function on V', i.e. $l: V' \to \Sigma_V$.

a) The set of *cut-descriptions* (over V) is $C(V) = V \times \Sigma_E \times \Sigma_V \times \{ \text{in, out} \}$. The set of *paste-descriptions* (over W) is $P(W) = (W \times \Sigma_E \times \{ \text{in, out} \}) \cup \{ \text{del} \}$. The symbols "in" and "out" indicate the direction of an edge whereas "del" denotes the deletion of an embedding edge. An *embedding description* is a pair $m = (c, p) \in C(V) \times P(W)$.

b) Let $(c, p) \in C(V) \times P(W)$ be an embedding description. The boolean function $fits_{h, l}$ determines the *fit of the cut-description* $c = (v', el', vl, d')$ to an edge $e = (s, el, t) \in V' \times \Sigma_E \times V'$: $fits_{h, l}(c, e) = el' = el$ and if $d' = $ in: $h^{-1}(s) = v' \wedge l(t) = vl$, if $d' = $ out: $h^{-1}(t) = v' \wedge l(s) = vl$.

The function $Fit_{h, l}$ determines those edges of a given set E which fit to the cut-part of an embedding description. They will be dangling edges.

$$Fit_{h, l}((c, p), E) = \{ e \in E | fits_{h, l}(c, e) \} .$$

c) Let $m = (c, p) \in C(V) \times P(V)$ be an embedding description with $c = (v', el', vl, d')$ and $p = (v, el, d)$. Let $E \subseteq V' \times \Sigma_E \times V'$ be a set of edges.

The *evaluation* of m applied to E under h and l determines a set of embedding edges which may connect an inserted and a rest graph:

$$eval_{h, l}(m, E) = \{ (w, el, h(v)) | w \in V_{emb}(m) \} , \text{if } d = \text{in}$$
$$= \{ (h(v), el, w) | w \in V_{emb}(m) \} , \text{if } d = \text{out}$$

where the set of embedding vertices $V_{emb}(m) \subseteq V'$ is defined as follows

$$V_{emb}(m) = \{ t | (s, el, t) \in Fit_{h, l}(m, E) \} , \text{if } d = \text{in}$$
$$= \{ s | (s, el, t) \in Fit_{h, l}(m, E) \} , \text{if } d = \text{out} \qquad \blacksquare$$

After the definition of an embedding description, the components of a graph rewriting rule are now formally introduced. A rule consists of two graphs and a set of embedding descriptions. The graphs were formerly called pre- and post-conditions, but in terms of rule-based graph rewriting they are adequately referred to by the rule's left- and right-hand side. The embedding description provides sufficient information to connect the inserted image of the right-hand side to the rest graph. So the insertion of an element to a list was already graphically stated as a rewriting rule.

Having a fast implementation as an objective, we do not stay with this straightforward definition. We apply, moreover, the idea of context known from string grammars. A context-sensitive rule may have a left-hand side in which the nonterminal symbol is surrounded by two arbitrary strings. The rule is applicable only when the whole left-hand side matches, but only the nonterminal symbol must be replaced. The context appears unchanged on the right-hand side of the rule.

We generalize the notion of context for graph rewriting systems. The context of a rule indicates that it must not be altered in a rewriting step. Take, for example, the insertion rule for lists. Our intuition says that neither the "list"- nor the "elem"-vertex of the left-hand side needs to be replaced in a rewriting step. The naive approach to a rewriting step, however, deletes the image of the left-hand side and replaces it by an image of the right-hand side. Thus it performs several redundant operations. If we indicate the context explicitly we may guide the implementation and improve the performance.

For the indication of context, we cannot use the method of context-sensitive string grammars. We do not distinguish between non-terminal and terminal labels. Furthermore we intend to replace whole subgraphs at once and not only single vertices. We therefore must use another approach. It exploits the fact that up to now the vertices of both sides of a rule can be chosen arbitrarily. For the indication of context, we couple both graphs as follows: a vertex is in the context of a rule if it appears in the vertex set of both sides, i.e. in their intersection. Since the context vertices must not be touched in the implementation of a rewriting step, they must not change their label. Hence the labelling functions must be consistent, i.e. equal on the intersection of the vertex sets.

The list insertion example with explicit context is shown in figure 7.The vertices 6 and 7 appear in both graphs. Thus they express the context of the rule. Similarly, the intersection of the edge sets yields a set of context edges. It is empty in the given example.

Definition 2.2.2 (g_l, g_r, M) , GRAPH REWRITING RULE

Let $g_l = (V_l, E_l, l_l)$ and $g_r = (V_r, E_r, l_r)$ be graphs with $l_l(v) = l_r(v)$ for all $v \in V_l \cap V_r$ and $M \subseteq C(V_l) \times P(V_r)$ be a set of embedding descriptions. A *graph rewriting rule* is the tuple $r = (g_l, g_r, M)$. The graph g_l is the *left-hand side*, g_r is the *right-hand side*, and M is the *set of embedding descriptions* of the rule. Since the labelling functions l_l and l_r are equal on the intersection $V_l \cap V_r$, the *labelling function l of the rewriting rule r* can be defined as $l(v) = l_l(v)$ for $v \in V_l$ and $l(v) = l_r(v)$ for $v \in V_r$. ∎

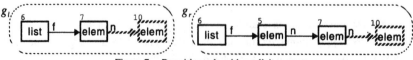

Figure 7   Rewriting rule with explicit context

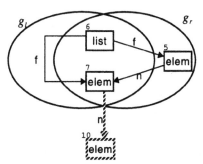

Figure 8   Graphical indication of context

For notational convenience, the components of the left-hand and right-hand side of a rule are indexed by l or r instead of g_l or g_r respectively. Thus V_r and l_r are the vertex set and the labelling function of the right-hand side respectively. Furthermore, we introduce the following convention for context sets and their complement. Let $r = (g_l, g_r, M)$ be a rewriting rule. The set of *context vertices* is $V_c = V_l \cap V_r$. The corresponding complementary sets are $V_{\bar{l}} = V_l \backslash V_c$ and $V_{\bar{r}} = V_r \backslash V_c$. The set of *context edges* is $E_c = E_l \cap E_r$. The complementary sets are $E_{\bar{r}} = E_r \backslash E_c$ and $E_{\bar{l}} = E_l \backslash E_c$.

If we explicitly want to visualize the context of a rewriting rule we use the convention as shown in figure 8. Each ellipse contains the corresponding side of the rewriting rule. In the intersection of both lie the context vertices 6 and 7. The "f"-edge between both vertices is not in the context. Thus it is drawn not as a straight line between its endpoints but also appears outside the context area. The graphical indication of context is not very much suited for the precise representation of embedding descriptions concerning context vertices. The example shows one embedding edge depicting the cut- and paste-description at the same time. Additional mechanisms must be used when embedding edges are passed between context vertices. We do not refine this representation any further, but use it only when it allows a unique interpretation. The precise presentation of rewriting rules will be according to figure 7.

The rewriting rule is a static specification of a graph transformation. After its definition we approach the definitions of the dynamics of graph rewriting. Thus we must specify how the rule interacts with a graph to transform it. As in any rewriting system, we first of all must define the applicability of a rule. In the introduction we already mentioned that the pre-condition of a rule must hold for a given graph. The validity of the condition is formally expressed as the existence of a graph isomorphism. If there is a subgraph isomorphic to the left-hand side, the rule is applicable.

After the definition of the rewriting rule, we can approach the definition of applicability.

Definition 2.2.3 APPLICABILITY

Let $r = (g_l, g_r, M)$ be a rewriting rule. Let g be a graph. The rewriting rule r is *applicable* to g iff there exists a graph isomorphism $\hat{h}$ such that $\hat{h}(g_l) \subseteq g$. ∎

At the beginning of the section, we listed the four phases of a graph rewriting step. The goal of the first phase was to determine an isomorphic subgraph. This goal is already achieved by the test for applicability. A rewriting rule is applicable only if there is a isomorphism from the left-hand side into the graph to be transformed. This graph is called *host graph* from now on because it hosts the rewriting step. The following definition of a rewriting step reflects the remaining three phases in terms of set operations.

Additionally we introduced a graph rewriting step as a cut and paste operation on a graph. Our definition provides a refinement. The context information given in the rewriting rule will be explicitly recognized. Thus not the complete left-hand side, but only the part not in the context is removed. Similarly only non-context components of the right-hand side are inserted.

The vertices which are required for the image of the right-hand side are provided by the set W. Since W must contain only new vertices, the vertex map of the left-hand side can be extended straightforwardly. The overall map h relates vertices of both sides to the graph.

The set of edges of the result graph depends on both sides of the rule and the set of embedding descriptions. The following edges are deleted from the host graph: left-hand side edges not in the context, edges incident to a deleted vertex (to avoid an incorrect result graph), and edges which fit to a cut-description. Edges are inserted in the graph if they appear on the right-hand side and not in the context, or if they are determined by the evaluation of an embedding description. Note that in fact not the edges and vertices of the rule but their images under h are deleted or inserted.

Let us now define the effect of a rewriting step, which is the basic operation in graph rewriting systems.

Definition 2.2.4 $g \to_h^r g'$, GRAPH REWRITING STEP

Let $r = (g_l, g_r, M)$ be a rewriting rule applicable to the host graph g and let $\hat{h}_l$ be a graph isomorphism such that $\hat{h}_l(g_l) \subseteq g$. Choose a vertex set W disjoint from V with $|W| = |V_r|$ and extend h_l to an injective map $h: V_l \cup V_r \to V \cup W$ such that $h(v) = h_l(v)$ for $v \in V_l$ and $h(v) \in W$ for $v \in V_r$. The graph g' is the result of *rewriting g with r under h*, in symbols $g \to_h^r g'$, iff

(i) $V' = [V \setminus h(V_l)] \cup W$,

(ii) $l'(v) = l_r \circ h^{-1}(v)$ for all $v \in W$ and $l'(v) = l(v)$ for all $v \in V' \setminus W$,

(iii) $E' = [E \setminus (inc_g(h(V_l)) \cup h(E_l) \cup \bigcup_{m \in M} Fit_{h,l}(m, Emb))] \cup$
$$h(E_r) \cup Emb_{ins},$$

where the set of inserted embedding edges Emb_{ins} is determined by the evaluation of the paste-description, $Emb_{ins} = \bigcup_{m \in M} eval_{h,l}(m, Fit_{h,l}(m, Emb))$, and the set of embedding edges connecting the image of the left-hand side with the rest graph is $Emb = inc_g(h(V_l)) \cap inc_g(V \setminus h(V_l))$.   ■

In figure 9 we give an example of a graph rewriting step. The application of the rewriting rule inserts an "elem"-vertex to the host graph. The rewriting step first must determine an isomorphic subgraph. This graph is indicated by the shaded box. That subgraph is in general to be removed, but only the "f"-edge must actually be deleted.

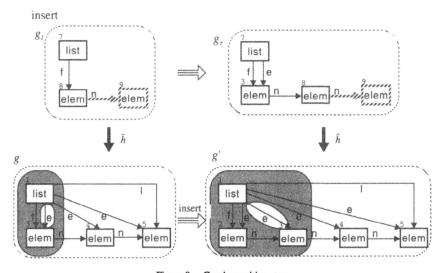

Figure 9   Graph rewriting step

The rest of the subgraph is the image of the context consisting of the two vertices 7 and 8. The edge $(1, e, 3)$ is an inner edge. It is not altered during the rewriting step, since both endpoints belong to the context. Because the "list" vertex is not deleted, no dangling edges occur as a result of a deletion. Hence they are identically embedded, i.e. also not altered during the rewriting step. The rule has one explicit embedding description which fits to the "n"-edge incident to vertex 3. This edge will be replaced by an identical edge in the final phase of the rewriting step; but before an isomorphic image of the right-hand side will be inserted in the rest graph. Because of context information, only an image of vertex 3 must be inserted together with the incident edges. The rest of the image of the right-hand side was not removed before.

Let us inspect the effect of the context in more detail. Consider the interpretation of an embedding description. Not all edges between the image of the left-hand side and the rest graph, i.e. of the set *Emb*, are deleted; only those which fit to an embedding description. What happens to the remaining edges of *Emb*? If they are incident to a deleted vertex they are also removed to obtain a well-defined graph. If they are incident to a context vertex, they remain in the graph. In this case they represent an *identical embedding*, i.e. the edge between the context vertex and the rest graph is not altered.

The same situation arises for edges between context vertices. The notion of applicability allows that not all edges between images of context vertices correspond to an edge of the left-hand side. Thus they are not known by the rule. They also remain in the host graph. Those edges are called *inner edges*.

Based on the definition of a rewriting rule, a graph rewriting system and related notions can be defined.

Definition 2.2.5   GRAPH REWRITING SYSTEM, DERIVATION, GRAPH LANGUAGE

Let Σ_V, Σ_E be alphabets. Let g_0 be a graph over Σ_V, Σ_E and R be a set of rewriting rules.

a) A *graph rewriting system* over the set of vertex labels Σ_V and the set of edge labels Σ_E with initial graph g_0 and a set of rules R is the tuple $gg = (\Sigma_V, \Sigma_E, g_0, R)$.

b) The graph g_n can be *derived* from a graph g_1 if there are rewriting rules $r_i \in R$, graphmorphisms $\hat{h}_i$ and graphs g_i such that $g_i \to_{h_i}^{r_i} g_{i+1}$ for $i = 1...n - 1$. In this case, there exists a *derivation* of g_n from g_1, in symbols $g_1 \to^* g_n$.

c) The *graph language* $L(gg)$ is defined as $L(gg) = \{g | g_0 \to^* g\}$.   ∎

We do not distinguish between terminal and non-terminal labels. Consequently, the set of graphs defined by a graph rewriting system, i.e. the generated language, is the set of all derivable graphs.

A graph rewriting system specifying the operations for a priority queue will be as follows. For the sake of simplicity, we distinguish between only two priorities, high and low. Furthermore there is a vertex accessing the first and the last element by an "f"- and an "l"-edge respectively. Since the queue may appear in a larger graph, any element is also explicitly referred to by an "e"-edge. Hence

$$\Sigma_V = \{\text{queue, high, low}\} \text{ and } \Sigma_E = \{\text{f, l, e}\}.$$

The initial graph represents the empty queue.

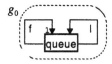

For each priority we have two insert operations, one for the empty queue and one for a non-empty queue. Here we show only the "high" operations.

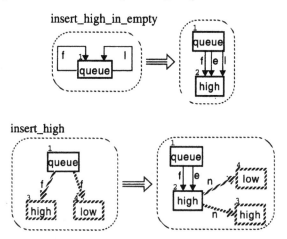

In the operation "insert_high" we exploit the fact that at any time there is exactly one first element in the queue. Hence only one of both embedding descriptions denotes an element. Furthermore the vertex 1 is in the context. Thus all other incident edges remain due to the identical embedding.

There are also two operations for removal for each priority. Again we only show the operations for high priority.

remove_high

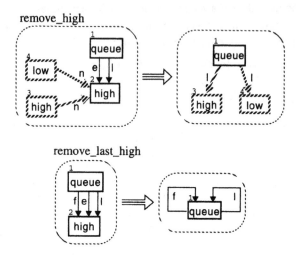

remove_last_high

When an element with high priority is inserted in the queue, it must be propagated to its right position. The correct ordering is obtained by subsequent application of the rewriting rule "swap".

swap

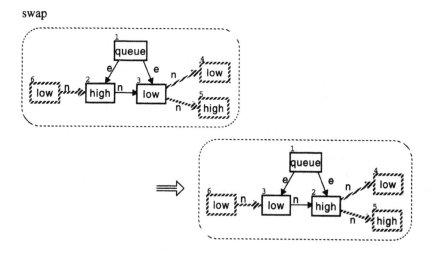

The given rewriting rules specify the operations which are required to maintain a priority queue for two priorities. A graph which can be derived by the rewriting system models the state of a queue (see for instance figure 10).

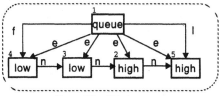

Figure 10   Priority queue

2.3   An Abstract Machine for Labelled Subgraph Matching

The test whether a rule is applicable to a graph can be realized by solving the subgraph isomorphism problem for labelled graphs. Analogous to pattern matching in term rewriting, we use the notion *labelled subgraph matching* for that specific task. The labelled subgraph matching problem can be solved by construction of an isomorphism for each connected component of the left-hand side. When the construction succeeds for each component, a graph morphism is found. It relates the left-hand side to a subgraph of the host graph.

A sequential algorithm may construct the set of possible isomorphisms by traversing the left-hand side. The first step of the algorithm in this setting determines the set of vertices isomorphic to an initial vertex. In each subsequent step, the algorithm tests whether an edge can be mapped to an edge incident to a current image. If it is possible, the current vertex maps are expanded. They are propagated to the next step. In this approach all partial subgraphs determined by a set of intermediate mappings have the same inverse image. To decide applicability of a rewriting rule, the algorithm traverses the left-hand side and finally constructs all possible isomorphisms from the left-hand side into the host graph. If there is at least one, the rule is applicable.

Up to now the algorithm for subgraph matching is free to choose the traversal order by interpreting the left-hand side. Like most interpreters, the algorithm has to perform a lot of bookkeeping to control the traversal. We can save this time by precomputing the traversal order and providing the algorithm with an explicit search strategy. The data which represent such a search strategy are a so-called *connected enumeration* of the left-hand side. The elements of the enumeration are successively drawn by the algorithm and control its execution. The main principle of our algorithm is the extension of partial handles. Thus the enumeration must ensure that for all edges there is one adjacent edge preceding it in the enumeration. Otherwise, an extension would be impossible, since both endpoints are unknown. Obviously, the initial edge deserves special treatment. The root of a connected enumeration is one vertex incident to the initial edge.

Definition 2.3.1 CONNECTED ENUMERATION WITH ROOT VERTEX

Let g be a graph with $q = |E|$.

a) A sequence (e_i) of edges $e_i \in E$, $i = 1...q$ is an *enumeration* of E iff

$$E = \{e_i | i = 1...q\}.$$

b) An enumeration (e_i), $i = 1...q$ of E is a *connected enumeration* iff

for all e_i with $i > 1$ there is an adjacent edge e_j with $j < i$.

Any vertex $v \in inc_g(e_1)$ may be choosen as the *root vertex* of (e_i), $i = 1...q$. ■

The connected enumeration of the left-hand side and the host graph is the input for the abstract machine for labelled subgraph matching. The machine performs a breadth first search for a graph isomorphism which maps a graph g' onto a subgraph of g. Thus it can decide the applicability of a rewriting rule by construction of the corresponding graph morphism.

In general, there are several connected enumerations for a graph. Take for example the left-hand side graph of the rewriting rule "remove_high".

remove_high

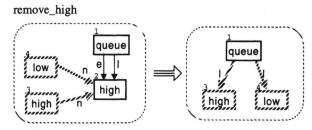

To determine an isomorphic subgraph, the vertices 1 and 2 must be mapped onto vertices of the host graph. A connected enumeration now can have one of both vertices as its root. Independent of that choice, again two alternatives are possible: either the "e"- or the "l"-edge. And lastly the remaining edge completes the enumeration.

In any sequential test for applicability we find *handles*. These are subgraphs of a host graph which are isomorphic to a subgraph of the left-hand side. If they correspond to proper subgraphs of the left-hand side they are called partial and may be completed to a *full handle*. In that case the corresponding rewriting rule is applicable to the host graph. A step in the sequential application test is mostly an extension of the vertex map which is the base of the graph morphism between left-hand side and the host graph. This morphism is partial for partial handles.

Definition 2.3.2   PARTIAL, FULL HANDLE

Let $r = (g_l, g_r, M)$ be a rewriting rule. Let $g = (V, E, l)$ be a graph. Any graph $g_p \subseteq g$ for which there exists a graph isomorphism $\hat{h}: g_l \rightarrow g$ with $g_p \subseteq \hat{h}(g_l)$ is a *partial han-dle*. If $g_p = \hat{h}(g_l)$, then g_p is a *full handle*. A partial handle $g_p = (\{v\}, \varnothing, l)$ with $v \in V$ is an *initial handle*.   ∎

We prepare the definition of the abstract machine by the definition of its basic opera-tions. For the specification of the machine's operation, we assume that the graph is given in a frame-based data structure. Each frame stores the direct neighbourhood of a vertex. Each slot of a frame contains a list of isomorphic edges incident to the vertex represented by the frame. Isomorphic edges have the same edge label, same direction, and the labels of the incident vertices are equal too. With the frame data structure we can directly address incident edges by their labels and direction.

Take for example the list graph shown in figure 2 on page 11. A part of the internal representation of that graph is presented in figure 11. Each frame has one segment for incoming and one for outgoing edges. Each segment again provides segments for any vertex label, and finally the slots for the edges of a certain edge label. In our example, there are only *single entry slots*. This does not hold true for the internal representation of the priority queue presented in figure 10 (see page 24). The frame storing the infor-

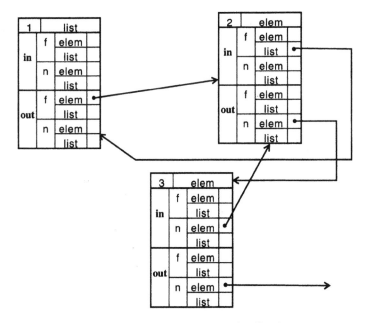

Figure 11   Frame representation of vertices

mation for vertex 1 labelled by "queue" carries several pointers in its slots for "e"-edges pointing to "high" and "low" vertices. These slots have *multiple entries*.

The abstract machine maintains a set of morphisms. The final set should contain all morphisms which map the left-hand side into the host graph. Therefore the machine performs one of two main operations depending on the edge currently drawn from the input enumeration. The operation is either a simple check or an extension. The machine executes a simple check when the images of both endpoints of an edge are already found. In that case, it selects those morphisms from the current set which are defined for that edge, i.e. the corresponding partial handles must contain an image of the edge. When the image of one endpoint is not determined already, the machine tries to extend the current handles. Therefore it looks up the corresponding slots determined by the edge's label and direction.

Definition 2.3.3   BASIC OPERATIONS OF THE ABSTRACT MACHINE

Let g and g' be two graphs.

a) Let $\hat{h}: g_1 \to g_2$ be a graph isomorphism induced by a partial vertex map $h: V_{g_1} \to V_{g_2}$. The graph isomorphism $\hat{h}'$ extends $\hat{h}$ *along an edge* $e \in E_1$ iff for $e = (s, el, t)$

(i)   either $s \notin dom(h)$ or $t \notin dom(h)$,

(ii) $\exists v \in V_2$ such that in case $s \notin dom(h)$: $(v, el, h(t)) \in E_2$ or in case $t \notin dom(h)$: $(h(s), el, v) \in E_2$,

(iii) $h'v|_{dom(h_v)} = h_v$,

(iv)   if $s \notin dom(h)$: $h'(s) = v$, if $t \notin dom(h)$: $h'(t) = v$.

Hence $\hat{h}(g_1) \subseteq \hat{h}'(g_1)$.

b) Let A be a set of partial graph isomorphisms $\hat{h}: g' \to g$. The operations *check* and *extend* compute another set of graph isomorphisms with respect to an edge $e' \in E'$ as follows:

$$check\,(A, e') = \{\hat{h} \in A | h(e) \in E\}$$
$$extend\,(A, e') = \{\hat{h}' | \hat{h}' \text{ extends } \hat{h} \in A \text{ by } e'\}$$ ∎

Single and multiple entry slots make an important difference for the performance of the abstract machine. The run time of the matching algorithm depends strongly on the number of entries. The check can be performed in unit time for single entry slots. In case of multiple entries, the algorithm must scan the list of entries to find the possible

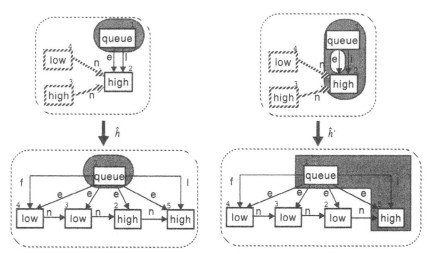

Figure 12   Extension of morphism $\hat{h}$ to $\hat{h}'$ along the edge $(1, l, 5)$

images of the given edge. Thus this check takes time dependent on the number of entries. In case we have to extend a match and the respective slot has multiple entries, the extension is performed for each entry and each current handle. Thus multiple extensions must be constructed.

Provided with the basic operations, we now can define the abstract machine for the labelled subgraph matching as the following algorithm.

Algorithm 2.3.4   ABSTRACT MACHINE FOR LABELLED SUBGRAPH MATCHING

Let g and g' be two graphs. The abstract machine executes the following algorithm.

INPUT: g, a connected enumeration (e_i), $i = 1 \ldots q$ of E' with root vertex $v' \in V'$

OUTPUT: a set of graphmorphisms $\hat{h}$ with $\hat{h}(g') \subseteq g$.

1.   **INITIALIZE** $A_0 := \{\hat{h} \mid \exists v \in V, l(v) = l'(v'), h(v') = v\}$

2.   **SET** $W_0 := \{v'\}$

3.   **FOR** $i = 1 \ldots q$ **DO**
         LET $(s, el, t) = e_i$
         IF $s, t \in W_{i-1}$
               THEN $A_i = \text{check}(A_{i-1}, e_i)$
               ELSE $A_i = \text{extend}(A_{i-1}, e_i)$
         ENDIF
         SET $W_i := W_{i-1} \cup \{s, t\}$

4.   **OUTPUT** A_q ■

We now prove the correctness of the algorithm for labelled subgraph matching.

Lemma 2.3.5   CORRECTNESS OF LABELLED SUBGRAPH MATCHING

Let g and g' be two graphs. Let (e_i), $i = 1...q$ be a connected enumeration of E' with root vertex $v' \in V'$. Let A be the output of the abstract machine of algorithm 2.3.4 for input g, (e_i), $i = 1...q$, and v'. For all $\hat{h} \in A$ it holds that

$$\hat{h}(g') \subseteq g.$$

Proof. We adopt the terminology of algorithm 2.3.4 and prove that $\hat{h}(g') \subseteq g$ holds by induction over $i \in \{1,..., q\}$. By definition of A_0 it holds that $\hat{h}_0(g_0) \subseteq g$ for all initial morphisms $\hat{h}_0 \in A_0$ and $g_0 = (\{v'\}, \varnothing, l')$.

Let $i \in \{1,..., q-1\}$, $\hat{h}_i \in A_i$, and $(s, el, t) = e_{i+1}$ the next edge of the connected enumeration. Assume now that $\hat{h}_i(g_i)$ is a partial handle for $g_i = (W_i, \{e_j | j = 1...i\}, l')$, i.e. $\hat{h}_i(g_i) \subseteq g$. Let $\hat{h}_{i+1} \in A_{i+1}$ be an extension of $\hat{h}_i$.

In case $s, t \in W_i$ it holds for all $\hat{h}_{i+1} \in A_{i+1}$ that $h_{i+1}(e_{i+1}) \in E$. Since $\hat{h}_{i+1}$ extends $\hat{h}_i$ by the mapping of e_{i+1} it follows that $dom(h_{V,i}) = dom(h_{V,i+1}) \setminus \{s\} = W_i$ and $dom(h_{E,i}) = dom(h_{E,i+1}) \setminus \{e_{i+1}\}$. With the induction hypothesis $\hat{h}_i(g_i) \subseteq g$ it follows that $\hat{h}_{i+1}(g_{i+1}) \subseteq g$.

Now, without loss of generality, let $s \notin W_i$. Since $\hat{h}_{i+1}$ extends $\hat{h}_i$ by e_{i+1} it follows by the definition of the operation "extend" that $dom(h_{V,i}) = dom(h_{V,i+1}) \setminus \{s\} = W_i$ and $dom(h_{E,i}) = dom(h_{E,i+1}) \setminus \{e_{i+1}\}$. For $\hat{h}_{i+1}$ it holds that $h_{i+1}(s) \in V$ and $h_{i+1}(e_{i+1}) \in E$. Hence $\hat{h}_{i+1}(g_{i+1}) \subseteq g$ and the proof is complete.   ∎

The runtime of the abstract machine is determined by steps 1 and 3 of the algorithm. The analysis of step 3 depends on the edge being processed. Let us determine the run time for the ith loop with edge $e_i = (s, el, t)$ for $i \in \{1,..., q\}$. In the case that both endpoints are included in the current match one check is performed for each handle. Let $n_{h(t), i}$ and $n_{h(s), i}$ be the number of entries in the respective slot of vertices $h(t)$ and $h(s)$ for all morphisms $\hat{h} \in A_{i-1}$. Hence the number of tests is

$$\sum_{\hat{h} \in A_{i-1}} n_{h(t), i} \quad \text{or} \quad \sum_{\hat{h} \in A_{i-1}} n_{h(s), i}$$

depending on the vertex at which the existence of the edge is checked.

In case extensions are performed, assume without loss of generality that $s \notin W_{i-1}$, i.e. the machine extends the current handles by possible images of s. Again let $n_{h(t), i}$ be the number of entries in the respective slot of vertices $\{h(t)|\ h \in A_{i-1}\}$. When the respective slot in the image of t is not empty, i.e. $n_{h(t),\,i} > 0$, the algorithm extends all handles of A_{i-1}. For each item of a slot, an extension must be defined. The number of extensions in the ith step is then

$$\sum_{\hat{h} \in A_{i-1}} n_{h(t),\,i}.$$

To determine the overall run time, let $p = |V'|$ and $q = |E'|$ the order and the size of the given subgraph. In step 1, $|V|$ comparisons are necessary to find all initial handles. In the further execution of the abstract machine, the remaining $p - 1$ vertices must be mapped onto an image in the graph g. The mappings are constructed by the extension of current handles in step 3. As a consequence, the existence of $q - (p - 1)$ edges must be checked. Without loss of generality, assume a connected enumeration which drives the matching such that the extensions are performed and afterwards the existence of the remaining edges is checked. Assume further that only source vertices must be found. Let $n_{h(t),\,i}$ be defined as above. The overall run time of the labelled subgraph matching is then

$$|V| + \sum_{i=1}^{p-1} \left(\sum_{\hat{h} \in A_{i-1}} n_{h(t),\,i} \right) \text{extensions} + \sum_{i=p}^{q} \left(\sum_{\hat{h} \in A_{i-1}} n_{h(t),\,i} \right) \text{checks}.$$

There is a special property of the matching algorithm. It relates the number of extensions to the run time caused by extensions. An execution of the algorithm is non-branching if the input is such that the number of handles does not increase in any iteration. This is a restriction particular for the extension steps, since checks per definition do not increase the number of morphisms. In case the set of initial morphisms has only one element, the non-branching execution of the machine computes a unique full handle if there is a match at all.

Definition 2.3.6   NON-BRANCHING EXECUTION

Let g and g' be two graphs. Let (e_i), $i = 1...q$ be a connected enumeration of E' with root vertex $v' \in V'$. The abstract machine for the labelled subgraph matching with input g, (e_i) and v' *executes non-branching* iff for all $i \in \{1,..., q-1\}$ and any $\hat{h}_i \in A_i$ there exists at most one extension $\hat{h}_{i+1} \in A_{i+1}$.   ■

For non-branching matchings we can calculate the number of extensions which are performed in an execution.

Lemma 2.3.7   NUMBER OF EXTENSIONS FOR NON-BRANCHING MATCHINGS

Let g and g' be two graphs with $p = |V'|$ and $q = |E'|$. Let (e_i), $i = 1...q$ be a connected enumeration of E' with root vertex $v' \in V'$. Let $m = |A_0|$ be the number of initial handles.

If the labelled subgraph matching algorithm executes non-branching it performs

$$m \cdot (p - 1) \quad \text{extensions.}$$

Proof. Since the labelled subgraph matching algorithm executes non-branching, it follows that for all $i = 1...q$ and any $\hat{h}_i \in A_i$ that there exists at most one extension $\hat{h}_{i+1} \in A_{i+1}$. Hence the algorithm performs an extension only on a single entry slot. Thus it holds that either $n_{h(s), i} \leq 1$ or $n_{h(t), i} \leq 1$ depending on the direction of the extension. The matching algorithm would otherwise branch. Furthermore it holds that $|A_{i+1}| \leq |A_i|$ for all $i = 1...q$ -1, hence $|A_i| \leq |A_0| = m$ for $i = 1...q$. Let us assume that the elements of the enumeration are such that the mapping extends partial handles only by the target of an edge. For the number of extensions then follows

$$\sum_{i=1}^{p-1} \left(\sum_{\hat{h} \in A_{i-1}} n_{h(s), i} \right) \leq \sum_{i=1}^{p-1} (|A_i|) \leq \sum_{i=1}^{p-1} (|A_0|) \leq m \cdot (p - 1) . \qquad \blacksquare$$

We do not explore here the run time of the matching algorithm for other specific conditions formally, but mention just one special property which will be important for the next chapter. Lemma 2.3.7 states that in case that the algorithm performs non-branching the number of extensions is bound by $m \cdot (p - 1)$. If we chose the root vertex of the input enumeration such that it has at most one image in the host graph, the number of extensions is bound by $p - 1$. The complete run time of the abstract machine now depends still on the checks for the existence of the $q - (p - 1)$ edges. If these checks can now be performed on vertices which have at most one entry in the slot for the respective edge, the algorithm performs $q - (p - 1)$ checks. We may assume that a single check and a single extension take one unit of time. Thus the algorithm takes time linear in the size of the enumeration when the extensions and checks are performed on single entry slots and there is exactly one initial handle. The remaining question now is how to select an appropriate connected enumeration.

2.4 Summary and Related Work

In this chapter we defined a basic formalism for *graph rewriting systems* following the algorithmic approach. Since we are interested in the transformational view on graph grammars, we defined graph rewriting systems as a set of *rewriting rules* together with an *initial graph*.

Because we will develop methods for static analysis of graph rewriting systems, our formalism has a *small number of ingredients*. They are

- embedding descriptions,
- graph rewriting rules,
- the notion of applicability,
- the graph rewriting step, and
- the graph rewriting system.

The major characteristics of a rewriting rule are *explicit context information* and the use of *embedding descriptions*. The context of a rewriting rule is given by those vertices and edges which occur on both sides. For the definition of a graph rewriting step and its implementation, it follows that context objects need not be touched. The embedding descriptions specify the connection between the image of the right-hand side and the former neighbours of the image of the left-hand side.

We recalled the labelled subgraph matching problem and specified an *abstract machine* for its solution if it exists. The main idea is the transformation of the subgraph into a search strategy given as a *rooted, connected enumeration* of the subgraph. This sequence controls the operation of the abstract machine. The frame-based representation for host graphs served for the analysis of the run time of the machine. If the machine executes *non-branching*, the run time of the machine is of polynomial order with degree 2.

The algorithmic definition of graph rewriting systems was introduced by [Nag79] and has been used by many others who deal with graph rewriting systems for modelling. In the project "Incremental Programming Support ENvironment" (IPSEN), algorithmic graph rewriting systems served as specification formalism [En86], [Nag86b], [EnSch89]. The main goal for IPSEN was the specification and implementation of a software development environment. Schürr extended the graph rewriting formalism to the specification language PROGRES which contains several non-standard structures [Schü90], [Schü94].

The usage of context information is also realized in Göttler's definition of graph rewriting systems [Gött88]. He used the graphical X-notation to denote the context graph of a rewriting rule. The X-notation is a good attempt to improve the performance of a graph rewriting step by explicit syntactical information. A closer inspection of Göttler's formalism, though, reveals a lack of clarity concerning the handling of edges incident to context vertices. They can be deleted, inserted, or untouched in a rewriting step. Göttler's graphical representation denotes the operation on those edges by drawing the edges with different lines. This problem appears also for our graphical representation of the context of a graph rewriting rule. Thus we decided not to indicate context vertices by a specialized graphical representation but to use the identification of vertices. Hence the semantics of the rule is still given as an intuitively clear cut-and-paste operation. Additional information to speed up the implementation is given by the identification of elements of both vertex sets.

3 UBS-Graph Rewriting Systems — Matching Subgraphs in Constant Time

The previous chapter provides an abstract machine solving the isomorphic subgraph problem. The machine inputs a host graph and a rooted connected enumeration. It controls the execution of the machine such that it computes all isomorphic subgraphs. In general there are several rooted connected enumerations of a graph. All may control the machine which will compute the same set of isomorphic subgraphs for each enumeration. The execution time, though, will be different and depend on the chosen enumeration. The apparent question now is: which enumeration of a subgraph provides an efficient computation of the isomorphic subgraphs?

The execution time analysis of the last chapter shows that the enumeration must be selected based on the host graph. If the enumeration controls the machine such that extensions and checks are performed only on single-entry slots, then the execution time depends on the number of initial handles and the length of the connected enumeration. The length is equal for all enumerations of a graph. The selection of an appropriate connected enumeration must thenconsider

(i)   the number of initial handles and

(ii)   the single-entry slots.

Consequently the implementation of an application test in graph rewriting might be realized in three steps: 1) analyse the current host graph; 2) select an appropriate enumeration of the left-hand side; and 3) compute the set of isomorphic subgraphs with the abstract machine. For a fast implementation of graph rewriting, this approach is not feasible. Each time the host graph, which might be arbitrarily large, must be scanned. Hence the rewriting step may be arbitrarily slow.

Thus a fast implementation of a graph rewriting system must not select a connected enumeration in each rewriting step. The search strategy for each rule moreover should be selected prior to the actual graph rewriting process. At that time, however, it is not known which rule is applied to which host graph. Thus the connected enumerations must be selected with respect to all derivable graphs. Only then we can ensure an optimal execution time for any host graph. Consequently a proper selection requires information such as the number of initial handles and the single-entry slots of any derivable graph.

In most applications the language generated by a graph rewriting system is of infinite size. Thus it is impossible to determine the properties of all derivable graphs by inspection. The only basis for the selection is instead the graph rewriting system itself. The analysis of the initial graph and the rewriting rules must derive a sufficient amount of information. The method we apply for the analysis is abstract interpretation.

The goal of abstract interpretation is to determine properties of the result of a computation by analysis of the static computation rules. Some information on the result of the computation, then, is available without performing the computation. In our case we will derive properties of the graph language without generating it. The basic idea of this method is to abstract the computation rules such that they compute an abstract value instead of the standard one. The rule of signs may serve as an example. Here we have an arithmetical expression such as

$$(3 + 4) * (-4).$$

We want to know whether the expression denotes a positive or a negative value, i.e. the sign of the expression's value. For the abstract interpretation we must find abstractions for the basic values and the operations such that the abstract interpretation computes the required information. In our example we abstract positive integers to the abstract value pos and negative integers to neg. Also, we specify abstract arithmetical operations $*$ and $+$ as follows:

$$
\begin{array}{ll}
neg * neg = pos & pos + pos = pos \\
pos * neg = neg & neg + neg = neg \\
pos * pos = pos & pos + neg = ?
\end{array}
$$

Note that in the case of the abstract sum of pos and neg the abstract value cannot be definitely determined. This reflects the characteristic of the standard interpretation where the sum of a positive and a negative value may be either positive or negative. Take for instance

$$3 + (-4) \text{ and } 3 + (-2).$$

This case illustrates the gap between standard and abstract interpretation. Not all information derived by standard interpretation is available from abstract interpretation. In general the abstract interpretation provides only an approximation of the standard values.

Let us now compute the abstract interpretation of

$$(3 + 4) * (-4).$$

It performs as follows:

$$(pos + pos) * neg = pos * neg = neg$$

Hence we know that the value of the expression must be negative although we have not computed the real result.[1]

With respect to the selection of an appropriate connected enumeration, we must develop two abstract interpretations of graph rewriting systems. The first must provide good candidates for root vertices. The initial handles determined in the initialization of the abstract machine are the images of the root vertex of the input connected enumeration. An initial handle is selected only by its label. Thus the *image is unique* if its label is unique in the host graph. The first abstract interpretation computes a lower approximation for the set of vertex labels which are unique in all derived graphs. Thus we can assert the singularity of initial handles.

The second abstract analysis derives a sufficient condition for single entry slots. The analysis of so-called *strong V-structures* determines those slots of all frames which have definitely at most one entry.

Hence we have a criterion at hand to select connected enumerations. We implement this criterion in a procedure. It computes an appropriate enumeration with respect to the results of the abstract interpretation. Whenever the computation succeeds for an input left-hand side, an enumeration is generated which controls the abstract machine such that it runs in time linear to the length of the enumeration. Hence we can statically decide whether the application test for all rules of a rewriting system takes time linear to the size of the left-hand side. The graph rewriting systems which satisfy our condition form the class of UBS rewriting systems.

In addition to the analysis of unique vertex labels and strong V-structures, this chapter contains two further analyses. The first one is very similar to the unique vertex label analysis. It determines the unique edge labels of a graph rewriting system. This analysis is not directly addressed to the efficient subgraph isomorphism problem, but improves the strong V-structure analysis.

The purpose of the second additional analysis is also not directly addressed to the efficient subgraph isomorphism problem, but reduces the storage requirements of the abstract machine. In the frame-based implementation, each frame holds a slot for any combination of labels. Labels, though, are mostly assigned in a very specific manner because they carry semantic information from the modelled system. In the priority queue example, for instance, no "high" element must be the source of an "e"-edge. Only the "queue" vertex must refer to its elements by an edge of that type. Hence the outgoing "e"-slots in each "high"-frame are unnecessary. The analysis of *label triples* considers exactly that problem. A label triple contains the label information provided for an edge, namely the labels of the incident vertices and the label of the edge itself. The abstract interpretation now computes an upper approximation of the set of label

---

1. Abramsky and Hankin provide an introduction into and a collection of applications of abstract interpretation [AbHa87].

triples occurring in the language. Only for these labels, a frame slot must be provided. All other slots can be safely removed. Consequently less memory is required by the abstract machine.

The label triple analysis also serves two other purposes. First of all, we can determine dead rules and dead embedding descriptions, i.e. rules and descriptions which never can be applied. Hence we are able to reduce the number of rules and embedding descriptions without changing the generated language. The second purpose is on a meta-level. The abstract interpretation of strong V-structures bears two sources of complexity, the structure of the interpretation itself and the subject of the interpretation, i.e. strong V-structures. In the section on the abstract interpretation with respect to strong V-structures we want to concentrate on the conditions in which strong V-structures are generated. We do not want to introduce the complex procedure of abstract interpretation at the same time. Thus we present the abstract interpretation with respect to label triples in advance. In the analysis of strong V-structures, we can then focus our attention on the subject of the analysis.

This chapter provides several analyses on graph rewriting systems. First, we study unique labels and determine lower approximations. Second, we develop an abstract interpretation framework which determines an approximation of the set of label triples generated by a graph rewriting system. Third and finally, based on this framework, we give a method to compute the set of strong V-structures which may be generated by a graph rewriting system. Based on this approximation we can assert that the abstract machine for the subgraph isomorphism problem takes time linear to the length of the enumeration.

3.1 Unique Labels — Singularities in Derived Graphs

3.1.1 Unique Vertex Labels

Looking to the abstract machine for the subgraph isomorphism problem in detail, we observe that an initial partial handle is a vertex. The execution time analysis has shown that there must be at most one initial handle. Otherwise several vertices of the host graph are selected as initial handles and the applicability of the rule is tested for several areas of the host graph. Hence the machine takes more than linear time.

A vertex label of a graph rewriting system is unique if there is a single occurrence of it in all derivable graphs. The existence of a unique label has a consequence for the application of a rewriting rule. If there is a single vertex on the left-hand side tagged with a label which is unique in all sentential forms, all partial handles must contain an image of that vertex. We will prove this property in corollary 3.1.5.

In this analysis we use the following definition of unique vertex labels.

Definition 3.1.1 $uv(g)$, $uv(gg)$, UNIQUE VERTEX LABELS

a) Let g be a graph. The set of *unique vertex labels of g* is defined as

$$uv(g) = \{ ul \in l(V) |\text{ there is exactly one } v \in V \text{ such that } l(v) = ul \} .$$

b) Let $gg = (\Sigma_V, \Sigma_E, g_0, R)$ be a graph rewriting system. The set of *unique vertex labels of gg* is defined as: $uv(gg) = \bigcap_{g \in L(gg)} uv(g)$. ∎

The second definition is not constructive since it is given in terms of a graph language. If we want to determine $uv(gg)$, we may perform an abstract interpretation. It is based on the following observation: according to the definition, all sentential forms have one set of unique vertex labels in common. Thus these labels must occur in the initial graph too. For an approximation of the set of unique vertex labels of a graph rewriting system, we must consider the effect of any rewriting rule. The basic idea of the characterization is as follows: no rule must alter the set of unique vertex labels of a sentential form by deleting, introducing, or duplicating the occurrence of a unique label. Thus, we determine the set of so-called *invariant* labels of a rewriting rule. Each invariant label occurs exactly once on each side of the rule if it occurs at all. Thus the execution of a rewriting step has no effect on the unique labels of the host graph.

We define the set of invariant vertex labels of a rewriting rule. They occur only once on both sides of a rewriting rule.

Definition 3.1.2   *invar*, INVARIANT VERTEX LABELS OF A REWRITING RULE

Let $r = (g_l, g_r, M)$ be a rewriting rule. The set of *invariant vertex labels invar(r)* is defined as: $invar(r) = uv(g_l) \cap uv(g_r)$. ∎

We give an algorithm which performs an abstract interpretation of a graph rewriting system. It computes a lower approximation of the set of unique vertex labels of a graph rewriting system. It is based on the invariant labels of all rewriting rules and depends on the unique labels of the initial graph.

Algorithm 3.1.3   ABSTRACT INTERPRETATION OF UNIQUE VERTEX LABELS

Let $gg = (\Sigma_V, \Sigma_E, g_0, R)$ be a graph rewriting system.

INPUT: R

OUTPUT: $UV(gg)$

1.   **INITIALIZE** $UV(gg) := uv(g_0)$

2.   **FOR** $ul \in UV(gg)$ **DO**
           FOR $r \in R$ **DO**
               IF not $[ul \in l_r(V_l \cup V_r) \Rightarrow ul \in invar(r)]$
                   THEN $UV(gg) := UV(gg) \setminus \{ul\}$
               ENDIF
           END
       END

3.   **OUTPUT** $UV(gg)$ ∎

The abstract interpretation of the set of unique vertex labels takes polynomial time. It depends on the number of rules times the product of the number of vertices on both sides. Figure 13 gives an example of the algorithm. We have given a graph rewriting system with initial graph and three rewriting rules. The vertex labels are denoted by the shades of the vertices. In the initial graph, we find two candidates for a unique label, namely ■ and ■. All other labels occur at least twice. Now we inspect the set of rules for each label. From the right-hand side of the second rule, it follows that ■ is not an invariant label. Hence it cannot be unique for the rewriting system. A close look at all three rules reveals that ■ is invariant for all rules. Thus it is the only member of $UV(gg)$.

The example rewriting system representing a priority queue has a single unique vertex label. The initial graph contains only one vertex. Hence its label "queue" is the only candidate. Inspecting each rewriting rule shows that a "queue" vertex appears on both sides of each rule exactly once. Thus "queue" is an invariant vertex label and hence a unique label of the rewriting system.

We now prove the correctness of the interpretation.

Theorem 3.1.4   CORRECTNESS OF THE ABSTRACT INTERPRETATION

Let $gg = (\Sigma_V, \Sigma_E, g_0, R)$ be a graph rewriting system. The set $UV(gg)$ is a lower approximation of the set of unique vertex labels $uv(gg)$:

$$UV(gg) \subseteq uv(gg).$$

Proof. Let $ul \in UV(gg)$. Let $g \in L(gg)$ be a sentential form. We prove $ul \in uv(g)$ by induction over the length of the derivation of g.

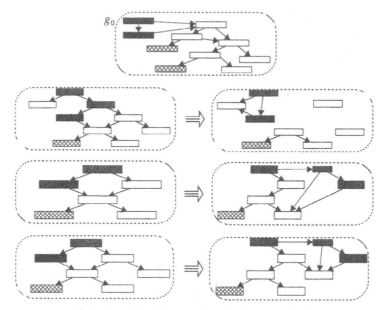

Figure 13   Abstract Interpretation of unique vertex labels

For the initial graph g_0 it holds by definitionthat $ul \in uv(g_0)$. Now let g' be derivable in n steps from g_0 and $ul \in uv(g')$. Let r be a rewriting rule with labelling function l_r and applicable to g'. Let g be a result graph. In case $ul \in l_r(V_l \cup V_r)$ it follows by construction of $UV(gg)$ that ul is an invariant label. Thus there exists a vertex v on the right-hand side with $l_r(v) = ul$ and $ul \in l(g)$. Since ul is an invariant label, it further follows that there is no other vertex $v' \in V_r$ with $v \neq v'$ and label ul. Hence, the rewriting step keeps the number of occurrences of ul invariant and $ul \in uv(g)$. In case $ul \notin l_r(V_l \cup V_r)$, the rewriting step does not affect that vertex of g labelled with ul, and does not introduce another vertex with label ul. Thus $ul \in uv(g)$ holds again. ■

The approximation is optimal if all rules are applicable to at least one sentential form. For that case, we can show that for all rules $r \in R$ with labelling function l_r and all $ul \in uv(gg)$, it holds that

$$ul \in l_r(V_l \cup V_r) \Rightarrow ul \in invar(r).$$

The proof proceeds as follows. Let r be a rewriting rule with $ul \in l_r(V_l \cup V_r)$. Let $g, g' \in L(gg)$ be two graphs with $g \rightarrow^r g'$. From the stated premises it follows that $ul \in uv(g) \cap uv(g')$. We first prove that $ul \in l_r(V_l)$. If we assume that $ul \notin l_r(V_l)$, then ul

$\in l_r(V_r)$, and graph g' has at least two vertices labelled by ul. This contradicts $ul \in uv(g')$. From $ul \in l_r(V_l)$ it follows that r must be applied to a subgraph of g containing a vertex labelled by ul. Since $ul \in uv(g')$, there must also be a vertex on the right-hand side labelled with ul. Furthermore there must not exist any other vertex in the left- or right-hand side of the rule labelled with ul. Thus $ul \in invar(r)$.

For the general case, it is undecidable whether a rule is applicable at all. Thus we cannot assume that all rules are applicable. This assumption, however, was a major premise for the proof. As a consequence the approximation in general is not sharp.

The next corollary relates theorem 3.1.4 to the labelled subgraph matching. Each unique vertex label addresses exactly one vertex of any sentential form. We prove that these vertices may serve as unique initial handles for any morphism used in a rewriting step.

Corollary 3.1.5

Let $gg = (\Sigma_V, \Sigma_E, g_0, R)$ be a graph rewriting system. Let r be a rewriting rule. Define the set of *unique vertex labels of* r as:

$$UV(r) = UV(gg) \cap invar(r).$$

a) Let $g \in L(gg)$ be a graph. The restriction of its labelling function l to the set of unique labelled vertices $l_{ul} = l|_{uv(gg)}$ is bijective:

$$l_{ul} \circ l_{ul}^{-1}(ul) = ul \text{ for all } ul \in uv(gg).$$

b) Let $r \in R$ be a rewriting rule with $UV(r) \neq \varnothing$ and labelling function l_r. Let $v \in V_l \cup V_r$ be a vertex with a unique label, i.e. $l_r(v) \in UV(r)$. Let $g \in L(gg)$ be a graph to which r is applicable. For all monomorphisms $\hat{h}: g_l \to g$ there is one and only one vertex $w \in V$ with $h(v) = w$.

Proof.

a) Let $g \in L(gg)$ be a graph. Let $v_1, v_2 \in \{v \in V | l(v) \in uv(gg)\}$ be two uniquely labelled vertices with $ul = l(v_1) = l(v_2) \in uv(gg)$. Definition 3.1.1 states that for all $ul \in uv(gg)$ there exists exactly one vertex $v \in V$ with $l(v) = ul$. Thus $v_1 = v_2$ and the proposition follows.

b) Let $r \in R$ be a rewriting rule with $UV(r) \neq \varnothing$ and labelling function l_r. Let $v \in V_l \cup V_r$ be a vertex with $l_r(v) = ul \in UV(r)$. Since $UV(r) \subseteq UV(gg)$ follows for all $g \in L(gg)$, the existence of exactly one $w \in V$ with $l(w) = ul$. Choose a graph $g \in L(gg)$ such that r is applicable to g. Thus there is a monomorphism $\hat{h}: g_l \to g$. All graph morphisms are label-preserving. Hence, $l(h(v)) = l_r(v) = ul \in UV(gg)$. With theorem 3.1.4, it follows from **a)** that $h(v) = w$. ∎

In the implementation of a graph rewriting system, we can exploit the knowledge of unique vertex labels by applying corollary 3.1.5. It states that the labelling function is bijective for all vertices of a sentential form which are uniquely labelled. Thus we can use the inverse function restricted to $UV(gg)$ to point to those vertices in the graph which are uniquely labelled. The set of all such vertices forms a unique base for all morphisms in the application of any rewriting rule. They can be stored explicitly in the abstract machine. Thus, as a consequence of part **b)**, the initialization step of the machine is improved. If the root vertex of a connected enumeration has a unique label, the initial handle can be directly determined form the base of uniquely labelled vertices of the host graph. Hence the initialization step must not scan the whole host graph.

The analysis is also valid for rewriting rules with more than one connected component. We check the labelled subgraph matching for each component individually. If there is a morphism for each component which does not overlap with some other, the rule is applicable. Thus in case there is at least one uniquely labelled vertex per component, the matching algorithm has an initial handle for each component. By this means, we can define rewriting rules which relate subgraphs far away from each other.

3.1.2 Unique Edge Labels

Similar to unique vertex labels, we can determine the existence of unique edge labels. The result of this analysis can merely be applied to the algorithm for labelled subgraph matching. It moreover gives another insight into the properties of the graphs being generated by a rewriting system. We will use the approximation derived here to sharpen the analysis of strong V-structures which is performed in section 3.3.

The definitions and propositions for unique edge labels are basically the same as for vertex labels. Due to the fact that an embedding description may alter an edge label during a rewriting step, we have to consider embedding descriptions too.

Unique edge labels of a graph and a rewriting system are defined similar to definition 3.1.1.

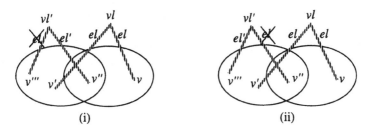

Figure 14   Edge labels invariant to a set of embedding descriptions

Definition 3.1.6 $ue(g)$, $ue(gg)$, UNIQUE EDGE LABELS

a) The set of *unique edge labels of a graph g* is defined as

$$ue(g) = \{ul \in \Sigma_E \mid \exists! s, \exists! t \in V \text{ such that } (s, ul, t) \in E\}.$$

b) The set of *unique edge labels of a graph rewriting system gg* is defined as:

$$ue(gg) = \bigcap_{g \in L(gg)} ue(g).$$ ∎

We approximate $ue(gg)$ by defining the set of *invariant edge labels* of a rewriting rule. In this definition, the invariance of the embedding descriptions of a rule must be taken into account. Whenever an edge of a host graph fits into a cut-description, it is deleted in the respective rewriting step. Thus as long as there is no edge with the same label inserted by the corresponding paste-description, the number of occurrences of the edge label changes. Hence for an invariant edge label, it must first of all hold that whenever it appears in a cut-description, it must be present in the corresponding paste-description as well. Furthermore all other embedding descriptions must respect the invariance. Thus there must be no other description either deleting (case (i)) or inserting (case (ii)) an edge with label *el*. Figure 14 exemplifies these conditions. The embedding description which may contain an invariant edge label is depicted to the right. For any other embedding description, either the cut- or the paste-description contains no edge label *el*. If either restriction is violated, the label *el*, which was unique in the host graph, may not be unique in the result graph.

Definition 3.1.7   *invel*, INVARIANT EDGE LABELS

a) The set of edge labels *invariant* to a set of *embedding descriptions M* is given by

$invel(M) = \{el \mid \exists (c, p) \in M \text{ with } c = (v', el, vl, d'), p = (v, el, d) \text{ and there is no}$
$(c', p') \in M \text{ with (i)} \quad c' = (v''', el, vl', d'''), p' = (v'', el', d'')$
$\text{or (ii)} \quad c' = (v''', el', vl', d'''), p' = (v'', el, d'') \}$

b) The set of *invariant edge labels of a rewriting rule r* is

$$invel(r) = \{ el \in [ue(g_l) \cap ue(g_r)] \cup invel(M)|$$

$$el \in \bigcup_{m \in M} elab(m) \Rightarrow el \in invel(M)$$

$$\text{and} \quad el \in elab(g_l) \cup elab(g_r) \Rightarrow el \in ue(g_l) \cap ue(g_r) \} .$$

where the function *elab* returns the set of edge labels of an embedding description or a graph respectively. ∎

Lemma 3.1.8

Let r be a rewriting rule. Let g be a graph such that r is applicable to g. Let g' be a result graph, i.e. $g \rightarrow^r g'$. For the invariant edge labels of r it holds:

$$ue(g) \cap invel(r) \subseteq ue(g').$$

Proof. Let $\hat{h}$ be a graph morphism such that $g \rightarrow^r_h g'$. Let $ul \in ue(g) \cap invel(r)$. Thus there is a single edge $(s, ul, t) \in E$ and $ul \in [ue(g_l) \cap ue(g_r)] \cup invel(M)$.

In case $ul \in ue(g_l) \cap ue(g_r)$, there must be an edge $(s', ul, t') \in E_l$ and s' and t' are mapped to s and t respectively. If the edge (s, ul, t) is in the context, it is deleted in the rewriting step. Since $ul \in ue(g_r)$, there is another single edge (s'', ul, t'') inserted. We must now prove that no other edge with label ul is inserted in the rewriting step. Assume that $(a, ul, b) \in h(E_r) \cup Emb_{ins} \backslash \{ (s'', ul, t'') \}$. If $(a, ul, b) \in h(E_r)$, there must be a second edge in E_r labelled by ul in contradiction to $ul \in ue(g_r)$. If $(a, ul, b) \in Emb_{ins}$, there must be a paste-description with label ul. Hence $ul \in elab(M)$. By the definition of $invel(r)$, it follows that $ul \in invel(M)$. Thus the corresponding cut-description c contains ul too. Since $ul \in ue(g_l)$, it follows that c cannot fit to an edge of g. Thus $(a, ul, b) \notin Emb_{ins}$. Hence $ul \in ue(g')$.

In case $ul \in invel(M)$, let $(c, p) \in M$ be an embedding description with $c = (v', ul, vl, d')$ and $p = (v, ul, d)$. If c fits to the edge $(s, ul, t) \in E$ under the morphism h, then this edge is the only one to which c fits. Thus p inserts only one edge with label ul. Let (s'', ul, t'') be that edge.

Again, we must show that no other edge with label ul is inserted during the rewriting step. Assume that there is an edge $(a, ul, b) \in h(E_r) \cup Emb_{ins} \backslash \{ (s'', ul, t'') \}$.

If $(a, ul, b) \in h(E_r)$, it follows that $ul \in ue(g_l)$ according to the definition of $invel(r)$. Thus there must be a further edge with label ul in g and $ul \notin ue(g)$. If $(a, ul, b) \in Emb_{ins}$ there must exist an embedding description $(c', p') \neq (c, p)$ such that p' has ul as the edge label. By definition of $invel(M)$ it follows that c' must have the edge label ul too. Since c' fits to an edge of g different to (s, ul, t), it follows that $ul \notin ue(g)$.

Hence $ul \in ue(g')$. ∎

Again, we give an abstract interpretation of a graph rewriting system. It approximates the set of unique edge labels of a graph rewriting system.

Algorithm 3.1.9   ABSTRACT INTERPRETATION OF UNIQUE EDGE LABELS

Let $gg = (\Sigma_V, \Sigma_E, g_0, R)$ be a graph rewriting system.
INPUT: R
OUTPUT: $UE(gg)$

    1.   **INITIALIZE** $UE(gg) := ue(g_0)$

    2.   **FOR** $ul \in UE(gg)$ **DO**
            FOR $r \in R$ **DO**
                   IF not $ul \in [ue(g_l) \cap ue(g_r)] \cup elab(M) \Rightarrow ul \in invar(r) \}$
                       THEN $UE(gg) := UE(gg) \setminus \{ul\}$
                 ENDIF
            END
        END

    3.   **OUTPUT** $UE(gg)$ ■

Theorem 3.1.10   CORRECTNESS OF THE ABSTRACT INTERPRETATION

Let gg be a graph rewriting system. The set $UE(gg)$ is a *lower approximation* of the set of unique edge labels $ue(gg)$:

$$UE(gg) \subseteq ue(gg) .$$

Proof. Let $ul \in UE(gg)$. Let g be a sentential form of gg. We prove $ul \in ue(g)$ by induction over the length of the derivation of g. For $n = 0$ it follows that $g = g_0$ and $ul \in ue(g)$. Now let g be a graph derivable in n steps from g_0. As a hypothesis, assume $ul \in ue(g)$. Thus there is an edge $e = (s, ul, t) \in E$. Let r be a rewrite rule applicable to g and let g' be a result graph, i.e. $g \to^r g'$. In case the unique edge label ul occurs on any side or any embedding description of r it follows by definition of $UE(gg)$ that $ul \in invel(r)$, and with lemma 3.1.8 that $ul \in ue(g')$. In the other case, the rewrite step cannot delete or introduce an edge labelled with ul. Thus the edge e is also in E' and $ul \in ue(g')$.   ■

3.2 Label Triples — Detecting Dead Rules and Saving Memory

In the last section we considered unique labels. Unique vertex labels form a constituent part of any full handle for rewriting. Thus they should be chosen as an initial handle in any test for the applicability of a rewriting rule. In this section, we direct our attention to an extended set of labels. We consider labels assigned to the constituent components of an edge, i.e. we study possible combinations of the label of an edge with the labels of its endpoints. We call this structure a *label triple*.

The abstract interpretation presented in this section computes an upper approximation of the set of label triples of a graph rewriting system. Hence we know which label triples are definitely not generated. This information is valuable for

- the determination of dead rules and superfluous embedding descriptions and
- a reduction of the memory allocation in an implementation of the abstract machine for labelled subgraph matching.

Dead rules and embedding descriptions are never applicable to a derivable graph or an embedding edge respectively. They are included in a graph rewriting system mostly by a mistake such as a typing error. In this way labels, are accidentally introduced in a specification. If such a label occurs in a left-hand side, this error can be detected by our analysis. If no other rule inserts this label into a graph, then the faulty rule is never applicable because it requires the wrong label. Thus it is a *dead rule*. If a faulty label occurs on the right-hand side of a rule, the dead rule analysis does not help directly; but the manual inspection of the upper approximation reveals that the rewriting system may derive a graph containing the unintended label. Based on the information on dead rules and superfluous embedding descriptions, we can reduce a given graph rewriting system.

The second application of the label triple analysis concerns the space requirements of the abstract machine. Up to now, each frame provides a slot for each possible combination of labels and edge directions. Based on the upper approximation of label triples we can safely refine the allocation scheme. Each label triple which is not in the approximating set does not appear in any host graph. Hence the internal data structure does not need to provide a slot.

3.2.1 Definition and Properties of Label Triples

The basic structure of the abstract analysis is a label triple. Its components are the label of a given edge and the labels of its endpoints. The direction of the edge is significant.

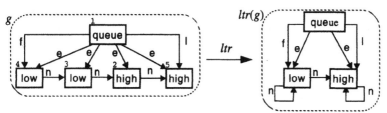

Figure 15   Label triples of the priority queue

Definition 3.2.1   *LTR*, *ltr(g)*, *ltr(gg)*, LABEL TRIPLES

a) The set $LTR = \wp(\Sigma_V \times \Sigma_E \times \Sigma_V)$ is the *domain of label triples*.

b) The set of *label triples of a graph g* is

$$ltr(g) = \{ (l(s), el, l(t)) \mid (s, el, t) \in E \} .$$

c) The set of *label triples of a graph rewriting system gg* is

$$ltr(gg) = \bigcup\nolimits_{g \in L(gg)} ltr(g).$$ ∎

The label triple view of a graph abstracts a graph to the set of "neighboured" labels. Figure 15 shows the label triples of an instance of a priority queue. The graph *ltr(g)* lists all label triples occurring in *g*. A vertex with label "low" can be incident to edges of four different types. Edges with label "f" or "e" must be incoming, whereas a "low" vertex can be source and target of a "n"-edge. From the abstraction follows also that "f"- and "n"-edges must be rooted in a "queue" vertex.

The abstraction function corresponding to the applicability of a rewriting rule is defined as follows. Later on it will serve in the computation of the upper approximation.

Definition 3.2.2   *ltr*-APPLICABILITY

The rewriting rule *r* is *ltr-applicable* to a set of label triples $lt \in LTR$ iff $ltr(g_l) \subseteq lt$. ∎

Lemma 3.2.3   APPLICABILITY IMPLIES *ltr*-APPLICABILITY

If a rewriting rule *r* is applicable to a graph *g*, then *r* is *ltr*-applicable to *ltr(g)*.

Proof. Let *g* be a graph and *r* be a rewriting rule applicable to *g*. Thus there is a graph isomorphism $\hat{h}$ with $\hat{h}(g_l) \subseteq g$. The fact $ltr(\hat{h}(g_l)) \subseteq ltr(g)$ completes the proof.   ∎

Hence *ltr*-applicability is consistent with the notion of ordinary applicability. Whenever a rule is applicable to a graph *g*, *ltr*(*g*) must contain all label triples of the left-hand side. Obviously, although the label triples requested for *ltr*-applicability are present, the rule may not be applicable to *g* in terms of ordinary rewriting. When we apply lemma 3.2.3 to all sentential forms of a graph rewriting system, we can infer whether a rewriting rule is dead, i.e. never applicable.

Corollary 3.2.4   DEAD RULE

Let $gg = (\Sigma_V, \Sigma_E, g_0, R)$ be a graph rewriting system. Let *r* be a rewriting rule. The following proposition holds: If $ltr(g_l)$ is no subset of $ltr(gg)$ then *r* is not applicable to any derivable graph $g \in L(gg)$.

Contrapositive proof. Let $ltr(g_l)$ be no subset of $ltr(gg)$. There is a label triple $lt \notin ltr(g)$ for all $g \in L(gg)$. From lemma 3.2.3 the proposition follows.   ■

3.2.2   Approximation of the Set of Label Triples

To apply the given properties of label triples, we must develop an abstract interpretation over the domain of label triples. We therefore record the effect of every rewriting rule on the label triples of a sentential form. The effect of an ordinary rewriting step in terms of label triples is twofold. First, there are label triples introduced by insertion of the right-hand side of the rule. Second, as a consequence of the evaluation of embedding descriptions, embedding edges are inserted and may introduce further label triples. In general there are edges deleted. Since, though, we are interested in an upper approximation, we do not remove the corresponding label triples. Thus abstract rewriting is monotone increasing.

How does a rewriting step contribute to the set of label triples by introduction of embedding edges? The label triples of inserted embedding edges can statically be determined by inspection of the corresponding paste-descriptions. However, note that the insertion of embedding edges in an ordinary rewriting step is conditional. It depends on the existence of an edge on which the cut-description fits (see definition 2.3.2). The definition of the *ltr*-evaluation must reflect this behaviour.

Definition 3.2.5   *ltr-fits*, *ltr*-EVALUATION

Let V and W be two vertex sets and l_V, l_W be labelling functions with $l_V\colon V \to \Sigma_V$ and $l_W\colon W \to \Sigma_V$

a) The boolean function *ltr-fits*$_{l_v}$ determines the *ltr-fit of a cut-description* $c = (v, el, vl, d) \in C(V)$ to a label triple *lt*. It is defined as follows for $d = $ out: $ltr\text{-}fits_{l_v}(c, lt) = [lt = (l_V(v), el, vl)]$ and for $d = $ in: $ltr\text{-}fits_{l_v}(c, lt) = [lt = (vl, el, l_V(v))]$.

b) Let *ltr* $\in$ *LTR* be a set of label triples. The *ltr-evaluation* of an embedding description $m = (c, p) \in C(V) \times P(W)$ with $p = (v, el, d)$ applied to *ltr* is defined

$$ltr\text{-}eval_{l_w}(m, ltr) = \{ (vl, el, l_w(v)) \mid \exists lt \in ltr \text{ with } ltr\text{-}fits_{l_v}(c, lt)\} , \text{ if } d = \text{out}$$

$$ltr\text{-}eval_{l_w}(m, ltr) = \{ (l_w(v), el, vl) \mid \exists lt \in ltr \text{ with } ltr\text{-}fits_{l_v}(c, lt)\} , \text{ if } d = \text{in}.$$

The graphical notation is $lt' \leadsto^m lt$ and $ltr \leadsto^m ltr\text{-}eval_{l_w}(m, ltr)$ respectively.   ■

The *ltr*-evaluation of an embedding description reflects the behaviour of an embedding description in ordinary rewriting. The following lemma states that whenever an embedding edge is inserted into a rewritten graph, a corresponding label triple is added to the actual set of label triples if not contained already. Since the fitting condition is relaxed in the *ltr*-embedding, the abstract embedding more likely inserts a label triple than an embedding edge during rewriting.

Lemma 3.2.6   THE EVALUATION OF EMBEDDING DESCRIPTION IMPLIES *ltr*-EVALUATION

Let g be a graph. Let r be a rewriting rule with labelling function l_r applicable to g. Let $\hat{h}$ be an injective graph morphism with $\hat{h}\colon g_l \to g$ and g' be the result of rewriting g by r under $\hat{h}$. Let $m = (c, p) \in M$ be an embedding description. For all edges $e = (s, el'', t) \in E$ it holds that $fits_{h,l}(c, e) \Rightarrow ltr\text{-}eval_{l_r}(m, \{l(s), el', l(t)\}) \subseteq ltr(g')$.

Proof. Let $c = (v', el', vl, d')$ and $p = (v, el, d)$ with wlog $d' = d = $ out. Let $e = (s, el'', t) \in E$ be an edge which satisfies $fits_{h,l}(c, e)$. Thus the label triple of e fits to c, i.e. $l(s) = l_r(v')$, $el' = el''$, and $l(t) = vl$. By definition of the rewriting step it follows that an edge $e' = (s', el, t) \in E'$ is inserted by evaluation of m. Hence $l(s') = l_r(v)$. It follows that $ltr\text{-}eval_{l_r}(m, \{l(s), el', l(t)\}) = \{ (l_r(v), el, vl) \} = ltr(e') \subseteq ltr(g')$.   ■

Next we define the abstract rewriting step.

Definition 3.2.7   *ltr*-REWRITING STEP

Let *ltr* be a set of label triples. Let *r* be a rewriting rule *ltr*-applicable to *ltr*.

The label triple set *ltr'* is the result of *ltr*-rewriting *ltr* with *r* iff

$$ltr' \;=\; ltr \cup ltr(g_r) \cup \bigcup_{m \in M} ltr\text{-}eval_i(m, ltr).$$

An *ltr*-rewriting step is denoted by $ltr \leadsto^r ltr'$.   ∎

Note that *ltr*-rewriting increases the size of the rewritten set of label triples. A more straightforward definition could be given by taking neither applicability of a rule nor the fit of an embedding description into account. In this case, the analysis would be done only on the right-hand side and the paste-descriptions of the rule. The result would be the union over all label triples of the right-hand sides and all label triples of eventually inserted edges. We do not only concentrate our analysis on the inserted parts of a rewriting rule but also study the left-hand side.

The definition of the *ltr*-rewriting step completes the calculus of abstract interpretation. Now we can perform *abstract derivations* to determine the set of label triples of an arbitrary sentential form given an ordinary derivation. Still we do not know anything about *ltr(gg)*, the set of label triples of all sentential forms. We will give a linear time algorithm that computes an upper approximation of *ltr(gg)*. To show the correctness of this algorithm, we prove that the *ltr*-abstraction of a graph rewriting system is confluent.

To prepare the proof, we show the following for any two rewriting rules, which are *ltr*-applicable to a set of label triples *ltr*: The result of an *ltr*-derivation which alternately applies both rules is independent of the choice of the initial rule. In the lemma, we inspect two rules r_1, r_2 and derivations in a 1,2- and a 2,1-order. A 1,2-derivation initially applies rule r_1 to a given set of label triples and afterwards r_2 and so on. In the 1,2-order derivation, the label triple sets ltr_{21}^i and ltr_{212}^i are the intermediate derivation results. In the 2,1-order they are ltr_{12}^i and ltr_{121}^i. We show that the 1,2-derivation has the set ltr_{12}^n as its fixpoint. Furthermore we show that a 2,1-derivation requires at most $n + 1$ iterations to find the fixpoint $ltr_{12}^n \subseteq ltr_{21}^{n+1}$.

Lemma 3.2.8   REORDERING OF *ltr*-DERIVATIONS

Let $ltr \in LTR$ be a label triple set. Let $r_j = (g_{l,j}, g_{r,j}, M_j)$ with $j = 1, 2$ be two rewriting rules both *ltr*-applicable to *ltr*. Let l_j be the corresponding labelling function. Let $ltr_{21}^i, ltr_{212}^i, ltr_{12}^i, ltr_{121}^i \in LTR$ for $i \geq 0$ be label triple sets such that $ltr_{21}^0 = ltr_{12}^0 = ltr$ and there exist alternating derivations $ltr_{21}^i \leadsto^{r_2} ltr_{212}^i \leadsto^{r_1} ltr_{21}^{i+1}$ and

$ltr_{12}^i \leadsto^{r_1} ltr_{121}^i \leadsto^{r_2} ltr_{12}^{i+1}$.

The 1,2-order derivation has the fixpoint ltr_{12}^n with $ltr_{12}^n \subseteq ltr_{21}^{n+1}$.

Proof. Note that $ltr^i_{12} \subseteq LTR$, $i \geq 0$. Since LTR is finite and ltr-rewriting increases the size of the rewritten set of label triples, there is a minimal number n for which rewriting ltr^n_{12} by r_1 and r_2 is stable, i.e. $ltr^n_{12} = ltr^{n+1}_{12}$.

Now we have to show that $ltr^n_{12} \subseteq ltr^{n+1}_{21}$ and to complete the proof. We prove this inclusion by induction over i.

Base step: $i = 0$: let $lt \in ltr^0_{12}$. Since $ltr^0_{12} = ltr^0_{21}$ and ltr-rewriting is monotone follows $lt \in ltr^1_{21}$.

The induction hypothesis assumes $ltr^{i-1}_{12} \subseteq ltr^i_{21}$: We have to prove that any $lt \in ltr^i_{12}$ is an element of ltr^{i+1}_{21}. By definition it holds that

$$ltr^i_{12} = ltr^{i-1}_{121} \cup \bigcup_{m \in M_2} ltr\text{-}eval_{l_2}(m, ltr^{i-1}_{121}) \text{ with}$$

$$ltr^{i-1}_{121} = ltr^{i-1}_{12} \cup \bigcup_{m \in M_1} ltr\text{-}eval_{l_1}(m, ltr^{i-1}_{12}).$$

Choose a label triple $lt \in ltr^i_{12}$. In case that $lt \in ltr^{i-1}_{12}$ it follows by the hypothesis that $lt \in ltr^i_{21} \subseteq ltr^{i+1}_{21}$. In case that $lt \in ltr^{i-1}_{121} \backslash ltr^{i-1}_{12}$ there exists a label triple $lt' \in ltr^{i-1}_{12}$ and an embedding description $m \in M_1$ such that $lt' \sim>^m lt$. By hypothesis $lt' \in ltr^i_{21} \subseteq ltr^i_{212}$, and m ltr-fits on an element of ltr^i_{212}. Thus $ltr^i_{212} \sim>^m (ltr^i_{212} \cup lt) \subseteq ltr^{i+1}_{21}$.

In case that $lt \in ltr^i_{12} \backslash ltr^{i-1}_{121}$ it follows that $lt \in \bigcup_{m \in M_2} ltr\text{-}eval_{l_2}(m, ltr^{i-1}_{121})$. Thus there is an embedding description $m \in M_2$ and a label triple $lt' \in ltr^{i-1}_{121}$ such that $lt' \sim>^m lt$.

Now we have to determine the origin of the label triple lt' in a 2,1-order derivation. If $lt' \in ltr^{i-1}_{12}$ it follows from the induction hypothesis that $lt' \in ltr^i_{21}$. Furthermore ltr-application of r_2 to ltr^i_{21} results in ltr^i_{212} which therefore contains lt. With $ltr^i_{212} \subseteq ltr^{i+1}_{21}$ it follows that $lt \in ltr^{i+1}_{21}$. If otherwise $lt' \notin ltr^{i-1}_{12}$ must lt' result from an ltr-embedding. Thus there is an embedding description $m' \in M_1$ and a label triple $lt'' \in ltr^{i-1}_{12}$, such that $lt'' \sim>^{m'} lt'$.

Now the proof of $lt \in ltr^{i+1}_{21}$ is reduced to the proof that the label triple lt'' is an element of ltr^i_{21}. Thus we have to trace back the history of ltr-embedding evaluations which produce lt. When we have reconstructed this sequence for 1,2-derivations we need to shift the sequence by at most one derivation step such that the rules are applicable in a 2,1-derivation. Since the last label triple introduced by the 1,2-order derivation is lt, the shift causes $lt \in ltr^{i+1}_{21}$, i.e. lt is also generated by a 2,1-order derivation.

Now we go into the details. Let m_{id} be an embedding description with no effect on any label triple, i.e. for all label triple sets ltr, $ltr \sim>^{m_{id}} ltr$. Let $m^k_j \in M_j \cup \{m_{id}\}$ for $j =$

1,2 and $k = 1...i$ be those embedding descriptions which form a sequence (m_1^k, m_2^k), $k = 1...i$ causing lt''. Note that $m_1^i = m'$ and $m_2^i = m$.

Let $lt_0 \in ltr \cup ltr(g_{r,1}) \cup ltr(g_{r,2})$ be that label triple which initiated the derivation of lt'' under (m_1^k, m_2^k), $k = 1...i$. In case $lt_0 \in ltr \cup ltr(g_{r,1})$ consider the modified sequence $m_{id}, m_1^1, (m_2^k, m_1^{k+1}), m_2^i, m_{id}$ for $k = 1...i - 1$ of length $2(i + 1)$. This sequence derives lt'' from lt_0 in a 2,1-order. Thus $lt \in ltr_{21}^{i+1}$. In case $lt_0 \in ltr(g_{r,2}) \setminus ltr \cup ltr(g_{r,1})$ it follows that $m_1^1 = m_{id}$. Now consider the sequence $m_2^1, m_1^2, (m_2^k, m_1^{k+1})$, m_2^i, m_{id} for $k = 1...i - 1$ of length $2i$. Again, this sequence derives lt'' from $lt_0 \in ltr(g_{r,2})$ in a 2,1-order. Thus $lt \in ltr_{21}^i \subseteq ltr_{21}^{i+1}$, even in the case that $lt' \notin ltr_{12}^{i-1}$.

Now the induction hypothesis is proven for all cases and the proposition follows. ∎

From the lemma follows that abstract ltr-rewriting is confluent. Hence an arbitrary order of abstract rewriting steps leads to the same result.

Corollary 3.2.9 ltr-REWRITING IS CONFLUENT

Let ltr be a set of label triples. Let r_1, r_2 be two rewriting rules both ltr-applicable to ltr. There exists a label triple ltr' and ltr-derivations such that

$$ltr \sim>^{r_1} ltr_1 \sim>^* ltr' \text{ and } ltr \sim>^{r_2} ltr_2 \sim>^* ltr'.$$

Proof. By lemma 3.2.8 it follows that there exist two numbers n, m and label sets $ltr_{12}^n, ltr_{21}^{n+1}$, ltr_{21}^m and ltr_{12}^{m+1} being derived from ltr such that $ltr_{12}^n \subseteq ltr_{21}^{n+1}$ and $ltr_{21}^m \subseteq ltr_{12}^{m+1}$. The sets ltr_{12}^n, ltr_{21}^m are fixpoints of the ltr-derivation. Without loss of generality assume $n \leq m$. Thus $ltr_{21}^{m+1} = ltr_{21}^m \subseteq ltr_{12}^{m+1} = ltr_{12}^n \subseteq ltr_{21}^{n+1}$. From $ltr' = ltr_{21}^{n+1} = ltr_{12}^n$ the proposition follows. ∎

The major consequence of this corollary is that, given an ltr-rewriting system and an initial set of label triples, there is an ltr-unique normal form. It is a set of label triples which can be produced by repeating the ltr-application of rewriting rules in an arbitrary order. In this case no further rule contributes to the set when it is rewritten. We use this property in the following algorithm which applies the abstract interpretation to calculate an approximation of $ltr(gg)$.

Algorithm 3.2.10   ABSTRACT INTERPRETATION OF $ltr(gg)$

Let $gg = (\Sigma_V, \Sigma_E, g_0, R)$ be a graph rewriting system.
INPUT: g_0, R.
OUTPUT: $LTR(gg)$, a set of label triples.

1.   **SET** $LTR(gg) := ltr(g_0)$

2.   **INITIALIZE** the set of potential embedding descriptions: $PM := \varnothing$

3.   **REPEAT**
           $LTR(gg)$ is stable := True
           FOR ALL $r = (g_l, g_r, M) \in R$ ltr-applicable to $LTR(gg)$ **DO**
                 $LTR(gg) := LTR(gg) \cup ltr(g_r)$
                 $PM := PM \cup M$
                 $R := R \setminus \{r\}$
                 $LTR(gg)$ is stable := False
           FOR ALL $(c, p) = m \in PM$ such that there is a $lt \in LTR(gg)$
                                    satisfying $ltr\text{-}fits(c, lt)$ **DO**
                 $LTR(gg) := LTR(gg) \cup ltr\text{-}eval(m, LTR(gg))$
                 $PM := PM \setminus \{m\}$
                 $LTR(gg)$ is stable := False
        UNTIL $LTR(gg)$ is stable

4.   **OUTPUT** $LTR(gg)$ ■

The approximation of $ltr(gg)$ selects a specific ltr-derivation. It is given by the ltr-applicability of rules selected in the first **FOR**-loop and the ltr-fit of embedding descriptions selected in the second.

   Multiple applications of a rewriting rule are taken into account as follows: Only the first ordinary application of r adds the label triples of g_r. Any further application of r can alter the set of label triples only by the evaluation of embedding descriptions. Thus, the rewriting rule r can be excluded from R after its first application, as long as its embedding descriptions are collected in PM. The same argument of a single contribution holds for the ltr-evaluation of an embedding description. An embedding description cannot contribute to $LTR(gg)$ a second time. Thus it can be removed from PM.

   The algorithm needs linear time bounded by the number of rules plus the number of all embedding descriptions. Termination is guaranteed. Either $LTR(gg)$ is stable or the algorithm enters at least one for-loop. In this case at least one $r \in R$ or $m \in PM$ is removed from the set. Thus the number of elements decreases while looping. Since there is only a finite number of embedding descriptions added to PM, the termination property is not affected.

Next, we show that this algorithm correctly computes an upper approximation of $ltr(gg)$.

Theorem 3.2.11   CORRECTNESS OF ALGORITHM 3.2.10

Let $gg = (\Sigma_V, \Sigma_E, g_0, R)$ be a graph rewriting system. Let $LTR(gg)$ be the output of algorithm 3.2.10 with input g_0 and R. The following property holds:

$$ltr(gg) \subseteq LTR(gg).$$

Proof. Since ltr-rewriting is confluent, the algorithm computes the ltr-normal form of the initial graph. Lemma 3.2.3 states that an ltr-rewriting step is performed more likely than an ordinary one. With definition 3.2.7 follows that the ltr-application of a rewriting rule approximates the set of label triples of the result graph. Thus ltr-derivation is an upper approximation of the label triples of any derivable graphs. For any sentential form g the inclusion $ltr(g) \subseteq LTR(gg)$ holds, and the proposition follows. ■

Based on the relation stated in theorem 3.2.11, we can give a definition of a reduced graph rewriting system. Corollary 3.2.4, which we proved earlier in this section, provides only a theoretical property because the finite enumeration of a language is impossible, in general. By means of the upper approximation computed in algorithm 3.1.9 we have an effective decision procedure for dead rules. We exploit the abstract interpretation in the definition of a reduced graph rewriting system.

Definition 3.2.12   REDUCED GRAPH REWRITING SYSTEM

Let gg be a graph rewriting system. Let $LTR(gg)$ be the set of label triples computed by algorithm 3.1.9 with input g_0 and R. The reduced set of embedding descriptions M is $red(M) = \{ (c, p) \in M \mid \neg \exists lt \in LTR(gg)$ such that $ltr\text{-}fits(c, lt)\}$.
We can define for any rewriting rule $r \in R$ the *reduced rewriting rule* $red(r)$ by

$$red((g_l, g_r, M)) = (g_l, g_r, M \setminus red(M)).$$

Furthermore we define the *reduced rule set* as

$$red(R) = \{red(r) \mid r \in R \text{ is } ltr\text{-applicable to } LTR(gg)\}.$$

Finally we define the *reduced graph rewriting system* as

$$red(gg) = (\Sigma_V, \Sigma_E, g_0, red(R)).$$ ■

Theorem 3.2.13   EQUALITY OF THE REDUCED GRAPH REWRITING SYSTEM

Let gg be a graph rewriting system. The following equality holds:

$$L(gg) = L(red(gg)).$$

Proof. Let $g \in L(gg)$ be a sentential form. Hence there is a sequence of rewriting rules (r_i), $i = 0...(n-1)$ and a sequence of sentential forms (g_i), $i = 0...n$ such that r_i is applicable to g_i and $g_n = g$. With lemma 3.2.6 it follows that all embedding descriptions which fit to an edge also fit to the corresponding label triple. Thus g can be derived by the sequence of reduced rewriting rules $(red(r_i))$, $i = 1...n$. Since all $red(r_i)$ are still applicable to the sentential form g_i it follows by definition that $red(r_i) \in red(R)$ and as a consequence $g \in L(red(gg))$.

The inclusion $L(red(gg)) \subseteq L(gg)$ is true because $red(R) \subseteq R$ and for all $r \in R$ holds $red(M) \subseteq M$. ∎

3.3 Strong V-Structures — The Branching Points

This section completes the development of a sufficient condition for constant-time execution of the labelled subgraph matching. In section 2.4 we exposed the reasons for the combinatorial explosion of the matching algorithm, and two main factors appeared. First there may be several initial handles for the root vertex; second the connected enumeration of the left-hand side may be such that there are alternative extensions of a partial handle. The algorithm branches and processes multiple partial handles at one expansion step. In this case the algorithm must match the next edge of a given enumeration several times. Those two properties make the computation time explode.

We have also observed that there are mostly different enumerations of a graph. The sufficient condition now motivates the selection of an appropriate enumeration, if it exists.

Figure 16 gives an example for a host graph for which a multiplying and a non-multiplying connected enumeration exist. The study of that graph provides a first impression of the problem. We have to perform the labelled subgraph matching for a left-hand side g_l and a host graph g. Assume that the algorithm has proceeded to the subgraph g'. Only edges incident with g' are candidates for the next extension step. At this stage we have two alternatives. We could test the existence of an edge labelled with "b" joining the image of vertex 2 with a vertex labelled by "C". The other alternative is a match for edge $(1, e, 3)$. The selection of the first alternative causes three extensions and thus three partial handles which have to be analysed further. Two of them cannot be completed, but this fact will not be observed before the next extension step. If we try to extend g' following the second alternative, we are lucky because we find a singular extension. Furthermore we can complete the handle in one additional step.

Obviously we do not want to rely on fortune when we select a connected enumeration for a given rule. Thus we look for a procedure to distinguish "good" from "bad" enumerations. The closer analysis of the example given in figure 16 provides a hint for this distinction. The graph g has a characteristic property leading to a multiplication of partial handles when extending the edge $(2, b, 3)$. The graph contains three edges on which the extension of g' is possible. These edges, all incident to vertex 12, extend the partial handle $\hat{h}(g')$. In graph theoretical terms, there exists a number of non-trivial automorphisms for these edges. Pairs of these edges form automorphic semipaths of length 2. Such a path consists of two isomorphic edges which are incident in one of their endpoints. Whenever a graph contains such an automorphism, the matching algorithm for a rewriting rule may take non-linear time.

The example also includes the key property for the solution of the "multiplication problem". We have seen that there is one enumeration initiated in vertex 1 which performs a non-multiplying search, although there are local automorphisms in g. When we choose enumeration $((1, e, 3), (2, b, 3), (1, a, 2))$ and initiate the labelled subgraph matching at vertex 1, we do not fall into the automorphism trap: we traverse the host graph g in a deterministic manner without multiplication of partial handles. Thus the important information for the selection of a non-multiplying connected enumeration is the non-trivial automorphisms on semipaths of length 2 in the host graph.

When we apply this conclusion to graph rewriting systems, we must infer information on any sentential form g. Only with the knowledge of the automorphisms of all sentential forms can we decide whether a connected enumeration controls the abstract machine such that it executes non-branching. Thus we have to analyse all graphs

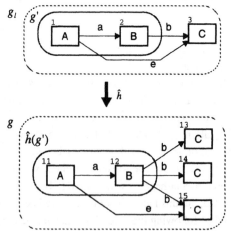

Figure 16 Graph causing multiplying and non-multiplying connected enumerations

generated by a given graph rewriting system. The major result of abstract interpretation will be an approximation for a set of automorphisms present in any sentential
form. We give a procedure which, based on this information, decides whether the
matching of a rewriting rule can be tested in constant time.

3.3.1 Strong V-Structures and Matching in Constant Time

We give an example for a general automorphic semipath of length 2 in the graph g of
figure 17. The center vertex x is connected to vertices y and automorphic semipath of
length z both with label vl_2. The incident pairs of edges have the same direction and
label. When the matching algorithm extends the current partial handle $\hat{h}(g_l)$ by vertex
1 it creates two full handles.

We characterize automorphic semipaths of length 2 by the labels of their components and define strong V-structures. Since the identification of vertices is of no
interest for any sentential form of a graph rewriting system, this characterization is
sufficient. We have chosen the adjective "strong" because the labels of the
automorphic non-center vertices will be significant also. We can perform a similar
analysis on so-called "weak" V-structures. They cover only labels and direction of the
edges and the label of the center vertex.

Let us now enter the technical part where we first give the main definitions.

Definition 3.3.1   *SVS, svs(g), svs(gg),* STRONG V-STRUCTURES, INSTANCE

a) The set of all *strong V-structures* over alphabets Σ_v, Σ_E is

$$SVS = \wp(\Sigma_V \times \Sigma_V \times \Sigma_E \times \{\text{in, out}\}).$$

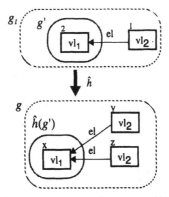

Figure 17   Extensions of a match in presence of an automorphic semipath of length 2

b) Let g be a graph. A pair of edges $(e, e') \in E^2$ is an *instance* of a strong V-structure $vs = (vl_1, vl_2, el, d)$ iff there are vertices $x, y, z \in V$, $y \neq z$ such that $l(x) = vl_1, l(y) = l(z) = vl_2$ and $e = (x, el, z)$, $e' = (x, el, y)$ if $d =$ out or $e = (z, el, x)$, $e' = (y, el, x)$ otherwise.

c) The set of *strong V-structures of a graph g* is given by

$$svs(g) = \{vs \in SVS| \exists (e, e') \in E^2 \text{ instance of } vs\} .$$

d) The set of *strong V-structures of a graph rewriting system gg* is

$$svs(gg) = \bigcup_{g \in L(gg)} svs(g). \qquad \blacksquare$$

The edges $((z, el, x), (y, el, x))$ of graph g in figure 17 form an instance of the strong V-structure (vl_1, vl_2, el, in). We give a characterization of instances and relate unique labels to strong V-structures.

Lemma 3.3.2   COMPONENT EDGES OF AN INSTANCE ARE INCIDENT AND ISOMORPHIC

Let g be a graph. For all pairs of edges $(e, e') \in E^2$ it holds that:

(e, e') is an *instance* of a strong V-structure $vs \Leftrightarrow e$ and e' are incident and isomorphic.

Proof. "$\Leftarrow$" Let $e = (s, el, t) \in E$ and $e' = (s', el', t') \in E$ be two edges incident and isomorphic. From the incidence it follows that one endpoint of e is identical to an endpoint of e'. Since the direction of the edges is fixed, either $s = s'$ or $t = t'$ follows. Wlog assume $s = s'$. From the isomorphism it follows further that $l(t) = l(t')$ and $el = el'$. Hence (e, e') is an instance of $(l(s), l(t), el, \text{out})$.

"$\Rightarrow$" follows by definition of instance. $\blacksquare$

Lemma 3.3.3   STRONG V-STRUCTURES AND UNIQUE LABELS

Let gg be a graph rewriting system and $vs = (vl_1, vl_2, el, d) \in svs(gg)$. The following properties hold for the labels: $vl_2 \notin uv(gg)$ and $el \notin ue(gg)$.

Proof. by inspection of corollary 3.1.5 and definition 3.1.1. $\blacksquare$

The strong V-structures of a graph are closely related to the data structure which was proposed for the abstract machine for the labelled subgraph matching. For each vertex of a graph g in the frame representation, and from the knowledge of $svs(g)$ it follows whether a slot has definitely at most one entry. For all instances (e, e') of a strong V-structure (vl_1, vl_2, el, d), it holds that e and e' are isomorphic with respect to their center vertex. Thus the slot of the center vertex determined by vl_2, el and d contains at least e and e', and thus it is a multiple entry slot. In the opposite case, when we know that g contains no strong V-structure (vl_1, vl_2, el, d), we can be sure that the slot vl_2, el, d for all vertices labelled by vl_1 has at most one entry. By means of the set of strong V-structures of a graph rewriting system, we are able to extend the knowledge of slots with at most a single entry to all derivable graphs.

Lemma 2.3.7 stated the number of extensions. Hence with the additional knowledge of the strong V-structures, we can decide in advance whether the labelled subgraph matching executes without branching. Furthermore we can check whether the algorithm takes time linear in the length of the enumeration. Therefore we relate connected enumerations to strong V-structures. A connected enumeration bypasses a set of strong V-structures when it controls the abstract machine in such way that all extensions and all checks can be performed on single entry slots. The definition of a bypassing connected enumeration is static in the sense that it does not refer to an execution of the labelled subgraph matching. We can, however, check for a given enumeration whether it bypasses a set of strong V-structures. We will later show that bypassing is a major condition for matching in constant time.

Definition 3.3.4   BYPASSING CONNECTED ENUMERATION

Let g be a graph and $q = |E|$. Let (e_i), $i = 1...q$ be a connected enumeration of E with root vertex v. Let $W_i = \bigcup_{j=1...i} inc_g(e_j)$ be the sets of vertices which are found by the prefix of length i for $i = 1...q$ and $W_0 = \{v\}$. Let svs be a set of strong V-structures. The *connected enumeration* (e_i), $i = 1...q$ bypasses svs iff for all $e_i = (s, el, t)$,

    in case $s \notin W_{i-1}$: $(l(t), l(s), el, in) \notin svs$,

    in case $t \notin W_{i-1}$: $(l(s), l(t), el, out) \notin svs$,

    in case $s, t \in W_{i-1}$:   either $(l(t), l(s), el, in) \notin svs$.

                    or $(l(s), l(t), el, out) \notin svs$ ■

Note that whenever a connected enumeration is bypassing a set of strong V-structures svs it bypasses any subset of svs.

The next lemma shows how bypassing connected enumerations influence the execution of the labelled subgraph matching.

Lemma 3.3.5   THE ABSTRACT MACHINE DOES NOT BRANCH FOR BYPASSING
                CONNECTED ENUMERATIONS

Let g and g' be two graphs and let (e_i) $i = 1...q$ be a connected enumeration of E' with root vertex $v \in V'$. If (e_i) $i = 1...q$ bypasses $svs(g)$, then the labelled subgraph matching executes without branching.

Proof. We adopt the terminology of algorithm 2.3.4. Let $i \in \{1, ..., q\}$ and $e_i = (s, el, t)$. Where $s, t \in W_{i-1}$, the matching algorithm does not branch by definition.

Otherwise wlog let $s \notin W_{i-1}$ and $\hat{h}', \hat{h}'' \in A_i$ be two extensions of $\hat{h}_i \in A_{i-1}$. Hence $\hat{h}_i = \hat{h}'|_{dom(h_i)} = \hat{h}''|_{dom(h_i)}$ and $h'(s), h''(s) \in V\backslash rg(h_i)$ with $h'(e_i), h''(e_i) \in E$. Since the connected enumeration bypasses $svs(g)$ it follows that $(l(t), l(s), el, in) \notin svs(g)$. Hence $h'(s) = h''(s)$ and therefore $\hat{h}' = \hat{h}''$. ∎

With lemma 3.3.5 we have solved the first half of the task necessary to perform the applicability test in time linear to the length of the enumeration. We give a *sufficient condition for the non-branching execution* of the labelled subgraph matching. The remaining question is how we can perform the existence checks in constant time. We have laid the foundations with the definition of bypassing connected enumerations. When we inspect the matching algorithm, however, we observe a small gap between the definition of bypassing and the algorithm in the case where both endpoints are found and an existence check is to be performed. The algorithm has no means to determine the endpoint on which the check is performed. So there is an unlucky possibility that the abstract machine inspects a multiple entry slot, although the corresponding slot of the other endpoint has at most one entry.

To avoid this situation we must augment the enumeration and slightly modify the check operation of the matching to enforce the selection of the appropriate endpoint. We know that for all edges $e_i = (s, el, t)$ of a bypassing enumeration with $s, t \in W_{i-1}$, either s or t has a single entry slot. Thus we *augment the connected enumeration* with that additional information. Consequently we must modify the matching algorithm to take that additional information into account. With these adaptations we can prove that the modified matching algorithm performs in constant time for an augmented bypassing enumeration rooted in a uniquely labelled vertex.

Theorem 3.3.6   CONSTANT-TIME MATCHING FOR GRAPH REWRITING SYSTEMS

Let $gg = (\Sigma_V, \Sigma_E, g_0, R)$ be a graph rewriting system.

If for all $r \in R$ there exists an augmented connected enumeration of E_l bypassing $svs(gg)$ and rooted in a uniquely labelled vertex v, then

   (i)   all applications of a rewriting rule to a sentential form $g \in L(gg)$ match in constant time and

   (ii)   there is at most one graph isomorphism $\hat{h}$ with $\hat{h}(g_l) \subseteq g$.

Proof. Let $g \in L(gg)$ and $r = (g_l, g_r, M) \in R$ with $p = |V_l|$. Let $(e_i), i = 1...q$ be a connected enumeration of E' bypassing $svs(gg)$ and rooted in a uniquely labelled vertex.

By definition of $svs(gg)$, it follows that (e_i), $i = 1...q$ bypasses $svs(g)$ too. Thus from lemma 2.3.7, it follows that the matching algorithm executes without branching. This property also holds for the modified algorithm. Since the enumeration is rooted in a uniquely labelled vertex, the algorithm builds $p - 1$ extensions, each extension consuming constant time. By the augmentation of (e_i), $i = 1...q$, we can drive the modified matching such that each check is performed on a single entry slot. Thus each of the $q - (p - 1)$ checks takes constant time. Hence the whole matching needs time linear to q. Since R is a finite set of rewriting rules, we can define an instance of the modified matching algorithm for each rule. Each instance executes in constant time.

Since the abstract machine does not branch for a bypassing connected enumeration, it computes at most one isomorphic subgraph.   ∎

The sufficient condition for a constant-time matching motivates the definition of a class of graph rewriting systems.

Definition 3.3.7   UBS GRAPH REWRITING SYSTEM

A graph rewriting system gg is a *UBS graph rewriting system* if for all $r \in R$ there exists a connected enumeration which bypasses $svs(gg)$ and is rooted in a vertex with label $ul \in uv(gg)$.   ∎

Up to now the notion of bypassing has been merely a theoretical property of connected enumerations. To prove constant-time matching for a given rewriting system, two major open problems must be solved:

- Can we determine $svs(gg)$ although it is defined as a possibly infinite union of sets of strong V-structures?
- Can we construct a connected enumeration which bypasses $svs(gg)$ if it exists?

The fact that the word problem of graph languages is undecidable strongly influences the study of label triples, and it applies to the analysis of strong V-structures as well. Thus we give an upper approximation for $svs(gg)$. Theorem 3.3.6 is still applicable because any connected enumeration which bypasses an upper approximation still bypasses any subset.

Let us first develop a constructive test for the existence of a bypassing connected enumeration.

3.3.2 Determination of a Bypassing Connected Enumeration

We assume in this subsection that any left-hand side under consideration is connected and has at least one vertex with a unique label. Under these assumptions, we can decide the property of bypassing solving a well-known problem for directed graphs, the rooted spanning tree problem. We give a transformation to the rooted spanning tree problem for a left-hand side and a set of strong V-structures. We decide the existence of a bypassing connected enumeration by inspection of the graph symmetric to the left-hand side.

The shift to a symmetric graph reflects the assumed ability to search for an adjacent vertex independent of the direction of the joining edge. For an edge of the connected enumeration, the matching algorithm distinguishes whether it should extend the current partial handles by its source or its target. The direction of edges in the symmetric graph explicitly models the direction of matching. When the source is already matched, we traverse the graph along the original edge and extend the partial handles by the target vertex. Otherwise we traverse the graph along the additional symmetric edge and match the source of the original edge. Thus all edges of the symmetric graph have one interpretation: "try to match the target vertex". As a consequence, each connected enumeration must at least contain one edge of each pair of symmetric edges. This holds except for symmetric edges already included in the left-hand side. In this case both edges must be part of the connected enumeration by definition.

After modelling all possible enumerations by the symmetric graph, we implement the information on strong V-structures in the representation of the left-hand side. Some edges of the symmetric graph may be part of an instance of a strong V-structure. They must not be included in a bypassing connected enumeration. Thus they are removed from the symmetric graph. All remaining edges can be traversed without getting trapped in the instance of a strong V-structure. With this transformation, bypassing is equivalent to the existence of a directed spanning tree of the modified symmetric graph rooted in a uniquely labelled vertex. The edges of that tree make up the first part of the connected enumeration which bypasses the given set of strong V-structures. If the tree exists, the matching algorithm determines the images of all left-hand side vertices after processing that first part. Afterwards, we can check the existence of the remaining edges which are therefore put in the second part, still with respect to the set of strong V-structures.

Theorem 3.3.8   EXISTENCE OF A BYPASSING CONNECTED ENUMERATION

Let $gg = (\Sigma_V, \Sigma_E, g_0, R)$ be a graph rewriting system. Let $r \in R$ be a rewriting rule with labelling function l_r and $UV(r) \neq \emptyset$. Let $p = |V_l|$ and $q = |E_l|$. Let

$$\bar{E} = \{ (t, el, s) \mid (s, el, t) \in E_l \} \backslash E_l.$$

The elements of $\bar{E}$ complete g_l to a symmetric graph. Let

$$F = \{ (s, el, t) \in E_l \mid (l(s), l(t), el, \text{out}) \notin svs(gg) \}$$

$$\text{and} \quad \bar{F} = \{ (t, el, s) \in \bar{E} \mid (l(t), l(s), el, \text{in}) \notin svs(gg) \}$$

be the edge sets of the symmetric graph cleared with respect to $svs(gg)$.
If there are

(i)   a uniquely labelled vertex $u \in V_l$, $l_r(u) \in UV(r)$,

(ii)   a spanning tree $S(g_l, u)$ of $g_l = (V_l, F \cup \bar{F}, l_r)$ rooted in u, and

(iii)   for all $e = (s, el, t) \in E_l \backslash E_{S(g_l, u)}$ it holds that either
$(l(s), l(t), el, \text{out}) \notin svs(gg)$ or $(l(t), l(s), el, \text{in}) \notin svs(gg)$,

then there exists a connected enumeration of E_l bypassing $svs(gg)$.

Proof by construction. Let (t_i), $i = 1...p - 1$ be a connected enumeration of the spanning tree of g_l rooted in u. Let $W_i = \bigcup_{j=1...i} inc_{g_l}(t_j)$ for $i = 1...p - 1$ and $W_0 = \{u\}$. The enumeration (t_i), $i = 1...p - 1$ is defined such that for $t_i = (s, el, t)$ it holds that $t \notin W_{i-1}$. Now a connected enumeration (e_i), $i = 1...p - 1$ is built with $e_i = t_i$ if $t_i \in E_l$ and otherwise $e_i = (s, el, t)$ with $t_i = (t, el, s)$.

The enumeration (e_i), $i = 1...p - 1$ bypasses $svs(gg)$: let $i \in \{1, ..., p - 1\}$ be fixed. Since $inc_{g_l}(e_i) = inc_{g_l}(t_i)$, it follows that $W_i = \bigcup_{j=1...i} inc_{g_l}(e_j)$.

Let $e_i = (s, el, t)$. In case $e_i = t_i$: $t \notin W_{i-1}$, and by definition $t_i \in F$. Hence $(l(s), l(t), el, \text{out}) \notin svs(gg)$. In case $e_i \neq t_i$, it follows that $s \notin W_{i-1}$. By definition $t_i = (t, el, s) \in \bar{F}$, and $(l(t), l(s), el, \text{in}) \notin svs(gg)$. As a consequence, it follows that (e_i), $i = 1...p - 1$ is bypassing $svs(gg)$.

For all edges $e \in E_l \backslash \{e_i \mid i = 1...p - 1\}$ it holds that $inc_{g_l}(e) \subseteq W_{p-1}$. It follows from the premises that any of these edges can be checked bypassing $svs(gg)$. Hence we can add these edges to (e_i), $i = 1...p - 1$ and receive a complete connected enumeration of E_l, bypassing $svs(gg)$ completely. ∎

We give an example for the construction of theorem 3.3.8 in figure 18. The upper half shows the left-hand side and its transformed graph g_l. The grey edges, i.e. $\bar{E}$, are inserted in g_l to give a symmetric graph. They are also indicated by an "inverse" label.

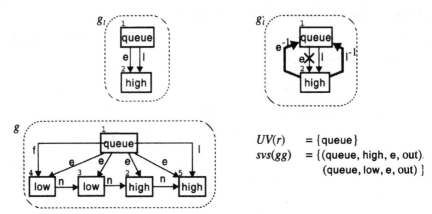

$$UV(r) = \{\text{queue}\}$$
$$svs(gg) = \{(\text{queue, high, e, out}),$$
$$(\text{queue, low, e, out})\}$$

Figure 18   Existence of a bypassing connected enumeration

The edge $(1, e, 2)$ is removed from g_i. If the abstract machine traverses the host graph along the edge $(1, e, 2)$ in its original direction, the search will branch, because the corresponding slot has possible multiple entries. Hence $\overline{F} = \{(1, e, 2)\}$. Note that we can still traverse the edge $(1, e, 2)$ in the opposite direction since the V-structure (high, queue, e, out) is not contained in $svs(g)$. We can find a spanning tree of the transformed graph rooted in the uniquely labelled vertex 1. In our example it consists of just the edge $(1, l, 2)$. This edge is the first part of the enumeration. The edge $(1, e, 2)$ completes the enumeration. It must be augmented with the information that the check for the existence of the edge must be performed in vertex 2. Then the modified algorithm for the labelled subgraph matching can execute the check by a constant-time look-up.

3.3.3 Conditions for the Introduction of Strong V-Structures

Now let us approach the main question: How can we compute a non-trivial upper approximation of $svs(gg)$? Well, again with abstract interpretation, but now with respect to strong V-structures. Similarly to the approximation of $ltr(gg)$ we must define abstract notions of the fit and evaluation of embedding descriptions, applicability and the rewriting step; but the abstraction is not as easy as for label triples. The introduction of a label triple is a local action and can therefore be directly observed from the rewriting rule. An instance of a strong V-structure, on the contrary, can be created under various conditions. Since a rewriting rule may add an incident edge to any vertex, this edge may complete an edge already in the graph to an instance.

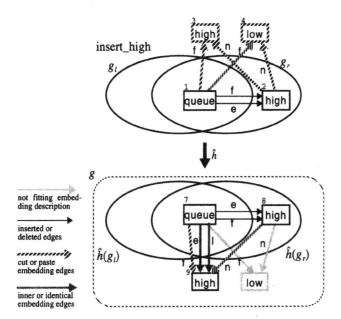

not fitting embed-
ding description

inserted or
deleted edges

cut or paste
embedding edges

inner or identical
embedding edges

Figure 19   Application of "insert_high" to a priority queue with one element

Take for example the application of the rule "insert_high" to the priority queue with one element of high priority as shown in figure 15. In this figure we explicitly denote the context of the rule. It consists of the vertex 1. The two embedding descriptions change the embedding of the vertices which according to the cut-description had been the first element of the queue. They become now the second element and are referred to by an "n"-edge from the inserted vertex. In the application to graph g, only the embedding of the "high" vertex is performed. It is also identically embedded with the "e"- and "l"-edges.

This particular rewriting step introduces a new strong V-structure in the graph, namely

$$\text{(queue, high, e, out)}.$$

Not any application of "insert_high" will introduce a new strong V-structure. Whenever it is applied to a queue with more than one "high"-element, that V-structure is already present.

Since we want to compute the set of strong V-structures which may be present in a graph language, we must determine the contribution of each rewriting rule. Because we must use a static analysis, we must find out which properties of a rule may cause a strong V-structure just by inspection of the rule. When we have determined these characteristics, we can compute the set of strong V-structures by abstract interpretation. Our analysis, for example, must tell that the insertion of an edge isomorphic to $(1, e, 2)$ may cause a strong V-structure, as it does it in the rewriting step of figure 15.

The abstract rewriting step must reflect all various situations in which an instance might be created. Thus the definition of *svs*-rewriting is not straightforward, but will take several steps. First of all, we will classify instances of strong V-structures caused by a rewriting step. The classification scheme lists all combinations of the three vertices incident to the instance of a V-structure with regions given by the definition of the rewriting step. For some classes there exist subclasses, because an edge of an instance might have two or more origins. We will show that the classification is complete, i.e. any instance of a strong V-structure which is introduced by a rewriting step belongs to at least one class. The classification is defined on dynamic properties, i.e. with respect to a rewriting step.

Second we map the properties of rewriting steps to characteristics of the rules which are applied. Hence we relate the dynamic conditions to a set of predicates which can be evaluated by inspection of the rewriting system with abstract interpretation. Thus we have to show that the predicates cover all dynamic conditions for the introduction of a strong V-structure, i.e. the static predicates must form a necessary condition for the dynamic characterization based on the classification. Consequently, any introduction of a strong V-structure must be related to at least one static condition.

The set of static predicates gives a first and rough approximation. In the third step we tighten this approximation, taking the left-hand side of a rule into account. Let us take for example the rule "swap" (see page 23). Here, instances of strong V-structures appear on both sides of a rule. By inspection of the right-hand side we must conclude that the application of the rule introduces that strong V-structure. If, though, we take the left-hand side into consideration, we observe that there must have been an instance of the V-structure in the host graph already, otherwise the rule is not applicable. As a consequence, it follows that the strong V-structure cannot be created by the application of the rule. So, by further analysis of the rewriting rules, we refine the set of necessary conditions for the existence of a strong V-structure in a result graph.

After these three steps, the necessary conditions for the introduction of a strong V-structure by a rewriting step are determined. In section 3.3.4 they are embedded in the abstract interpretation framework.

First we prove a small technical lemma. It states that for each instance of a strong V-structure introduced in a rewriting step there must be an edge as part of the instance which is inserted by that rewriting. In particular, that edge must be an element of $h(E_r) \cup Emb_{ins}$ with respect to the definition of the rewriting step. In the application of "insert_high", the edge $(1, e, 2)$ is an inserted edge. The lemma states a fundamental property which relates a new strong V-structure to the applied rewriting rule. We exploit this property throughout the rest of this section by assuming that for any instance of a new V-structure one edge must be caused by the applied rule. In the proofs of the following lemmata, we fix one edge, and consider the origin of the other edge of the instance. This technique allows us to structure the proofs.

Lemma 3.3.9   ONE EDGE OF A NEW INSTANCE MUST HAVE BEEN INSERTED

Let g be a graph and $r = (g_l, g_r, M)$ be a rewriting rule applicable to g. Let g' be the result of rewriting g by r under a graph morphism $\hat{h}$, i.e. $g \rightarrow_{\hat{h}}^{r} g'$. Let $vs \in svs(g') \setminus svs(g)$ be a new strong V-structure. For any instance $(e, e') \in E'^2$ of vs, it holds that either e or $e' \in h(E_r) \cup Emb_{ins}$.

Proof. Let $(e, e') \in E'^2$ be an instance of vs. Assume $e, e' \notin h(E_r) \cup Emb_{ins}$. By definition of the rewriting step, it follows that $e, e' \in E$ and that (e, e') is already an instance of vs in g in contradiction to the premises.   ∎

We apply the lemma in the following classification of new strong V-structures. An instance of a strong V-structure is obviously a symmetric relation, i.e. whenever a pair (e, e') is an instance, the pair (e', e) is one also. With lemma 3.3.9 we break the symmetry, since we fix one edge to be contributed by the rewriting rule. The other edge may now be from the rest graph or inserted too. In the latter case, the instance may appear in two classes, one for each inserted edge.

The classification is first of all determined by the location of the vertices of an instance. It is refined by the origin of the second edge. The resulting classification is sufficient for the rest of the section because all possible situations of the introduction of a new V-structure are covered.

Figure 20 shows the images of the left- and the right-hand side of an applied rewriting rule for each class. In the intersection of the ellipses lie the context vertices. The graphical representation of class 7, for instance, reads as follows. It shows an instance (e, e') with $e = (x, el, y)$ and $e' = (x, el, z)$. Vertex x is the image of a context vertex, i.e. $x \in h(V_c)$. Vertices y and z are both inserted by the rewriting step, i.e. $y, z \in h(V_r)$. Hence both edges e and e' are inserted by the rewriting step also.

Let us further consider class 18, which is refined to three subclasses. Here, x is again the image of a context vertex. From the assumption in lemma 3.3.9 it follows that the edge (x, el, y) is inserted by an embedding description, and no further restriction on (x, el, y) is given. Because x is a context vertex it can be identically embedded, i.e. stay connected to vertex z during the rewriting. The edge e', though, might also be introduced by an embedding description which may or may not be different to the description causing e.

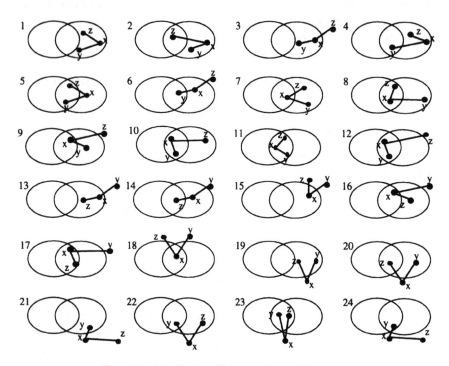

Figure 20   Classification of instances of strong V-structures

The instance $((7, e, 9), (7, e, 8))$ shown in the example of figure 15 falls into class 9. The "queue" vertex is in the context. The "high" vertex 8 is inserted, i.e. an element V_i, whereas vertex 9 is in the rest graph. Thus we have the situation depicted in class 9. With respect to the subclassification, we must consider whether the edge $(7, e, 9)$ is an identically embedding -, or an inner edge. Since the former holds, it follows that the instance belongs to subclass 9b.

Lemma 3.3.10   CLASSIFICATION OF NEW STRONG V-STRUCTURES

Let g be a graph and $r = (g_l, g_r, M)$ be a rewriting rule applicable to g. Let g' be the result of rewriting g by r under a graph morphism $\hat{h}$, i.e. $g \to_h^r g'$. Let $vs = (vl_1, vl_2, el, d)$ be a new strong V-structure of g', i.e. $vs \in svs(g')\backslash svs(g)$. Let $(e, e') \in E'^2$ be an instance of vs with vertices $x, y, z \in V'$ such that $l(x) = vl_1$, $l(y) = l(z) = vl_2$ and if $d =$ out: $e = (x, el, y)$, $e' = (x, el, z)$, or if $d =$ in: $e = (y, el, x)$, $e' = (z, el, x)$.

Let wlog $e \in h(E_i) \cup Emb_{ins}$.

We denote the instance (e, e') graphically as $x \hspace{-0.3em}\begin{smallmatrix} \bullet\, y \\ \bullet\, z\end{smallmatrix}$.

a) The pair (e, e') is member of one of the classes shown graphically in figure 20.

b) If the nature of e' according to the definition of the rewriting step is considered the classes 8, 9, 11, 12, 17, 18, and 20 split into 2 or 3 subclasses.

Proof.

a) The vertex set V' can be divided into three disjoint subsets

$$V' = h(V_i) \cup h(V_c) \cup (V \backslash h(V_r)).$$

By a combinatorial argument, it follows that there are 27 different distributions of x, y, and z on the subsets. Since $e \in h(E_r) \cup Emb_{ins}$ it follows that either x or y must not be an element of $V \backslash h(V_r)$. Thus the three classes with $x, y \in V \backslash h(V_r)$ and arbitrary z must not appear, and we have 24 possible distributions of x, y, and z - hence 24 classes for instances of a new strong V-structure.

b) In case the edge e' is an embedding edge, we distinguish whether it was introduced by the same embedding description as e or not. This leads to a subdivision of classes 15, 18, and 20 into 15a, 18a, and 20a or 15b, 18b, and 20b respectively.

In classes 8, 11, and 17 the edge e' is either a context or an inner edge. The first case is covered by subclasses 8a, 11a, and 17a, whereas the latter leads to subclasses 8b, 11b, and 17b.

For classes 9, 12, 18, and 20 the edge e' is either introduced by an embedding description, or was already an edge of graph g and part of the identical embedding. Thus these classes split into 9a, 12a, 18a, and 20a; or 9b, 12b, 18c, and 20b respectively.

Inspection of the definition of the rewriting step shows that the case analysis of e' is complete, that the listed classes are subdivided properly, and that the origin of e' is unique in all other classes.   ∎

The classification given by lemma 3.3.10 covers only new strong V-structures. This restriction reflects the fact that we want to analyse the effect of a rewriting step on the set of strong V-structures of a given graph. Furthermore the classification is defined for new instances caused in a rewriting step. To enable an abstract interpretation we must relate the dynamic properties to static ones, i.e. to predicates defined on rewriting rules instead of rewriting steps.

We define four predicates on a set of strong V-structures and a rewriting rule. According to their domain, they can be evaluated statically by inspection of a given graph rewriting system. Each static predicate covers the introduction of a strong V-structure. There are four main cases.

    (i)   the right-hand side contains a complete instance already,

(ii)   the image of a right-hand side edge causes the introduction of an instance,

(iii)   an inserted embedding edge completes an edge lying in the subgraph in-
        duced by the image of the right-hand side's vertices, or

(iv)   an inserted embedding edge forms a new instance together with an edge of
        the rest graph.

The static predicates, which will be given in definition 3.3.11, determine the particular
strong V-structure which might be introduced. So for the edge $e = (1, e, 2)$ of
"insert_high" (see figure 15), it holds that

$$e \in E_i \cap inc_{g_r}(V_c).$$

Hence according to $V2$ the introduced strong V-structure must be (queue, high, e, out)
if it is introduced at all. Also the embedding description related to vertex 3 may
introduce the strong V-structures (high, high, n, out) and (high, high, n, in) according
to $V3$ and $V4$ respectively.

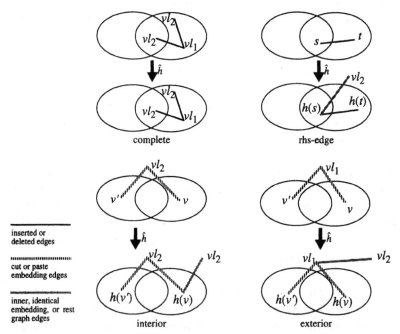

Figure 21   Static predicates

Definition 3.3.11   STATIC PREDICATES

Let R be a set of rewriting rules and let d^{-1} = out iff d = in and vice versa. The *static predicates over SVS and R V1, V2, V3,* and *V4* are defined for a strong V-structure $vs = (vl_1, vl_2, el, d)$ and a rewriting rule $r = (g_l, g_r, M)$ with labelling function l as follows:

(complete) $V1(vs, r) \equiv vs \in svs(g_r),$

(rhs-edge) $V2(vs, r) \equiv \exists\,(s, el, t) \in E_r \cap inc_{g_r}(V_c)$ such that

$$l(s) = vl_1, l(t) = vl_2, s \in V_c, \text{ if } d = \text{out}$$

$$l(t) = vl_1, l(s) = vl_2, t \in V_c, \text{ if } d = \text{in}$$

(interior) $V3(vs, r) \equiv \exists\,(c, p) \in M$ such that $c = (v', el', vl_2, d')$

$$\text{and } p = (v, el, d) \text{ with } l(v) = vl_1,$$

(exterior) $V4(vs, r) \equiv \exists\,(c, p) \in M$ such that $c = (v', el', vl_1, d')$

$$\text{and } p = (v, el, d^{-1}) \text{ with } l(v) = vl_2. \quad\blacksquare$$

The following lemma relates the static predicates defined above to instances of strong V-structures. It sets up the key correspondence between the dynamic classification and the static properties represented by the predicates $V1$ to $V4$. If a predicate is true, then the application of the rewriting rule may introduce a new strong V-structure. We apply the classification lemma for the proof.

From the classification lemma it follows that any new instance belongs to a class or subclass. Furthermore the instance is produced by a certain characteristic of the applied rewriting rule. These characteristics are expressed by the static predicates. By inspection of the instances of a given class, we can deduce properties of the rewriting rules which must have been present to produce the instances. Especially we can deduce whether one of the static predicates must have been valid. In those cases, the corresponding entry of the table contains a mark. The subclassification applies to the deduction as follows: if we can prove the validity of a static predicate only for the instances of a subclass, we enter a bracketed mark in the table.

Lemma 3.3.12   STATIC PREDICATES AND CLASSES

Let g be a graph and $r = (g_l, g_r, M)$ be a rewriting rule with labelling function l being applicable to g. Let g' be the result of rewriting g by r under a graph morphism $\hat{h}$, i.e. $g \to_h^r g'$. Let $vs \in svs(g') \backslash svs(g)$.

The entry (cl, Vi) is marked iff for *all instances* $(e, e') \in E'^2$ of vs which belong to class cl and with $e \in h(E_r) \cup Emb_{ins}$, the predicate $Vi(vs, r)$ is valid.

The entry (cl, Vi) contains a bracketed mark iff $Vi(vs, r)$ is valid for *some instances* $(e, e') \in E'^2$ of vs belonging to class cl and with $e \in h(E_{\vec{r}}) \cup Emb_{ins}$, the predicate $Vi(vs, r)$ is valid.

	1	2	3	4	5	6	7	8	9	10	11	12
V1	x	x		x	x		x	(x)		x	(x)	
V2							x	x	x	x	x	x
V3		x			x				(x)			(x)
V4												

	13	14	15	16	17	18	19	20	21	22	23	24
V1												
V2				x	(x)							
V3	x	x	x	x	x	x						
V4							x	x	x	x	x	x

Table 1: Validity of predicate Vi for class cl

Proof. Let $(e, e') \in E'^2$ be an instance of vs. We verify the marking of the table by inspection of the corresponding instances. We give two exemple arguments, one for the entries $(V1, 7)$ and $(V2, 7)$, and the other for entry $(V3, 9)$.

Let (e, e') be a member of class 7 and wlog $d = $ out. Hence $e = (x, el, y)$ and $e' = (x, el, z)$ for vertices $x \in V_c$ and $y, z \in V_{\vec{r}}$. Thus $e, e' \in E_{\vec{r}}$, and $vs \in svs(g_r) \equiv V1(vs, r)$ is true. In this case, it further holds that $e \in E_{\vec{r}} \cap inc_{g_r}(V_c)$ and $l(x) = vl_1$, $l(y) = vl_2$. Hence $V2(vs, r)$ is also true.

To prove the correctness of entry $(V3, 9)$ assume that (e, e') is a member of class 9. Again wlog let $d = $ out. Hence $e = (x, el, y)$ and $e' = (x, el, z)$ for vertices $x \in V_c$ and $y \in V_{\vec{r}}$. In lemma 3.3.9, assuming $e \in E_{\vec{r}} \cap inc_{g_r}(V_c)$, we proved that the edge e' was either inserted explicitly as a result of the evaluation of an embedding description (subclass 9a) or left in the graph as an edge being identically embedded (subclass 9b). In the first case $V3$ is true, otherwise it is not. Thus the entry is bracketed.

Other marks in the table follow from similar arguments. ∎

On page 69 we have shown that the instance of figure 15 belongs to class 9b. We have also discussed that for the edge $(1, e, 2)$ of the rule "insert_high", the static predicate $V2$ holds. Lemma 3.3.12 sets up this relation explicitly for all combinations of instances and properties of a rewriting rule. Whenever an instance is introduced by rewriting, at least one of the predicates must be valid for the corresponding V-structure. Hence the predicates form a set of necessary conditions for the introduction of new V-structures. As a consequence, when we determine those strong V-structures for which the predicates are valid for a given rule, we know that these V-structures are potentially introduced by rewriting using that rule. This consequence will be explicitly stated in the next theorem which relates the four static predicates to new strong V-structures.

Theorem 3.3.13   STATIC PREDICATES ARE NECESSARY FOR NEW STRONG
                      V-STRUCTURES

Let g be a graph and $r = (g_l, g_r, M)$ be a rewriting rule applicable to g. Let g' be the result of rewriting g by r under a graph isomorphism $\hat{h}$, i.e. $g \rightarrow_{\hat{h}}^{r} g'$. The following implication holds:

$$vs \in svs(g')\backslash svs(g) \Rightarrow V_{i=1}^{4} Vi(vs, r)$$

Furthermore, the predicates $V1$ to $V4$ form a minimal set, i.e. none of the predicates can be ignored.

Proof. Let $vs \in svs(g')\backslash svs(g)$. Thus there is an instance $(e, e') \in E'$ of vs belonging to some class $cl \in \{1, ..., 24\}$. From the table of lemma 3.3.12, it follows that for all classes cl at least one Vi, $i = 1...4$ is true for vs and r. Hence $V_{i=1}^{4} Vi(vs, r)$ is true.

For all proper, non-empty subsets $W \subseteq \{V1, ..., V4\}$, there exists a $vs \in svs(g') \backslash svs(g)$ such that $V_{P \in W} P(vs, r)$ is false. Assume $V1 \notin W$. Let (e, e') be an instance of vs and member of class 1. Thus $V_{i=1}^{4} Vi(vs, r)$ is true, but not $V_{P \in W} P(vs, r)$. From a similar argument, it follows that $V1 \vee V2 \vee V4$ and that $V_{i=1}^{3} Vi(vs, r)$ are false for instances of class 3 and class 9 respectively. To prove that $V2$ is a necessary element of the set, assume that (e, e') is an instance of vs and belongs to class 8. We assume further that $e \in h(E_r)$ and e' is an inner edge. Thus there is no strong V-structure in g, and only $V2$ is true.   ∎

The implication reduces any dynamic situation in which a strong V-structure can be introduced to a disjunction of four static predicates which must be satisfied. Thus the predicates indicate the potential introduction of a V-structure by application of a rule.

The static predicates are very weak. With the exception of $V1$, the predicates are defined over only one edge or one embedding description, although for the introduction of a strong V-structure, another appropriate edge must exist. There are occasions on which we also can extract necessary properties for the second edge of an instance. Furthermore we can determine whether the introduction of a strong V-structure depends on the existence of another one.

Refinements of the static predicates take these additional properties into account and extend the domain of the predicates to the left-hand side and the strong V-structures of the host graph. The latter extension is the reason for the use of abstract interpretation in the analysis of V-structures. We give refinements for all predicates except V1.

First we will state an obvious property of a rewriting rule which introduces a strong V-structure. No new V-structure may occur in the left-hand side. Otherwise the rule would neither be applicable nor the V-structure new. We state this property separately since it holds for all rules and V-structures. The refinements of the static predicates will follow.

Lemma 3.3.14

Let g, g', r, and h be as in lemma 3.3.12. For all $vs \in svs(g')\backslash svs(g)$ holds

$$vs \notin svs(g_l)$$

Proof. by contradiction. ∎

The static predicate $V2$ can partly be reduced onto $V1$ and $V3$, and partly be restricted by conditions related to the second edge. This edge can result from the evaluation of an embedding description. In this case, there must be a paste-description which replaces a cut-edge by an edge isomorphic to and incident with the first edge, or the second edge was in the host graph already, either as an inner edge, or belonging to an identical embedding. In this case, we cannot impose further restriction derived from the right-hand side, but we can cover the case in which the inserted edge is transferred from the left- to the right-hand side. This is a typical property of an application where referencing edges are shifted from one referred vertex to the other. Under these circumstances, the V-structure existed already in the host graph.

Lemma 3.3.15 REFINEMENT OF $V2$

Let g, g', r, and h be as in lemma 3.3.12. For all $vs \in svs(g')\backslash svs(g)$, it holds that

$$V2(vs, r) \Rightarrow V1(vs, r) \vee \overline{V2}(vs, r) \vee V3(vs, r)$$

where $\overline{V2}(vs, r) \equiv \exists\, (s, el, t) \in E_r \cap inc_{g_r}(V_c)$ with $s \in V_c$, $l(s) = vl_1$, $l(t) = vl_2$, if $d =$
out $t \in V_c$, $l(t) = vl_1$, $l(s) = vl_2$, if $d =$ in

and   1) $\exists\, (c, p) \in M$: $c = (v', el', vl_2, d')$ and $p = (s, el, d)$, if $d =$ out,
$p = (t, el, d)$, if $d =$ in
or 2) $\neg\exists\, (s, el, t') \in E_i$ with $l(t') = vl_2$, if $d =$ out
$\neg\exists\, (s', el, t) \in E_i$ with $l(s') = vl_2$, if $d =$ in

Proof. Let $vs = (vl_1, vl_2, el, d) \in svs(g')\backslash svs(g)$ be a strong V-structure such that $V2(vs, r)$ is true. Any instance (e, e') with wlog $e \in h(E_r) \cup Emb_{ins}$ of vs falls into one of the classes 7-12, 16, or 17 according to lemma 3.3.9.

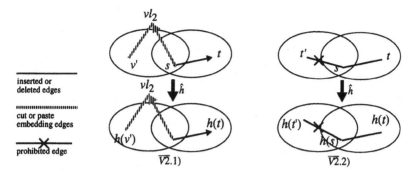

Figure 22   Refinements of V2

For classes 7 and 10, or 16 and 17, vs satisfies not only $V2(vs, r)$, but also $V1(vs, r)$ or $V3(vs, r)$ respectively. Thus assume that (e, e') belongs to classes 8, 9, 11, or 12. Hence both edges e and e' are incident to the same context vertex. Wlog let $d =$ out and $e = (x, el, y)$ be the inserted edge. Thus $e = h((s, el, t))$ for $s \in V_c$ and $t \in V_r$.

Case analysis on e' applies the subclassification for classes 8, 9, 11, and 12 as given in lemma 3.3.9: for $e' \in h(E_r)$ it holds that $vs \in svs(g_r)$. Thus $V1(vs, r)$ is true for subclasses 8a and 11a.

In case $e' \in E' \backslash h(E_r)$ we distinguish the origin of e'. If, on the one hand, $e' \in Emb_{ins}$, there is a $(c, p) \in M$ with $c = (v', el', vl_2, d')$ and $p = (s, el, \text{out})$. This case covers classes 9a and 12a and leads to the first additional restriction. If, on the other hand, e' is an inner edge or an identical embedding edge, we can derive the following restriction for the left-hand side: There must not be an edge $(s, el, t') \in E_i$ with $l(t') = vl_2$. Otherwise there exists an edge $e'' = (x, el, y') \in h(E_l)$ with $l(y') = vl_2$, and the pair (e', e'') would already have been an instance of vs in g. This second restriction covers subclasses 8b, 9b, 11b, and 12b.

Thus for any instance (e, e') of a strong V-structure vs which is a member of classes 8, 9, 11, or 12, $\overline{V2}(vs, r)$ holds. Since the case analysis is complete, the proposed implication follows.   ∎

The static predicate V3 is refined also. It can either be reduced to $\overline{V2}$, or one of the given five further conditions must hold. Condition 1) reflects the same situation as the second restriction for V2. To be sure that an instance of a new V-structure is introduced, there must be no edge on the left-hand side isomorphic and incident to the inserted paste-edge. Otherwise this strong V-structure has already existed in the host graph.

A paste-edge may complete an inner edge. In this case at least one further context vertex with an appropriate label must exist (condition 2)).

In case there is a second embedding description which potentially refers to embedding vertices with the same label and inserts the same paste-edges, instances of a strong V-structure are introduced when both cut-descriptions fit in a rewriting step.

An embedding description can introduce a new V-structure by transformation of an old one (see condition 4). If a cut-description fits to two edges, they form an instance. The embedding vertices of the rest graph are connected to the image of a right-hand side vertex with respect to the paste-description. Since there is more than one embedding vertex the connecting edges make an instance also. This further condition is not statically decidable any more, but requires abstract interpretation.

Condition 5) is symmetric to the first restriction of $V2$ where a paste-edge completes an edge in the image of the right-hand side. Here we have the opposite dependency.

Figure 23 shows the five conditions defined for a rewriting rule and a set of strong V-structures. In contrast to the figures above we depict only the rule itself and not the application of the rule also. For cases 1) and 2) we include the inner or identical edge which may appear in a rewriting step in the presentation of the rule.

Lemma 3.3.16   REFINEMENT OF $V3$

Let g, g', r, and h be as in lemma 3.3.12. For all $vs \in svs(g')\backslash svs(g)$ it holds that

$$V3(vs, r) \Rightarrow \overline{V2}(vs, r) \vee \exists m \in M \text{ with } \overline{V3}(vs, r, svs(g), m)$$

where $\overline{V3}(vs, r, svs, (c, p)) \equiv c = (v', el', vl_2, d')$ and $p = (v, el, d)$ with $l(v) = vl_1$

and   1) $v \in V_c$ and $\neg\exists (v, el, t') \in E_i$ with $l(t') = vl_2$, if $d = $ out

$\neg\exists (s', el, v) \in E_i$ with $l(s') = vl_2$, if $d = $ in

or 2) $v \in V_c$ and $\exists w \in V_c\backslash \{v\}$ with $l(w) = vl_2$

or 3) $\exists (c', p') \in M$ such that $c' = (v'', el'', vl_2, d'') \neq c$ and $p = p'$

or 4) $(l(v'), vl_2, el', d') \in svs$

or 5) $\exists (v, el, t') \in E_{\overline{r}}$ with $l(t') = vl_2$, if $d = $ out,

$\exists (s', el, v) \in E_{\overline{r}}$ with $l(s') = vl_2$, if $d = $ in

Proof. Let $vs = (vl_1, vl_2, el, d) \in svs(g')\backslash svs(g)$ be a strong V-structure such that $V3(vs, r)$ is true. Any instance (e, e') with wlog $e \in h(E_{\overline{r}}) \cup Emb_{ins}$ of vs falls into one of the classes 3, 6, 9, 12, or 13-18 according to lemma 3.3.12.

For classes 9 and 12, it follows that whenever $V3(vs, r)$ is true, $V2(vs, r)$ is satisfied also. Classes 9 and 12 are covered by the implication $V2(vs, r) \Rightarrow \overline{V2}(vs, r)$ according to the proof of lemma 3.3.15. Thus $V3(vs, r)$ can in that case be reduced to $\overline{V2}(vs, r)$.

Thus assume that an instance (e, e') of vs belongs to classes 3, 6, 13-17, and 18. In all classes, there is one edge being inserted by an embedding description. Thus let wlog $e \in Emb_{ins}$ and let wlog for the further analysis $d = out$. For $e = (x, el, y)$ with $l(x) = vl_1$ and $l(y) = vl_2$ exists a $(c, p) \in M$ with $c = (v', el', vl_2, d')$ and $p = (h^{-1}(x), el, d)$. Hence there is a vertex $v = h^{-1}(x) \in V_r$ with $l(v) = vl_1$.

Now we have to consider four cases dependent on the location of $v \in V_c \cup V_r$ and the origin of $e' \in E' \subseteq h(E_r) \cup Emb_{ins} \cup E$.

In case $v \in V_c$ and $e' \in E$ holds that e' must be a context, inner, or identical embedding edge. If e' is a context or an identical embedding edge, the instance (e, e') must be in subclasses 17a or 18c. There must be no edge $e'' = (x, el, y')$ being an element of $h(E_i)$ with $e'' \neq e'$ and $l(v') = vl_2$. Otherwise, (e', e'') would be an instance of vs in g. Statically, we derive the condition that no edge (v, el, t') with $l(t') = vl_2$ must be a member of E_i, i.e. subcondition 1). For an inner edge e' the instance (e, e') belongs to class 17b. Hence there must be at least one vertex $v' \in V_c \setminus \{v\}$ with $l(v') = vl_2$ and subcondition 2) follows.

In case $e' \in Emb_{ins}$, we have two alternative origins of e'. First there may be a second $(c', p') \in M$ with $c = (v'', el'', vl_2, d'') \neq c$ and $p' = p$. This case covers subclasses

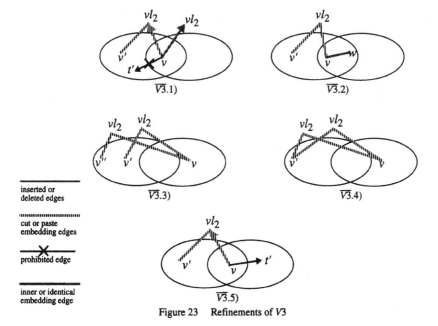

inserted or
deleted edges

cut or paste
embedding edges

prohibited edge

inner or identical
embedding edge

$\overline{V3}.1)$ $\overline{V3}.2)$ $\overline{V3}.3)$ $\overline{V3}.4)$ $\overline{V3}.5)$

Figure 23   Refinements of V3

15b and 18b and leads to condition 3). Or second, c fits to at least two edges from g represented by subclasses 15a and 18a. In this case there must $vs' = (l(v'), vl_2, el', d')$ be a strong V-structure in g, and subcondition 4) follows.

In case $v \notin V_c$ and $e' \notin Emb_{ins}$, it follows that $e' \in h(E_r)$. Classes 3, 6, 13, 14, and 16 are covered. Hence there is an edge $(v, el, t') \in E_r$ with $l(t') = vl_2$ and condition 5) is satisfied.

The case analysis is complete with respect to the classification lemma, and the proposed restriction follows. ∎

The refinement of the fourth static predicate detects the transfer of strong V-structures. In case an embedding description determines isomorphic cut- and paste-edges, no V-structure can be newly introduced.

Lemma 3.3.17   REFINEMENT OF $V4$

Let g, g', r, and h be as in lemma 3.3.12. For all $vs \in svs(g')\backslash svs(g)$, it holds that

$$V4(vs, r) \Rightarrow \exists m \in M \text{ with } \overline{V4}(vs, r, m)$$

where $\overline{V4}(vs, r, (c, p)) \equiv c = (v', el', vl_1, d'), p = (v, el, d^{-1})$ with $l(v) = vl_2$ and
$$l(v') \neq vl_2, el' \neq el, \text{ or } d' \neq d^{-1}$$

Proof. Let $(e, e') \in E'^2$ be an instance of vs. Let wlog $e \in Emb_{ins}$. Hence $e' \in E$.

Let wlog $d^{-1} = out$. Thus $e = (x, el, h(v))$ and $e' = (x, el, z)$. There is also an edge $e'' = (x, el', h(v')) \in E$ cut by c. Assume $l(v') = vl_2$, $el' = el$, and $d' = d^{-1}$. Thus (e', e'') is an instance of vs in g. Therefore either $l(v') \neq vl_2$, or $el' \neq el$, or $d' \neq d^{-1}$. ∎

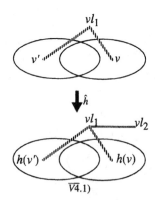

cut or paste
embedding edges

edge of the rest
graph

$\overline{V4}.1)$

Figure 24   Refinement of $V4$

We conclude with the following corollary, which combines these refinements with theorem 3.3.13.

Corollary 3.3.18

Let g be a graph and $r = (g_l, g_r, M)$ be a rewriting rule applicable to g. Let g' be the result of rewriting g by r under a graph morphism $\hat{h}$, i.e. $g \rightarrow_{\hat{h}}^r g'$. The following implication holds:

$$vs \in svs(g') \backslash svs(g) \Rightarrow V1(vs, r) \vee \overline{V2}(vs, r) \vee$$

$$\exists m \in M \text{ such that } \overline{V3}(vs, r, svs(g), m) \vee \overline{V4}(vs, r, m)$$

Proof. by inspection of the refinements and theorem 3.3.13.   ∎

This corollary concludes the section on the static analysis of strong V-structures. We have derived a disjunction of predicates which forms a necessary condition for the introduction of strong V-structures. With the help of this preparation, we can approach the calculation of an upper approximation of $svs(gg)$ by means of abstract interpretation in the next subsection.

By inspection of the predicates and their refinements, we derive guidelines for the design of graph rewriting systems generating a small set of strong V-structures. The guidelines generalize the detailed analysis based on the refined predicates. The pragmatics of the design of a graph rewriting system should include the following:

- few embedding descriptions,
- large label alphabets, and
- edges inserted together with vertices.

The first guideline addresses the introduction of strong V-structures by predicates $V3$ and $V4$. The smaller the set of embedding descriptions, the smaller the chance that a V-structure is created. As a second rule, use large alphabets to decrease the probability that two isomorphic edges or vertices occur in one rule. Thus the conditions 2) or 5) of $\overline{V3}$ might not be satisfied. Finally observe, that when inserted edges connect inserted vertices, we disable predicate $V2$. Especially, we insert no edges incident to a context vertex. Assume that an edge is needed in the lifetime of a vertex. We introduce that edge on creation of the vertex and park it, for example, as a loop incident to the vertex. When we use the edge, we do not create it, but just transfer from the left- to the right-hand side. Thus the second restriction of $\overline{V2}$ is applicable which detects that no new V-structure is introduced. Still, the designer with a detailed knowledge of the refined predicates will be able to construct rules with a minimal set of strong V-structures derived by the analysis.

3.3.4 Approximation of the Set of Strong V-Structures

We have laid the theoretical foundations for the static analysis of strong V-structures. Now we can mould them in terms of abstract interpretation. We will give an algorithm to compute an upper approximation for the set of strong V-structures of a graph rewriting system. Thus we give an affirmative and constructive answer to the first and major question posed at the beginning of this subsection: "Can we determine $svs(gg)$ although it is defined as a possibly infinite union of sets of strong V-structures?"

The procedure is similar to the calculation of reachable label triples. First, we define svs-applicability as well as an svs-evaluation of embedding descriptions for a given set of strong V-structures. The definition of svs-applicability is straightforward and reminds us of lemma 3.3.14.

Definition 3.3.19 SVS-APPLICABILITY

Let $r = (g_l, g_r, M)$ be a rewriting rule. Let $svs \subseteq SVS$ be a set of label triples. The rule r is svs-applicable to svs iff $svs(g_l) \subseteq svs$.   ■

The following lemma shows that svs-applicability is consistent with the definition of applicability in ordinary graph rewriting systems.

Lemma 3.3.20   APPLICABILITY IMPLIES SVS-APPLICABILITY

Let $r = (g_l, g_r, M)$ be a rewriting rule. Let g be a graph. The following proposition holds:

$$r \text{ is applicable to } g \implies svs(g_l) \subseteq svs(g)$$

Proof. For $svs(gg) = \varnothing$ the statement follows trivially. Thus let $vs \in svs(g_l)$ with an instance $(e, e') \in E_l^2$. Let r be applicable to g. For all injective graph morphisms $h: g_l \to g$ it follows that $(h(e), h(e')) \in E^2$ is an instance of vs in g. Thus $svs(g_l) \subseteq svs(g)$.   ■

Now we approach the formalisation of the effect imposed on a set of strong V-structures by the evaluation of an embedding description. We therefore will define the function svs-$eval$. In this definition, we apply the necessary conditions for the introduction of strong V-structures.

First we will define a tailored version of the $fits$-predicate known from ordinary graph rewriting systems. The definition of svs-applicability stated the requirement that a strong V-structure of the left-hand side must appear in the set of V-structures of the host graph. We transfer this requirement to embedding descriptions.

We know from lemma 3.3.5 that two edges which are incident and isomorphic form an instance of a strong V-structure. In case there is an edge on the left-hand side, isomorphic and incident to a cut-edge, the evaluation of the embedding description presumes the existence of a strong V-structure. We reflect this situation in the following definition. It is based on an extended graph anticipating the existence of a cut-edge. For all cut-descriptions c, extend the left-hand side by a potential cut-edge. When the cut-edge is part of an instance in the extended graph, the fit of the cut-description depends on the existence of the corresponding strong V-structure in any host graph.

Definition 3.3.21   *svs-fits*, svs-FIT OF AN EMBEDDING DESCRIPTION

Let $r = (g_l, g_r, M)$ be a rewriting rule with labelling function l. Let svs be a set of strong V-structures.

a) For an embedding description $(c, p) \in M$ with $c = (v, el, vl, d)$ define the *c-extension* of a graph g $ext(g, c) = (V \cup \{w\}, E \cup \{e\}, l')$
where $w \notin V$ is a vertex, the labelling is $l'(w) = vl$ and $l'|_V = l|_V$, and the edge e joins w and v, with $e = (v, el, w)$, if $d =$ out or $e = (w, el, v)$, if $d =$ in.

b) Let vs be a strong V-structure. The *cut-description c svs-fits to svs* iff in case there exists an instance of vs $(e, e') \in (E_{ext(g_r, c)} \backslash E_l) \times E_{ext(g_r, c)} \Rightarrow vs \in svs$.   ■

Now we can state the effect of the evaluation of an embedding description on a given set of strong V-structures. For that purpose we reflect the static predicates and their refinements.

Definition 3.3.22   *svs-eval*, svs-EVALUATION OF AN EMBEDDING DESCRIPTION

Let $r = (g_l, g_r, M)$ be a rewriting rule with labelling function l. Let svs be a set of strong V-structures. Let $m \in M$ be an embedding description.
The function *svs-eval* defines the *evaluation of m with respect to svs*:
If $svs\text{-}fits(c, svs)$:

$$svs\text{-}eval_l(m, svs) = \{vs| \overline{V4}(vs, r, m) \text{ is true for } vs = (vl, l(v), el, d^{-1})\}$$

$$\cup \{vs| \overline{V3}(vs, r, svs, m) \text{ is true for } vs = (l(v), vl, el, d)\},$$

otherwise $svs\text{-}eval_l(m, svs) = \emptyset$,
where $m = (c, p)$ with $c = (v', el', vl, d')$ and $p = (v, el, d)$.   ■

The predicates $\overline{V3}$ and $\overline{V4}$ are applied in the definition of *svs-eval*, since they deal with the effect of embedding descriptions. As a consequence we gain a constructive formulation of the introduction of strong V-structures by the evaluation of embedding descriptions. Next we will cope with predicates $V1$ and $\overline{V2}$, which cover the effect of the right-hand side. In the definition of the *svs*-rewriting step we combine them with $\overline{V3}$ and $\overline{V4}$. Overall we derive a constructive version of the necessary condition for the introduction of V-structures by execution of a rewriting step.

Definition 3.3.23   *SVS*-REWRITING STEP

Let *svs* be a set of strong V-structures. Let $r = (g_l, g_r, M)$ be a rewriting rule with labelling function l *svs*-applicable to *svs*.
The set of strong V-structures *svs'* is the *result of svs-rewriting svs by r* iff

$$svs' = (svs \cup \bigcup_{m \in M} svs\text{-}eval(m, svs)) \cup svs(g_r) \cup \{ vs |\ \overline{V2}(vs, r) \text{ is true} \} . \quad \blacksquare$$

We will now prove that *svs*-rewriting is consistent with respect to ordinary rewriting.

Lemma 3.3.24   CONSISTENCY OF *SVS*-REWRITING

Let g be a graph. Let $r = (g_l, g_r, M)$ be a rewriting rule applicable to g. *Let* g' be a graph such that there exists an injective graph morphism $\hat{h}$ with $g \rightarrow_h^r g'$.
Let *svs'* be the result of *svs*-rewriting $svs(g)$ by r. The following relation holds:

$$svs(g') \subseteq svs'.$$

Proof. Let $vs \notin svs(g')\backslash svs(g)$. From corollary 3.3.18 it follows that at least one of the refined static predicates is true. In case $V1(vs, r)$ is true, it follows that $vs \in svs(g_r) \subseteq svs'$. In case $\overline{V2}(vs, r)$, it follows that $vs \in svs'$. Let $m \in M$. In case $\overline{V3}(vs, r, svs(g), m)$ or $\overline{V4}(vs, r, m)$ are true, it follows that $vs \in svs\text{-}eval(m, svs)$ by definition. Hence $vs \in svs'$. $\quad \blacksquare$

We conclude this section with an algorithm to compute an upper approximation of $svs(gg)$. The algorithm delays the interpretation of embedding descriptions and the application of a rewriting rule until they are applicable. By this means, repetitive application of monotone abstract rewriting rules is implemented similar to algorithm 3.1.9. We give the basic structure of the algorithm which should in a real implementation respect the refinement of lemma 3.3.3, which rules out strong V-structures with unique edge or non-center vertex labels.

Algorithm 3.3.25 $SVS(gg)$, ABSTRACT INTERPRETATION OF $svs(gg)$

Let $gg = (\Sigma_V, \Sigma_E, g_0, R)$ be a graph rewriting system.

INPUT: g_0, R.

OUTPUT: $SVS(gg)$, a set of strong V-structures.

1.   **SET** $SVS(gg):=svs(g_0)$

2.   **INITIALIZE** the set of potential embedding descriptions: $PM:=\varnothing$

3.   **REPEAT**
       SVS is stable := True
       FOR ALL $r = (g_l, g_r, M) \in R$ svs-applicable to $SVS(gg)$ **DO**
         $SVS(gg):=SVS(gg) \cup svs(g_r) \cup \{vs|\ \overline{V2}(vs, r)\ \text{is true}\ \}$
         $PM:=PM \cup M$
         $R:=R\backslash\{r\}$
         $SVS(gg)$ is stable := False
       FOR ALL $m \in PM$ which svs-fits on $SVS(gg)$ **DO**
         $SVS(gg):=SVS(gg) \cup svs\text{-}eval(m, SVS(gg))$
         $PM:=PM\backslash\{m\}$
         $SVS(gg)$ is stable := False
       UNTIL $SVS(gg)$ is stable

4.   **OUTPUT** $SVS(gg)$ ∎

The complexity of the algorithm is linear in the sum of the number of rules and the number of embedding descriptions. Termination is guaranteed because the sizes of R and PM are monotonously decreasing.

   The correctness of algorithm 3.3.25 is proven is a similar way to theorem 3.2.11.

Theorem 3.3.26   CORRECTNESS OF ALGORITHM 3.3.25

Let gg be a graph rewriting system and $SVS(gg)$ be the output of algorithm 3.3.25.

$$svs(gg) \subseteq SVS(gg).$$

Sketch of Proof. The comparison of the definitions of *ltr*- and *svs*-rewriting reveals that *svs*-rewriting is also confluent. In detail, we have conditional rewriting caused by *svs*-applicability as well as the evaluation of embedding descriptions conditioned by the notion of *svs*-fit. Thus we can prove that reordering of two rewriting rules in an *svs*-derivation leads to the same result similar to lemma 3.2.8. Moreover *svs*-rewriting is monotone and increases the cardinality of the host set.

Hence *svs*-rewriting is confluent and algorithm 3.3.25 computes the *svs*-normal form of the initial graph. From lemma 3.3.24 the consistency of each *svs*-rewriting step follows. Thus for all sentential forms g, it holds that $svs(g) \subseteq SVS(gg)$, and the proposition follows from the definition of $svs(gg)$. ∎

The construction of a connected enumeration bypassing can exploit the upper approximation of strong V-structures. We noted already that an enumeration bypasses any subset of a set of strong V-structures. Thus when we can construct an enumeration bypassing the output of algorithm 3.3.25, it also bypasses the subset given by the theoretical definition of the set of strong V-structures of a graph rewriting system. Thus we have developed a complete constructive way to determine whether a rewriting system is constant-time matching.

3.4 Summary and Related Work

This chapter concentrated on the static analysis of graph rewriting systems. The application of these techniques, in particular the use of abstract graph rewriting, is novel in the area of graph rewriting systems. We presented three analyses which infer information on the generated graphs by inspection of the generating rewriting system.

Our approach follows a programming philosophy known from functional languages. Due to Milner's type inference calculus, explicit type declarations can be omitted by the programmer [Mil78]. The type of any object is inferred statically by its definition. We support this declarative style with our analyses. The programmer or designer of the graph rewriting systems does not need to declare properties of the generated graphs. He or she is advised by the results inferred by the analyses. Furthermore, no run-time checks are necessary to ensure properties which have been stated but were not checked statically.

The first static analysis determined lower approximations for the sets of unique vertex and edge labels of a given graph rewriting system. These sets are computable in polynomial time. As a corollary, we proved that the domain of the unique vertex labels of a rewriting rule must be contained in any full handle determined in the application of that rule. This improves the implementation of a graph rewriting system, since we know by static analysis which vertices must be unique. Hence they might be stored for direct access. Furthermore we have seen that the existence of at least one uniquely labelled vertex in each rule is necessary for constant-time matching. The corresponding notion of unique edge labels is exploited to sharpen the analysis on strong V-structures.

More sophisticated analysis could be performed by tracking dependencies between vertex edge labels respectively, and the introduction of equivalence classes of derivable graphs according to their set of unique labels. This analysis would comprise the dynamic anchor mentioned by Nagl [Nag79, p. 268]. Since we are mainly interested in the linear application of rewriting rules, our definitions are sufficient.

The next analysis, the study of label triples gives us an upper approximation for the set of label triples of all graphs derivable by a graph rewriting system. Based on this knowledge, we can reduce a given graph rewriting system without loss of generating power. This reduction is of interest, since any analysis will perform faster on graph rewriting systems with reduced size. The approximation of the label triples of a graph rewriting system reduces, furthermore, the space consumption of the abstract machine for the labelled subgraph matching.

The analysis of strong V-structures is the main contribution of this chapter. By means of this analysis, we are able to determine single entry slots in advance of an actual rewriting process. Thus we have a criterion at hand to select a connected enumeration as input for the labelled subgraph matching algorithm. We applied this criterion in the proof of the main theorem 3.3.8, which stated that enumerations bypassing the set of strong V-structures of a graph rewriting system and rooted in a uniquely labelled vertex perform a constant-time matching. We gave a constructive proof for the existence of a bypassing enumeration. The static analysis of strong V-structures is based on a classification of the instances of strong V-structures which are introduced in a rewriting step. The classification lemma is the main tool to prove a set of static predicates to form a necessary condition for the introduction of strong V-structures. The connection between static analysis and dynamic properties of a rewriting process is established by theorem 3.3.13. The refinement of the static predicates enables us to perform a more precise analysis. Finally we gave an algorithm which computes an upper approximation of strong V-structures.

As a side effect, it follows that the application of a rewriting rule for which a bypassing connected enumeration with uniquely labelled root exists has a deterministic result. We have seen in lemma 3.3.5 that the matching algorithm does not branch for a bypassing enumeration. Thus at most one graph morphism is found. The actual graph transformation on base of the morphism is deterministic. Hence when we have only one morphism, we can have no other choice, and the rewriting step has a deterministic result.

Each analysis can be sharpened by the results of the other ones. The reachability and V-structure analyses have a notion of abstract applicability. Thus whenever a rewriting rule turns out to be not abstractly applicable, it needs not to be considered by the other analyses. The unique label analysis has an influence on the strong V-structure analysis. lemma 3.3.3 states that a strong V-structure must contain nearly no unique label. Thus it might be possible to perform the analysis repeatedly until stable results are gained.

A lot of theoretical work has been done in the area of graph rewriting systems. Mostly it deals with context-free rewriting systems. For this class of systems, a context freeness lemma [DrKr91] is proved; and their relation to monadic second order logic [Cou91], [En91], fractal geometry [HaKr91], and term languages [EnHe91] is shown. For higher classes of graph rewriting systems, fewer theoretical results have been shown. There are, for example, parallelism and concurrency theorems in the algebraic framework [EKL91], or the hierarchy of classes given by Nagl [Nag79]. Kaul defined a subclass of context free graph grammars [Kau86]. For precedence graph grammars, the membership problem can be decided in polynomial time. All mentioned problems are treated for rewriting systems which are more restricted than ours.

Static analysis of programs is an old tool for optimization. Techniques like loop unrolling or peephole optimization are well-known operations on source and object code. The abstract interpretation of programs is a kind of static analysis developed in the last two decades. This analysis approach turned out to be a valuable means to determine dependencies between components of a program. Interest in this information grew in connection with the parallel implementation of logic as well as functional languages. The analysis of data dependency in logic programs, and of strict arguments in function definitions, unveiled cut-points for the parallelization. It was exploited for instance by Loogen and Burn [Loo90], [Bur87]. Without this information, parallelization could not provide sufficient speed-up.

Our approach to reduce the complexity of the labelled subgraph matching algorithm heavily exploits the application context. We thoroughly examine the possible inputs to the algorithm which are graphs generated by the rewriting system and the left-hand side of rules. Based on their strong interrelation, it is possible to derive our sufficient criterion for a constant-time matching rewriting system. Other approaches for the complexity reduction of the subgraph isomorphism problem do not have such fruitful soil. Corneil and Gotlieb, for example, give a procedure which is polynomial for most classes of graphs [CoGo70]. In a preprocessing step, a representative and a reordered representation of both input graphs is computed, and the problem is decided based on the transformed graphs. This procedure, however, gives an incomplete answer to the isomorphism problem. It may either give a positive or negative answer, or it must confess that it cannot decide. Because of preprocessing both graphs, it cannot be used in the implementation of graph rewriting systems. In each rewriting step, the transformations of the host graph must be calculated to eventually determine the morphism.

The RETE-algorithm proposed by Bunke et al. addresses the labelled subgraph matching problem for graph rewriting systems too [BGT91]. It is based on the observation that each rewriting step performs only local changes on the host graph. In a preprocessing step the system is analysed and the RETE-network created. Its topology represents the left-hand sides of the rewriting rules. The network is initialized by input of the initial graph. In each rewriting step, the possible matching subgraphs for a left-hand side can be selected by inspection of the network. After execution of the rewriting step, the information in the network is updated. This approach is not static, since at run time, the network is read and updated. We, on the contrary, preprocess the bypassing enumeration if it exists, and apply the rewriting rule without auxiliary updates.

The subsection on unique vertex labels formalizes a pragmatic property which is already mentioned by Nagl and Göttler [Nag79,p.189], [Gött88,p.97]. Nagl introduces the "stati-sche Verankerungsstruktur" (static anchor). Göttler uses a "Fixknoten" (fixed vertex) to define an application area of a rewriting rule and to force the application of subsequent rules to that area. The static anchor is used to program graph rewriting systems by means of graph rewriting systems only.

Bunke explicitly defines a class of so-called pivotal graph rewriting systems [Bun82]. They provide a set of pivotal vertex labels. In each derivable graph there must be exactly one label of that set. Bunke therefore uses rewriting rules which leave the number of pivotal labels invariant, i.e. one pivotal label must either remain or be replaced by another one in a rewriting step. We, on the contrary, define unique labels such that they are present in all derivable graphs. Thus a unique vertex label must not be replaced in a rewriting step. The combination of the periodic dependencies of pivotal labels and the existence of several unique labels in a graph rewriting system have not yet been discussed. They will certainly improve the static analysis of unique vertex labels.

The reachability problem for rules is known in the area of formal languages. Lewis II et al. give a procedure to determine unreachable non-terminals of a context-free string grammar [LRS76]. Those non-terminals do not appear in any string derived from the starting symbol. Our notion of reachable label triples covers exactly this notion of reachability; but the applicability of a graph rewriting rule does not only depend on the label triples of the host graph, but also on the structural properties. Thus our determination of reachable label triples cannot be as precise as the procedure given by Lewis II et al. In the context of graph rewriting our analysis is novel.

We share our interest in V-structures with Witt who studied locally unique graphs [Wit81]. This property is closely related to our notion of weak V-structures. He shows that by extension of the edge label alphabet, it is possible to create for any graph with bounded degree a homomorphic and locally unique image. Furthermore he proves the existence of a linearizable hull for each locally unique graph. In this context, a graph is linearizable iff each vertex of the graph has a unique address given as a list of edge labels. In contrast to our work on strong V-structures, he limits his studies to single graphs and not a whole language defined by a rewriting system.

The current implementation of the graph specification language PROGRES offers analyses too [NaSch90], [Schü91]. With respect to the declaration attitude of strongly typed imperative languages, the semantics of PROGRES requires, for example, the declaration of vertex and edge labels. Violations of this declaration requirement and inconsistent declarations are detected as well. Another property of PROGRES related to our work is edge label annotations. They prescribe for all edges of a given label an interval for the number of isomorphic edges incident with the target or source vertex. By this means, strong V-structures can be ruled out by annotations. The annotations are currently checked only for path-expressions by static analysis; however even the most obvious violation, the introduction of a strong V-structure on the right-hand side, is not recognized. To implement this approach correctly, run-time checks must be introduced when a static analysis like ours cannot ensure the correctness of the declarations.

The computation of a bypassing connected enumeration for the representation of a left-hand side is novel in the implementation of graph rewriting systems. Current implementations of unrestricted graph rewriting systems either choose an arbitrary enumeration (PROGRES, [Zün92]) or derive it from user information (chart-parser by Klauck, [KlMa92]). Löwe and Beyer implemented an interactie system for Algebraic Graph Grammars (AGG) system, the user gives the mapping of the left-hand side to the host graph [LöBe93]. In the implementation of context free graph rewriting systems by Himsolt, the user mostly selects the vertex to be rewritten [Him89].

4 Programmed Attributed Graph Rewrite Systems — An Advanced Modelling Formalism

Experiences with graph rewriting systems have shown that attribution and programming are the two additional concepts which provide a comfortable and structured specification formalism. The assignment of *attribute values* to vertices enables the representation of non-structural information in a graph. If these values would be encoded graphically, the resulting representation is hardly accessible to an intuitive understanding. Vertex and edge labels of ordinary graph rewriting systems are adequate representations of a small number of discrete states of graph components, but they are not able to designate an arbitrary number, or even a continuous space of values. The label alphabets, therefore, must be infinite and consequently a rewriting system must consist of an infinite number of rewriting rules. The traditional way to fix this lack of adequate representational power to use attributes.

The second major extension to our basic formalism is the use of *control structures* to build compound rule expressions. In the ordinary formalism, rewriting rules may be applied in an arbitrary order. Dependencies between rules must be encoded by specific vertex labels which block the application of rules to certain areas of the host graph. If vertex labels are assigned appropriately, an ordering can be enforced on the set of rewriting rules. The sophisticated labelling, though, introduces control information in the host graph which interferes with the structural representation. As a consequence, the intuitive interpretation of the graph is lost. The introduction of explicit programming separates the two areas of representation. The resulting specifications are easier to understand because two complementary formalisms are available.

For both extensions to our basic formalism we consider whether the theoretical results proven in the last chapter still apply. Thus we must also relate them to the ordinary formalism such that we can show that attributed and programmed graph rewriting systems may achieve constant-time matching as well.

This chapter now introduces attributed graph rewriting systems in a very general manner. We do not insist on a specific syntactical format, but define the underlying mathematical framework. The programmed graph rewriting systems, on the contrary, are specified in the traditional combination of syntactic and semantic definition.

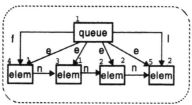

Figure 25   Priority queue redesigned

4.1 Attributed Graph Rewriting Systems — Extension I

In this subsection we give a mathematical description of the characteristic components of an attributed graph rewriting system. The extension of a graph rewriting systems covers all major components. We do not restrict ourselves to a specific syntactical format, but develop a general semantic framework for attributed graph rewriting systems. A variety of attribution formalisms can be mapped to our definitions.

The priority queue example from section 2.2 exhibits the problem that labels inadequately represent values of a large domain. For each priority "low" and "high", the rewriting system provides insertion and deletion rules. For any further priority class, we require extra rules. Also the number of embedding descriptions increases wherever they appear in a rewriting rule. The rule "remove_high", for instance, must provide an embedding description for each priority class, because the element preceding the terminating "high" vertex may be of any priority.

The introduction of attributes solves this problem. They allow a redesign by an attributed rewriting system with a fixed number of rules independent of the number of supported priority classes. An element of a priority queue is henceforth represented as an "elem"-vertex which carries its priority in an attribute. The priority queue shown in figure 10 we thus represent as shown in figure 26.

The two priorities are encoded as attribute values 1 and 2 respectively. They are shown on the top right edge of each element. Because the elements of the queue have the same label, we need only one rule to represent an operation. Also, only one embedding description is required to denote a neighboured vertex. The redesigned "remove" rule abstracts from the attribute value and considers only the structure of the graph.

remove

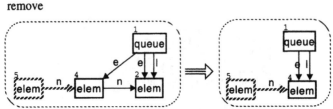

The refined rule "remove_last" can also be applied without respect to the priority of the last element.

remove_last

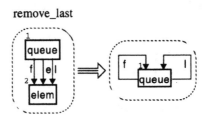

Hence the introduction of attributes enables the separate representation of structural and value-oriented properties.

The complete formalism for attributed graph rewriting systems provides three specific extensions to rewrite attributed graphs. Attribute values

- are input via parameters
- are assigned in a rewriting step and
- may provide an additional condition for applicability.

When we insert a new element to the priority queue, we must not only create a new vertex, but also set the attribute value. It is provided as a parameter given to the rewriting rule. The assignment then sets the attribute to the actual parameter value. The additional condition for the applicability of a rewriting rule is required, for instance, to realize the swap operation on the queue. Only elements which appear in the wrong order must be swapped. In the case of two priorities, we have expressed this condition by appropriate vertex labels. In the redesign, the labels are equal and the priorities are kept as attribute values. To apply "swap" only to wrongly ordered elements, the applicability of the operation must depend on the attribute values.

4.1.1   The Formalism

We begin by defining the basic extension, *attributed graphs*. Since vertices are the primary components of a graph, the attribution function is defined on vertices only. This design decision imposes no major restriction because attributes assigned to edges can be represented as vertex attributes too. The value of an attribute assigned to a vertex is the element of an arbitrary but fixed domain. It is accessed via the attribute's name and the corresponding vertex.

Definition 4.1.1   ATTRIBUTED GRAPH, ATTRIBUTE FUNCTION

Let $g = (V, E, l)$ be a graph. Let Σ_A be a finite, non-empty set, the set of *attribute names*. Let D be a set, the set of *attribute values*. A partial function $f: (V \times \Sigma_A) \rightarrow D$ is an *attribute function*. The extension of a graph g by the function f is the *attributed graph*

$$ag = (V, E, l, f) \, .$$

The graph g is the *underlying unattributed graph* of ag, $unatt(ag) = g$.   ∎

We have chosen D to be a plain set of values. This general definition can be refined by a type structure imposed on D.

When using attributed graphs as the basic objects, we must be able to compute the attribute function of the result graph. The application of an attributed rewriting rule should determine the new attribute function as well as structural changes. The changes to the attribute function must be specified by computation rules. In a rewriting step, we do not know the vertices of either the host or the result graph. They are accessible only via the morphism mapping both sides of an applied rule into the host and the result graph. Hence for the evaluation of computation rules, we assume the existence of that morphism. The computation rules can be given in terms of vertices occurring in rewriting rules, and they are evaluated in presence of a vertex mapping. Take, for example, the insertion rule of the priority queue. It must assign a value to an attribute of the inserted vertex. The inverse image of that vertex is, under any rewriting morphism, part of the right-hand side. Thus we can state a symbolic assignment of that value to an attribute of the right-hand side vertex.

Furthermore we want to compute attribute values depending on values of host graph attributes. The computation rule therefore must access vertices of the left-hand side to denote their images in a rewriting step. During the application of the rule, the references in the computation rules are dissolved by the graph morphism. According to the intuitive understanding of graph rewriting, the attributes of host graph vertices remain unchanged when they are not in the range of the rewriting morphism.

Attribute values must also be input to the attribute computation performed in a rewriting step. Formally, attribute values are introduced to a rewriting step as a list of actual parameters. Hence each rule definition holds a list of formal parameters which serve as place holders in computation rules. In a rewriting step, a list of actual parameters must be provided which substitutes the formal parameters.

The following two rules give examples for the use of parameters, assignments, and conditions on a syntactical level. The rule "insert" takes a parameter and assigns it to the "priority" attribute of the inserted element.

insert (n)

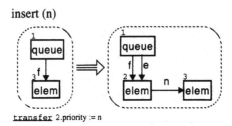

transfer 2.priority := n

The transfer statement serves in the sequel as the syntactical representation of a computation rule. The interpretation during a rewriting step will be as follows: assign the value of parameter n to the value attribute of the image of vertex 2.

Two elements of the queue are swapped if they are in the wrong order. Thus the rule "swap" must check the priorities of neighbouring elements. It must not be applied when the priority of the image of vertex 2 is lower than that of the image of 3.

swap

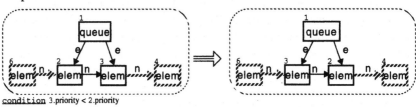

condition 3.priority < 2.priority

The definition of an attributed rewriting rule provides a semantics for the condition and the transfer statements.

We have determined four components which take part in the computation of the result graph's attribute function:

- a graph morphism accessing vertices of the host and the result graph,
- a list of actual parameters,
- the attribute function of the host graph, and
- computation rules which syntactically describe the attribute function
  of the result graph.

Only the last component is part of an attributed graph rewriting system as the syntactical specification of possible rewriting steps. The other three components are dynamic: they are different for each rewriting step, and they determine the evaluation of the result graph's attribute function with respect to the computation rules.

The semantic domain for computation rules is given by the general definition of an *attribute function transformation*. Such transformation computes the attribute function of the result graph based on the three dynamic components: the graph morphism, the vector of actual parameters, and the host graph's attribute function. Thus the semantics of a computation rule is given as an attribute function transformation.

The extension of graph rewriting to attributed graphs deserves an extended definition of applicability. The applicability of an attributed rewriting rule should be determined not only by structural properties, but also by attribute values. Therefore we define an *application predicate*. Similar to the attribute function transformation, it is defined in terms of the components of a rewriting step.

The attribute function transformation and the application predicate extend the ordinary graph rewriting rule to an *attributed rewriting rule*. Because we are interested in a general framework for attributed graph rewriting systems, we do not explicitly specify a syntactical representation. For our purpose, the definition on a semantic level is sufficient.

Definition 4.1.2   ATTRIBUTED GRAPH REWRITING RULE

Let $r = (g_l, g_r, M)$ be a rewriting rule.

a) Let D be a set of values and n a non-negative integer. A vector $par \in D^n$ is a vector of *actual parameters*.

b) Let par be an n-dimensional vector of actual parameters. Let $ag = (V, E, l, f)$ be an attributed graph such that r is applicable to $unatt(ag)$. Let $\hat{h}$ be a graph isomorphism with $\hat{h}(g_l) \subseteq unatt(ag)$. Let g' be the graph with $unatt(ag) \rightarrow_{\hat{h}}^r g'$. Any function aft with $aft(par, h, f) \in (V \times \Sigma_A) \rightarrow D$ is an *attribute function transformation*. Any function ap with $ap(par, h, f) \in \{true, false\}$ is an *application predicate*. The degrees of the functions aft and ap equal the dimension of par, i.e. $deg(atf) = deg(ap) = n$.

c) Let atr be an attribute function transformation and ap an application predicate both with degree n. The quintuple $ar = (g_l, g_r, M, aft, ap)$ is an *attributed rewriting rule* of degree n, i.e. $deg(ar) = n$. The rule r is the *underlying unattributed rewriting rule* of ar, $unatt(ar) = r$.   ∎

The transfer statement of the rule "insert" has the following semantics in terms of an attribute function transformation: the priority attribute of the image of vertex 3 must be set to the value of parameter n. All other attributes remain unchanged. Hence the semantics of

$$\underline{\texttt{transfer}}\ 3.\text{priority} = n$$

is defined for an arbitrary graph isomorphism $\hat{h}$, and an attribute function f as

$$aft((n), h, f)\ (v, a) \quad = n \qquad , \text{if } (v, a) = (h(3), \text{priority})$$
$$= f(v, a) \quad , \text{else.}$$

The condition which is stated in the "swap" rule accesses attributes of the host graph. Hence the application predicate must apply the graph morphism h to select the appropriate vertices of the host graph. Their attribute values are determined by the attribute function f. Consequently the application predicate has the following semantics:

$$ap(\varepsilon, h, f)\ (v, a) = f(h(2), \text{priority}) > f(h(3), \text{priority})$$

The definition of the attributed rewriting rule does not enforce an order in which application predicate and the attribute function transformation must be evaluated. Hence it might be possible to update the attributes of a graph by a transformation before the predicate of the applied rule is computed. Hence the predicate's value is based on wrong information. The definition of an attributed rewriting step must ensure the correct evaluation order.

In case the domain of values has a type structure, we must lay more interest in the shape of parameter vectors concerning type correctness. We decided, however, to use a quite simple attribution calculus which requires just equal degree of attribute function transformation and application predicate. Furthermore note that, according to the definition of the attribute function transformation, a global change of attribute values is possible. As a simplification, we assume that the transformation matches the intuition of locality in a graph rewriting step and performs updates only in the images of the right-hand side.

After the definition of the attributed rewriting rule, we extend the definition of the application condition. The application predicate prohibits the application of a rule even if there is an isomorphic subgraph. An attributed rewriting rule is *att-applicable* if the structural premises hold and the application predicate evaluates to "true". From the definition of the application predicate it follows that the *att*-applicability depends not only on the attributed graph but also on a vector of actual parameters.

Definition 4.1.3 *att*-APPLICABILITY

Let $ar = (g_l, g_r, M, aft, ap)$ be an attributed rewriting rule of degree n. Let $ag = (V, E, l, f)$ be an attributed graph and par be an n-dimensional vector of actual parameters. The attributed rewriting rule ar is *att-applicable* to the attributed graph ag and the vector of actual parameters par iff there is a graph isomorphism $\hat{h}$ such that $\hat{h}(g_l) \subseteq \hat{h}(unatt(ag))$ and $ap(par, h, f) = \text{true}$. ∎

Corollary 4.1.4   *att*-APPLICABILITY IMPLIES APPLICABILITY

Let *ar* be an attributed rewriting rule of degree *n*. Let *ag* be an attributed graph and *par* be an *n*-dimensional vector of actual parameters.

> *ar* is *att*-applicable to *ag* $\Rightarrow$ *unatt*(*ar*) is applicable to *unatt*(*ag*).

Proof. The proposition holds by the first condition of definition 4.1.3.   ∎

The effect of an *attributed rewriting step* is twofold: given an attributed host graph, the application of an attributed rewriting rule changes the underlying unattributed graph as defined in ordinary rewriting; additionally, the attribute function of the result graph is computed by application of the attribute function transformation.

Definition 4.1.5 $ag \rightarrow^{r}_{par,\,h} ag'$, *att*-REWRITING STEP

Let $ag = (V, E, l, f)$ be an attributed graph. Let *par* be an *n*-dimensional vector of actual parameters. Let $ar = (g_l, g_r, M, aft, ap)$ be an attributed rewriting rule of degree *n*, *att*-applicable to *ag* and *par*. Let $\hat{h}$ be a corresponding graph isomorphism. The attributed graph $ag' = (V', E', l', f')$ is the result of *rewriting ag with ar under par and h* iff

$$unatt(ag) \rightarrow^{unatt(ar)}_{h} unatt(ag') \text{ and } f' = aft(par, h, f).$$

An attributed rewriting step is denoted by $ag \rightarrow^{ar}_{par,\,h} ag'$.   ∎

The application of the attributed rewriting rule "insert (2)" to the redesigned priority queue (see figure 26) results in the graph shown in figure 26. The semantics of the transfer statement enforces that the priority attribute of the vertex 7 has the value 2.

The distinction between inherited and synthesized attributes known from attributed context-free string grammars is misleading in the context of attributed graph rewriting systems. Synthesized attributes usually refer to values which are computed later on in a derivation. Such a reference can be set up by a sequence of synthesized attributes, whose value depends on the proceeding one. No vertex carrying a synthesized attribute on which other attributes depend must be deleted until the dependency is

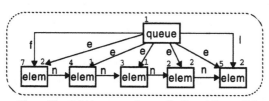

Figure 26   Priority queue after application of "insert (2)"

removed. Otherwise, the value of dependent attributes is undefined. The deletion of vertices makes synthesized attributes unsuitable for graph rewriting systems. In string grammars, the distinction makes sense as long as attributed abstract syntax trees are generated. They incorporate the complete information on the derivation. Each inner node in the tree represents a non-terminal symbol which has been rewritten to the sequence of symbols of the children nodes. No node is deleted during the derivation. Thus, definitions of synthesized attributes can be evaluated independently of existing dependencies.

Based on the definition of a rewriting rule, an *attributed graph rewriting system* and related notions can be defined.

Definition 4.1.6   ATTRIBUTED GRAPH REWRITING SYSTEM

Let Σ_V, Σ_E, Σ_A be alphabets. Let ag_0 be an attributed graph over Σ_V, Σ_E, Σ_A and $AR = \{ar_i | i = 1...n\}$ be a set of attributed rewriting rules over Σ_V, Σ_E, Σ_A.

a) An *attributed graph rewriting system* over the set of vertex labels Σ_V, the set of edge labels Σ_E, and the set of attribute names Σ_A with initial graph ag_0 and a set of rules AR is the tuple $agg = (\Sigma_V, \Sigma_E, \Sigma_A, ag_0, AR)$. The *underlying unattributed graph rewriting system* is $unatt(agg) = (\Sigma_V, \Sigma_E, unatt(ag_0), \{unatt(ar)| ar \in AR\})$.

b) The attributed graph ag_n can be *derived* from an attributed graph ag_1 if there are attributed rewriting rules $ar_i \in AR$, parameter vectors par_i of appropriate dimension $deg(ar_i)$, and graph isomorphisms $\hat{h}_i$ such that $ag_i \xrightarrow[par_i, h_i]{ar_i} ag_{i+1}$ for $i = 1... n - 1$. In this case there exists a derivation of ag_n from ag_1, denoted as $ag_1 \rightarrow * ag_n$.

c) The *attributed graph language* is defined as $L(agg) = \{ag| ag_0 \rightarrow * ag\}$. The underlying *unattributed language* is $unatt(L(agg)) = \{unatt(ag) | ag \in L(agg)\}$ ∎

4.1.2   Application of the Analyses

The analysis of chapter 3 was performed on ordinary rewriting systems. To relate the results to attributed graph rewriting systems, we study the generating power of an attributed and its underlying unattributed graph rewriting system. We show that the unattributed version of any attributed graph derived by an attributed system is also derivable in the unattributed rewriting system. This result corresponds to the intuitions that, first, attributed rewriting rules are less applicable than ordinary ones, and, second, the graphical part is identical.

Lemma 4.1.7

Let *agg* be an attributed graph rewriting system. It holds that

$$unatt(L(agg)) \subseteq L(unatt(agg)).$$

Proof. Let $ag \in L(agg)$ be an attributed graph. Thus there exists a derivation with attributed rewriting rules ar_i, parameter vectors par_i, and isomorphisms h_i $ag_i \to_{par_i, h_i}^{ar_i} ag_{i+1}$ for $i = 0...n$ such that $ag_{n+1} = ag$ and ag_0 is the initial graph. All ar_i are *att*-applicable to ag_i. From lemma 4.1.7 it follows that the unattributed rewriting rule $unatt(ar_i)$ is applicable to $unatt(ag_i)$. Thus the unattributed graph $unatt(ag)$ is also derivable from $unatt(ag_0)$ by ordinary rewriting. Hence $unatt(ag) \in L(unatt(agg))$. ∎

The analysis of unique vertex labels of an attributed rewriting system is performed by reduction to the unattributed system. We define first the set of unique vertex labels of an attributed graph rewriting system by reduction to the unique labels of the unattributed generated graphs. Then we prove a lower approximation for this set again by reduction to the unattributed case.

Definition 4.1.8 $uv(agg)$, UNIQUE VERTEX LABELS

Let *agg* be an attributed graph rewriting system. The set of *unique vertex labels of agg* is defined as $uv(agg) = \bigcap_{ag \in L(agg)} uv(unatt(ag))$. ∎

Theorem 4.1.9   APPROXIMATION OF $uv(agg)$

Let *agg* be an attributed graph rewriting system. Let $UV(agg) = UV(unatt(agg))$ be the result of the approximation algorithm for unique vertex labels applied on the unattributed rewriting system. Then $UV(agg)$ is an approximation of the set of unique vertex labels $uv(agg)$, i.e. $UV(agg) \subseteq uv(agg)$.

Proof. The unique vertex labels of an attributed rewriting system are defined as $uv(agg) = \bigcap_{ag \in L(agg)} uv(unatt(ag))$. Lemma 4.1.7 states that whenever an attributed graph is generated by an attributed rewriting system, its underlying graph is derivable by the unattributed rewriting system. Hence it follows for the intersection over all generated graphs that $\bigcap_{g \in L(unatt(agg))} uv(g) \subseteq \bigcap_{ag \in L(agg)} uv(unatt(ag))$. From theorem 3.1.4 it follows that $UV(gg)$ is a lower approximation of $uv(gg)$ for all unattributed rewriting systems. Hence it follows that $UV(agg) = UV(unatt(agg)) \subseteq uv(unatt(agg))$ $= \bigcap_{g \in L(unatt(agg))} uv(g)$. ∎

As a consequence, it follows that corollary 3.1.5 is applicable to attributed graph rewriting systems as well. Hence all morphisms from an attributed rewriting rule into an attributed host graph map vertices with the same unique label onto exactly one vertex of the host graph.

We extend the definitions of label triples and strong V-structures to attributed graph rewriting systems as well. The algorithms which perform an abstract interpretation still compute upper approximations when applied to the underlying unattributed rewriting systems. Hence the results on reachability and constant-time matching also hold for attributed graph rewriting systems.

Definition 4.1.10 $ltr(agg)$, $svs(agg)$, LABEL TRIPLES, STRONG V-STRUCTURES

Let agg be an attributed graph rewriting system.

a) The set of label triples of agg is defined as: $ltr(agg) = \bigcup_{ag \in L(agg)} ltr(unatt(ag))$.

b) The set of strong V-structures of agg is defined as:

$$svs(agg) = \bigcup_{ag \in L(agg)} svs(unatt(ag)).$$ ■

Theorem 4.1.11   APPROXIMATION OF $ltr(agg)$ AND $svs(agg)$

Let agg be an attributed graph rewriting system and LTR and SVS be the functions computed by algorithm 3.1.9 and algorithm 3.3.25. The following propositions hold.

$$ltr(agg) \subseteq LTR(unatt(agg))$$
$$svs(agg) \subseteq SVS(unatt(agg))$$

Proof. The set of label triples is defined as $ltr(agg) = \bigcup_{ag \in L(agg)} ltr(unatt(ag))$. Lemma 4.1.7 relates attributed rewriting systems to the underlying unattributed ones and it follows that $ltr(agg) \subseteq \bigcup_{g \in L(unatt(agg))} ltr(g) = ltr(unatt(agg))$. From theorem 3.2.11 we know that algorithm 3.1.9 computes an upper approximation, $ltr(unatt(agg)) \subseteq LTR(unatt(agg))$, and the first proposition follows.

A similar argument proves the second inclusion. ■

4.2 Programmed Graph Rewriting Systems — Extension II

A methodological principle of a specification by graph rewriting is the identification of system's operations with rewriting rules and valid states with derivable graphs. In ordinary graph rewriting, any rule can be chosen for the next application. Hence any operation might be triggered in the specified system. Should an operation be disabled in a certain system state, the corresponding rewriting rule must not be applicable to the representing host graph. The blocking of rewriting rules is mostly implemented using labels which represent parts of the system's state. So, for example, the graph may contain a vertex with a label such that certain rules are not applicable. They represent disabled operations. The rewriting rules are therefore extended to include vertices with this kind of state information. As a result, they are only applicable when the system is in the right state.

Blocking vertices, for example, control the applicability of rewriting rules. For the specification of complex systems the blocking mechanism turns out to be inconvenient. Not only the structural properties of the system must be covered by a specification, but also the various dependencies between operations must be represented. If that control information is included in the graphical representation as well, the resulting specification is hard to understand. *Control and structural information are represented by identical means* and are thus inseparable.

Several graph specification formalisms have been augmented with imperative control structures in order to cope with the different requirements for a graph specification. The graphical properties are represented by an ordinary graph rewriting system. The control information is represented by a *separate graph rewriting program*. Thus we follow the equation "Algorithms + Data Structures = Programs" stated by Wirth [Wir76]. The improved clarity has a particular advantage for two reasons:

(i)   sequences of operations can be directly mapped to control sequences based on the individual representation of each operation and

(ii)   the representation of a singular complex operation can be split into a number of various rules. Their application is controlled by a rewriting program.

Take again the priority queue as an example. Up to now, we have informally specified that whenever an element is inserted, it must be propagated to its correct position by the repeated application of "swap". We can enforce this behaviour using an additional label for the "queue"-vertex. The label indicates that the queue is not sorted. Hence when an element is inserted, the "queue"-vertex is replaced by a vertex with label "unsor". Thus the operation "insert" is blocked, but "swap" will be allowed. When "swap" is not applicable any more, the state of the queue is reset by "no_swap". The following three rules realize the described behaviour:

swap

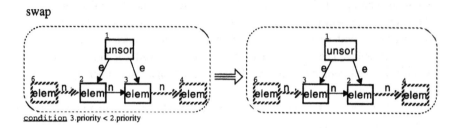

condition 3.priority < 2.priority

insert (n)   no_swap

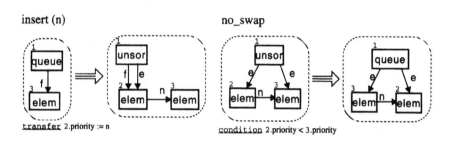

transfer 2.priority := n   condition 2.priority < 3.priority

Note that "swap" and "no_swap" are mutually exclusive. They apply to the same subgraph, but their conditions are inverse. The labels "unsor" and "queue" denote the two states of the queue, and enable two subsets of the specified rewriting rules. With control structures we can directly express the dependencies of the rewriting rules. Assume, for the moment, that ";" denotes the sequence of rewriting rules and that "loop ... end" applies a rule as long as it is applicable. Both control structures suffice for the statement of a compound rewriting rule "insertion". It inserts an element and propagates it to the appropriate place.

> insertion (n) = insert (n);
>   loop
>   swap
>   end

This section provides a sound definition of control structures like those used in the example above. From a theoretical point of view, the use of control structures does not increase the *generating power* of an ordinary graph rewriting system. Nagl proves that the ordinary formalism can already generate all enumerable graph languages [Nag79, p.61].

We will not introduce a large set of *control structures*, but restrict ourselves to a *basic set*. To prove the relevance of our approach, we reduce several control structures introduced by other authors into our basic set. This set provides constructors for

- sequential combination
- non-deterministic choice and
- conditional application of a rule or a rule expression.

The constructors combine simple rewriting rules, or rule expressions to compound rule expressions. Repeated application of a rule expression is realized by recursive calls to that expression. Therefore, the programming language contains definitions to bind rule expressions to names.

For the presentation of programmed graph rewriting systems, we use the terminology known from the *semantics of programming languages*. The presentation is founded on the set-theoretic formulation of ordinary graph rewriting systems. Both levels are linked by the semantics of a programmed graph rewriting system which uses the notions of applicability and rewriting step.

A programmed graph rewriting system is first of all defined as a syntactical object. The interpretation of the control structures provided is given by their semantics. We present two denotational semantics:

- the failure and
- the collection semantics.

They differ mainly in the semantic domain for a rule expression. The *failure semantics* interprets a rule expression as the relation between host and result graphs. Similarly, a rule expression may derive several result graphs when applied to a certain host graph. Thus it extends the intuitive semantics of a single rule to rule expressions, with one important difference: the semantics of a single rule is a set of host-result-graph pairs. If the rule is not applicable to a graph, then there is no element in the relation. When we define the semantics of a sequence of rewriting rules, this sequence may be partially executable for a given host graph. The failure semantics now records the partial execution and includes the pair of host and last result graphs in the relation. An all-or-nothing semantics, on the contrary, would only take fully successful application sequences into account. The failure semantics reflects the execution behaviour of an interpreter-based implementation. The interpreter inputs the graph rewriting program and determines the rewriting rule to be applied next. If that rule is successfully applied, the interpreter selects the next rule. If the application of the rule fails, the interpreter terminates. The program caused the application of a non-applicable rule. As long as the interpreter has no sophisticated features like backtracking, it has no other alternative than simply to fail.

The *collection semantics* not only determines a set of result graphs, but also reflects the derivation of the application of a rule expression. The semantics records all graphs which have been derived during the application. We provide the collection semantics to apply the analyses of chapter 3 to programmed graph rewriting systems. For that purpose, we must show that any graph derivable by a programmed graph rewriting system can be generated by the ordinary system also. Hence we must have a means to determine the set of derivable graphs explicitly. The failure semantics does not provide that information. It suppresses graphs which are generated during the derivation and sets up only the relation between an initial host and the final result graph. Thus we define the collection semantics additionally.

4.2.1 The Syntax

The syntactical definition of a programmed graph rewriting system contains ordinary rewriting rules as an integral part. The rewriting rules are provided by an underlying ordinary graph rewriting system in an arbitrary syntactical form. We introduce an abstract string grammar to define the set of programmed graph rewriting systems which can be built on top of an ordinary rewriting system. The relation between a programmed and an underlying ordinary graph rewriting system is defined by a syntactical rule reflecting ordinary rewriting rules. Another link between programmed and ordinary graph rewriting will be set up in the definition of semantic functions.

Definition 4.2.1   SYNTAX OF A PROGRAMMED GRAPH REWRITING SYSTEM

a) Let $gg = (\Sigma_V, \Sigma_E, g_0, R)$ be a graph rewriting system. A *programmed graph rewriting system* is derived by the following abstract string grammar with initial non-terminal <pgrs>:

             <pgrs> ::=<def>

             <def>   ::=<def> <def> |

                      <ident> = <exp>

             <exp>   ::=<exp> OR <exp> |

                      <exp> AND <exp> |

                      IF <rule> THEN <exp> ELSE <exp> |

                      SKIP | FAIL | <rule> | <ident>

             <rule>   ::= ... syntactical representations for all $r \in R$

             <ident> ::= ... a set of identifiers

All programmed graph rewriting systems derived from <pgrs> have gg as an *underlying ordinary rewriting system*.

b) The syntactic domains PGRS, DEF, EXP, RULE and IDENT are those sets of strings derived from <pgrs>, <def>, <exp>, <rules> and <ident>.   ■

A programmed graph rewriting system is first of all a set of definitions which bind rule expressions to identifiers. The rule expressions are either simple or compound. Simple expressions are a single rule, a rule expression call, or the constant expressions SKIP and FAIL. SKIP denotes the empty rewriting rule which is always applicable and performs no transformations, whereas FAIL is the rewriting rule which is never applicable. Compound expressions are built by the constructors AND, OR and IF-THEN-ELSE, which denote a sequence, a choice, and the conditional application of rules.

The underlying ordinary rewriting system is not uniquely defined because the initial graph does not appear in a programmed rewriting system. Thus any graph rewriting system with the same set of rules suffices as an underlying rewriting system. Furthermore, just a subset $R' \subseteq R$ may be used in the expressions of a specific programmed rewriting system. Hence it can also be derived by a string grammar which has a smaller rewriting system $(\Sigma_V, \Sigma_E, g_0, R')$.

4.2.2   The Failure Semantics

A denotational semantics of a syntactical domain like PGRS must provide a number of *semantic domains*. The defined *semantic functions* map the syntactic onto semantic domains, and thereby give a mathematical interpretation of the syntactic objects. These domains must be complete partial orders to provide a sound semantics even in the presence of recursive definitions of semantic functions. The flat domain for an enumerable set S is denoted by $S_\perp$. The bottom element of a semantic domain D is $\perp_D$. The failure and the collection semantics are both primitive, i.e. the definitions of semantic functions reflect the structure of the syntactic objects.[1]

The semantic domains for the failure semantics are as follows. Let G be the set of all labelled, directed graphs.

$$G_\perp = G \cup \{\perp_G\}$$
$$Exp = \wp(G_\perp \times G_\perp \times \{v, f\}_\perp)$$
$$Env = IDENT \rightarrow Exp$$

In the failure semantics, a *rule expression* is interpreted basically as the *relation between host and result graphs*. Furthermore it contains information on the status of the derivation denoted by the expression. The derivation might terminate during the evaluation of the expression because the application of a rule to an intermediate host graph failed. In this case, the application of the expression derives that intermediate graph on which no further rule must be applied. That status of the derivation is denoted by "**f**" for failed. In case the expression can be evaluated in total for a certain host

---

1. Fehr gives further details on denotational semantics [Fe89].

graph, the partial relation may be extended by further applications and is therefore viable, denoted by "**v**". The environment *Env* represents the bindings of expressions to identifiers which are set up by the definitions of a programmed graph rewriting system.

The four semantic functions which comprise the failure semantics are:

R: RULE $\rightarrow Exp$

E: EXP $\rightarrow Env \rightarrow Exp$

D: DEF $\rightarrow Env \rightarrow Env$

P: PGRS $\rightarrow$ IDENT $\rightarrow \wp(G_\perp) \rightarrow \wp(G_\perp)$

The semantic function for a single rewriting rule sets up the interface between the set theoretic and semantic formalisms.

$$R[|r|] = \{ (g, g', \mathbf{v}) \in Exp |\, g \rightarrow^r g' \}$$
$$\cup \{ (\mathbf{g}, \mathbf{g}, \mathbf{f}) \in Exp |\, r \text{ is not applicable to } g \}$$

The semantics of a rewriting rule distinguishes two cases depending on the first component which is a potential host graph. In case the rule is applicable, it derives one or more result graphs which may serve as host graphs for further applications. Thus the third component is set to "**v**" for viable. In case the rule is not applicable to a graph *g*, the derivation terminates with *g* as the final result. To pass this derivation state to the surrounding rule expression, the third component carries an "**f**" for failure. This information is used by the sequential combination and the conditional application.

The function *E* computes the relation denoted by an expression in a given environment ρ.

$$E[|e_1 \text{ OR } e_2|]\rho \quad = E[|e_1|]\rho \cup E[|e_2|]\rho$$
$$E[|e_1 \text{ AND } e_2|]\rho \quad = \{ (g, g', \mathbf{f}) \in E[|e_1|]\rho \}$$
$$\cup \{ (g, g'', s) \in Exp |\, (g, g', \mathbf{v}) \in E[|e_1|]\rho$$
$$\text{and } (g', g'', s) \in E[|e_2|]\rho \}$$
$$E[| \text{ IF } r \text{ THEN } e_1 \text{ ELSE } e_2|]\rho =$$
$$\{ (g, g', s) \in E[|e_1|]\rho |\, \exists g'' \in G:\, (g, g'', \mathbf{v}) \in R[|r|] \}$$
$$\cup \{ (g, g', s) \in E[|e_2|]\rho |\, (g, g, \mathbf{f}) \in R[|r|] \}$$
$$E[|id|]\rho \quad = \rho(id)$$
$$E[| \text{ SKIP } |]\rho \quad = \{ (g, g, \mathbf{v}) \in Exp \}$$

$$E[|\ \underline{FAIL}\ |]\,\rho \qquad = \{\ (g, g, \mathsf{f})\ \in\ Exp\}$$
$$E[|r|]\,\rho \qquad\quad = R[|r|]$$

Non-deterministic choice is defined as the union of the semantics of both subexpressions according to the intuitive understanding of that construct. The evaluation of a non-deterministic choice may end up with a failed or a viable derivation, depending on the chosen subexpression. Hence for a given host graph g, there may be triples $(g, g',$ $\mathsf{f})$ and (g, g'', v) included in the semantics of a non-deterministic choice. For the first triple, the corresponding derivation leads to a failing application to graph g', whereas a second derivation succeeds and generates the result graph g''.

An alternative definition for the non-deterministic choice would prefer viable derivations as long as they exist for a subexpression. The non-deterministic choice would fail for a host graph only when both subexpressions fail. This definition has the advantage that it preserves the *application dichotomy*, i.e. a rule or an expression is either applicable or not. On the other hand, any implementation of that definition requires some kind of backtracking. The implementation must recover from failed applications and find a viable derivation, if it exists. Since our interest lies in the efficient implementation of graph rewriting systems, we reject the latter definition.

The *sequential combination* of two rule expressions is the second compound expression of programmed graph rewriting systems. As mentioned above, the combination denotes a viable derivation when both expressions are applicable in sequence. Otherwise, the sequential combination fails. If the first expression is successfully applied and generates the graph g', then the result graph of the sequential combination is determined by the application of e_2 to g'.

The selector of a *conditional application* consists of a rule which is tested for applicability. In our semantics, it is not advisable to allow arbitrary rule expressions because the application dichotomy is not provided. A rule expression may evaluate to both viable and failed derivations for a single host graph. Thus the test for the applicability of a whole rule expression may have a non-deterministic result. This behaviour would not meet the intuition of a conditional branch.

The remaining definitions are related to simple rule expressions. Any expression identifier is replaced by the bound expression, if defined. Otherwise the identifier evaluates to the empty set as the bottom element of *Exp*. An application of $\underline{SKIP}$ does not alter the host graph and never fails. The constant expression $\underline{FAIL}$ also does not perform any derivation, but fails. The definition of an ordinary rewriting rule refers to the semantics defined by R.

The semantic functions for expression definitions and rewriting programs are based on the definitions above.

$$D[\![id_1 = e_1, ..., id_k = e_k]\!]\rho = \rho' \text{ where } \rho' = \rho\,[\tilde{e}_1/id_1, ..., \tilde{e}_k/id_k]$$
$$\text{and } \tilde{e}_i = E[\![e_i]\!]\rho' \text{ for } i = 1...k$$

$$P[\![d]\!]id \;\; G \;\;\;\;\; = \{g'|\,(g, g', s) \in (D[\![d]\!]\bot)\;\; id, g \in G\}$$

The semantic function D takes an arbitrary number of expression definitions and extends the given environment. Hence expression definitions have a scope. The recursive definition of rule expressions is mapped to a recursive call to expressions by the evaluation of $E[\![id]\!]\rho$. The definition of P assumes that all definitions of a programmed rewriting system are in the same scope. It returns all graphs which can be derived from an element of G by an application of the rule expression being bound to id.

In our approach, a programmed graph rewriting system defines a set of complex rule expressions which can be selected by the corresponding identifier. Hence a programmed rewriting system is a *module* which *provides a number of complex rule expressions*. With small extensions to the definition of P, explicit export declarations may restrict the access to internal expression definitions.

The generating aspect of rewriting systems can easily be simulated; therefore assume the definition of an identifier "main". The *language F* being generated by a programmed graph rewriting system *pgg* in the failure semantics is then defined as the application of "main" to the set $\{g_0\}$ where g_0 is the initial graph of the underlying graph rewriting system.

$$F_{g_0}(pgg) = P[\![pgg]\!] \text{ main } \{g_0\} \cup \{g_0\}$$

The failure semantics provides *algebraic properties* for the expression constructors <u>OR</u> and <u>AND</u>. Obviously, the definitions of <u>OR</u> and <u>AND</u> are such that the non-deterministic choice commutes for both subexpressions, whereas the sequential combination does not. Furthermore, we can prove that both constructors are associative - an important property for the equality of structured expressions. Choices with a large number of alternatives, as well as long sequences, can be hierarchically structured without change of the semantics.

Lemma 4.2.2   ASSOCIATIVE LAW

Let $e_1, e_2, e_3 \in EXP$ and $\rho \in Env$.

a) $E[\![e_1 \text{ } \underline{OR} \text{ } (e_2 \text{ } \underline{OR} \text{ } e_3)]\!]\rho = E[\![(e_1 \text{ } \underline{OR} \text{ } e_2) \text{ } \underline{OR} \text{ } e_3]\!]\rho$

b) $E[\![e_1 \text{ } \underline{AND} \text{ } (e_2 \text{ } \underline{AND} \text{ } e_3)]\!]\rho = E[\![(e_1 \text{ } \underline{AND} \text{ } e_2) \text{ } \underline{AND} \text{ } e_3]\!]\rho$

Proof.
a) follows from the associativity of the set union.

b) $E[\![e_1 \ \underline{AND} \ (e_2 \ \underline{AND} \ e_3 \ )\!]\!]\rho$

$= \{ (g, g', f) \in E[\![e_1\!]\!]\rho \} \cup \{ (g, g''', s) \in Exp | \ (g, g', v) \in E[\![e_1\!]\!]\rho$

$\qquad\qquad$ and $(g', g''', s) \in E[\![(e_2 \ \underline{AND} \ e_3 \ )\!]\!]\rho \}$

$= \{ (g, g', f) \in E[\![e_1\!]\!]\rho \} \cup \{ (g, g'', f) \in Exp | \ (g, g', v) \in E[\![e_1\!]\!]\rho$

$\qquad\qquad\qquad$ and $(g', g'', f) \in E[\![e_2\!]\!]\rho \}$

$\quad \cup \{ (g, g''', s) \in Exp | \ (g, g', v) \in E[\![e_1\!]\!]\rho \, , \ (g', g'', v) \in E[\![e_2\!]\!]\rho,$

$\qquad\qquad$ and $(g'', g''', s) \in E[\![e_3\!]\!]\rho \}$

$= \{ (g, g'', f) \in E[\![e_1 \ \underline{AND} \ e_2\!]\!]\rho \}$

$\quad \cup \{ (g, g''', s) \in Exp | \ (g, g'', v) \in E[\![e_1 \ \underline{AND} \ e_2\!]\!]\rho$

$\qquad\qquad$ and $(g'', g''', s) \in E[\![e_3\!]\!]\rho \}$

$= E[\![(e_1 \ \underline{AND} \ e_2) \ \underline{AND} \ e_3\!]\!]\rho$ $\qquad\qquad\qquad\qquad\qquad$ ∎

4.2.3   The Collection Semantics

The failure semantics models the input-output relation of a rule expression as the set of viable expression triples. Information on the intermediate states of a programmed derivation is not provided. On the contrary, our definition of the language generated by an ordinary graph rewriting system included all sentential forms, i.e. all intermediate graphs of a derivation. Only with this definition were we able to prove the sufficient condition for constant-time matching. The main theorem of chapter 3 applies to the application of any rewriting rule to any sentential form. Thus the knowledge of specific characteristics of all derivable graphs was necessary to prove constant-time matching. This requirement reveals that the failure semantics is insufficient to prove a constant-time matching theorem for programmed graph rewriting systems. For that purpose we introduce the *collection semantics*. It not only defines an input-output relation of rule expressions, like the failure semantics, but also collects those graphs which are generated during the evaluation of a rule expression. The collection of all intermediate graphs is one component of the collection semantics. The second component is the set of derivable graphs, similar to the result graphs of viable derivations.

The semantic domains are identical to those in the failure semantics (see page 106) with exception of *Exp*. In the collection semantics, an expression maps pairs of graph sets. The first component is the collection of prior host graphs and the second contains current host graphs on which a rule expression may be applied.

$$Exp = (\wp(G_\bot) \times \wp(G_\bot)) \rightarrow (\wp(G_\bot) \times \wp(G_\bot))$$

The signature of the semantic functions is the same as in the failure semantics.

$$R: \text{RULE} \rightarrow Exp$$
$$E: \text{EXP} \rightarrow Env \rightarrow Exp$$
$$D: \text{DEF} \rightarrow Env \rightarrow Env$$
$$P: \text{PGRS} \rightarrow \text{IDENT} \rightarrow \wp(G_\perp) \rightarrow \wp(G_\perp)$$

A rewriting rule updates the collection of past host graphs and computes the set of result graphs which serve as host graphs for any successive rule expression.

$$R[|r|]\,(C, H) = (C \cup H, \{g'| g \in H \text{ and } g \rightarrow^r g'\})$$

The interpretation of a rule expression is defined as follows:

$$E[|e_1 \text{ OR } e_2|]\rho\ S \quad = \ (C_1 \cup C_2, H_1 \cup H_2)$$
$$\text{where } (C_i, H_i) = E[|e_i|]\rho\ S \text{ for } i = 1,2$$
$$E[|e_1 \text{ AND } e_2|]\rho\ S = E[|e_2|]\rho\ (E[|e_1|]\rho\ S)$$
$$E[|\text{ IF } r \text{ THEN } e_1 \text{ ELSE } e_2|]\rho\ (C, H) =$$
$$(C \cup H, \pi_2(E[|e_1|]\rho\ (C, T)) \cup \pi_2(E[|e_2|]\rho\ (C, H\backslash T)))$$
$$\text{where } T = \{g \in H| r \text{ is applicable to } g\}$$
$$E[|id|]\rho\ (C, H) \quad = \ (C \cup H \cup C', H') \text{ where } (C', H') = \rho(id)\,(\varnothing, H)$$
$$E[|\text{ SKIP }|]\rho\ (C, H) = \ (C \cup H, H)$$
$$E[|\text{ FAIL }|]\rho\ (C, H) = \ (C \cup H, \varnothing)$$
$$E[|r|]\rho\ S \quad\quad\ = \ R[|r|]\ S$$

The semantics of the non-deterministic choice meets the intuition that all result graphs derived by either e_1 or e_2 may occur in a derivation. Consequently the intermediate graphs of the evaluation of both subexpressions are derivable in an execution of e_1 OR e_2. The sequential combination is defined as the composition of the functions denoted by the subexpressions. The conditional application branches dependent on the applicability of the rule r. This condition defines a subset $T \subseteq H$ of host graphs on which r is applicable. Elements of T serve as host graphs for the expression in the THEN branch whereas the second branch will be applied to the complementary set $H \setminus T$. A call to a rule expression applies that expression to the set of current host graphs. The graphs being derived during the application are collected in C' and therefore added to the collection. Thus even in the presence of a "non-terminating recursive call", the intermediate generated host graphs, are put into the collection. The expression invoked by $\rho(id)$ requires only the set of current host graphs because the current collection C is already saved.

The remaining semantic functions are defined as follows:

$$D[|id_1 = e_1,...,id_k = e_k|]\rho = \rho' \text{ where } \rho' = \rho\,[\tilde{e}_1/id_1, ..., \tilde{e}_k/id_k]$$

$$\text{and } \tilde{e}_i = E[|e_i|]\rho' \text{ for } i = 1...k$$

$$P[|d|]\,id\ H\ = (D[|d|]\bot)\,id\ (\varnothing, H)$$

The semantic function D is defined as in the failure semantics. The semantics of a program is a function of an identifier and an initial set. A program calls the expression denoted by id and applies it to the set of current host graphs H. Based on this definition, we can define a language generated by a programmed graph rewriting system pgg in the collection semantics and dependent on an initial graph g as:

$$L_{g_0}(pgg) = C \cup H \text{ where } (C, H) = P[|pgg|] \text{ main } \{g_0\}.$$

The languages defined by the two semantics are equal. This property can be proved by structural induction.

The collection semantics of a programmed graph rewriting system is closely related to the underlying ordinary graph rewriting system. Since both definitions cover all derivable graphs, it can be easily shown that the results of chapter 3 apply to programmed graph rewriting systems also.

Theorem 4.2.3   GENERATING POWER OF A PROGRAM AND ITS UNDERLYING
ORDINARY GRAPH REWRITING SYSTEM

Let pgg be a programmed graph rewriting system on top of the ordinary graph rewriting system $gg = (\Sigma_V, \Sigma_E, g_0, R)$.

a) $L_{g_0}(pgg) \subseteq L(gg)$.

b) Let $R = \{r_1, ..., r_k\}$ and let $p = $ "main $= (r_1$ OR ... OR r_k) AND main" be a programmed graph rewriting system on top of gg. It holds that $L_{g_0}(p) = L(gg)$

Proof.

a) Let $\rho = D[|p|]\bot$ be the environment defined by p. Let $g \in L_{g_0}(pgg) = C \cup H$ be a graph where the collection C and the set of host graphs H is given as the semantics of the identifier "main", $(C, H) = P[|pgg|]$ main $\{g_0\} = E[|\text{main}|]\rho\,(\varnothing, \{g_0\})$. If the environment is undefined for main, i.e. $\rho(\text{main}) = \bot_{Exp}$ then $C = H = \varnothing$ and the generated language is empty: $L_{g_0}(pgg) = \varnothing \subseteq L(gg)$. Otherwise, there is a definition "main $= e$" in pgg and $(C, H) = E[|e|]\rho\,(\varnothing, \{g_0\})$. We show the main proposition by structural induction, i.e. we show that from $C \cup H \subseteq L(gg)$ it follows that $C' \cup H' \subseteq L(gg)$ for all $(C', H') = E[|e|] \rho (C, H)$ determined by expression e.

Let $g \in C \cup H$.

If $e = \underline{FAIL}$: $C' \cup H' = C \cup H \cup \emptyset \subseteq L(gg)$.

If $e = \underline{SKIP}$: $C' \cup H' = C \cup H \cup H \subseteq L(gg)$.

If $e \in$ RULE: for all result graphs g' with $g \to^e g'$ and $g \in H \subseteq L(gg)$ it holds that $g' \in L(gg)$. Hence $C' \cup H' = C \cup H \cup \{g' | g \in H \text{ and } g \to^e g'\} \subseteq L(gg)$.

If $e \in$ IDENT the pair of resulting collection and host graphs is determined by the semantics of the identifier, $(C'', H'') = \rho(e) (\emptyset, H)$. Hence $(C', H') = E[|e|] \rho (C, H) = (C \cup H \cup C'', H'')$. If ρ is undefined for e, i.e. $\rho(e) = \perp_{Exp}$ it follows that $(C'', H'') = \perp_{Exp} (\emptyset, H) = \perp_{\wp(G_\perp) \times \wp(G_\perp)} = (\emptyset, \emptyset)$ and $C \cup H' = C \cup H \cup \emptyset \cup \emptyset \subseteq L(gg)$. Now let $\rho(e) = E[|e'|] \rho$. From structural induction and $\emptyset \cup H \subseteq C \cup H \subseteq L(gg)$ it follows that $C'' \cup H'' \subseteq L(gg)$ and hence $C' \cup H' \subseteq L(gg)$.

If $e = e_1 \underline{OR} e_2$: Let $(C_i, H_i) = E[|e_i|] \rho (C, H)$ be the result of the two subexpressions, $i = 1, 2$. From the induction hypothesis it follows that the results C_i, H_i are subsets of $L(gg)$. Hence $C' \cup H' = C_1 \cup C_2 \cup H_1 \cup H_2$ is also a subset of $L(gg)$.

If $e = e_1 \underline{AND} e_2$: Let $(C_1, H_1) = E[|e_1|] \rho (C, H)$ be the result of the first subexpression applied to (C, H) and $(C', H') = E[|e_2|] \rho (C_1, H_1)$ be the result of the second. From the induction hypothesis it follows first that $C_1 \cup H_1 \subseteq L(gg)$. Further with a second application of the hypothesis it follows that $C' \cup H' \subseteq L(gg)$.

If $e = \underline{IF} r \underline{THEN} e_1 \underline{ELSE} e_2$: Using structural induction it follows for both subexpressions e_i that $C_i \cup H_i \subseteq L(gg)$ with $(C_i, H_i) = E[|e_i|] \rho (C, T)$ for $i = 1,2$ and any subset $T \subseteq H$. By inspection of the definition $C' \cup H' \subseteq L(gg)$ is proved.

b) Let $e = (r_1 \underline{OR} \dots \underline{OR} r_k)$ be the first subexpression of p. By definition it holds that $L_{g_0}(p) = C \cup H$ with $(C, H) = P[|p|] \text{ main } \{g_0\} = (D[|p|] \perp) \text{ main } (\emptyset, \{g_0\})$. The environment $\rho = D[|p|] \perp$ is defined for main as $\rho(\text{main}) = E[|e \underline{AND} \text{main}|] \rho$, and undefined otherwise, $\rho(x) = \perp_{Exp}$. Hence $(C, H) = E[|e \underline{AND} \text{main}|] \rho (\emptyset, \{g_0\})$. Let H and H_j be sets of graphs with $R[|r_j|] (\emptyset, H) = (H, H_j)$ for $j = 1 \dots k$. By definition of R it follows that $H_j = \{g' | \exists g \in H \text{ such that } g \to^r g'\}$. The semantics of subexpression e is then $E[|e|] \rho (\emptyset, H) = (H, \cup_{j=1 \dots k} H_j)$. We can now define a sequence of host graph sets H_i by $H_0 = \{g_0\}$ and $E[|e|] \rho (\emptyset, H_i) = (H_i, H_{i+1})$ for $i \geq 0$. Because e is a non-deterministic choice of rule applications it holds that

$$H_{i+1} = \{g' | \exists g \in H_i \text{ such that } g \to g'\} \qquad (*)$$

With application of the definition of E, the graph rewriting program "main" evaluates as follows: $E[|e\ \underline{AND}\ \text{main}\ |]\rho\ (\varnothing, H_i)\ =\ E[|\text{main}|]\rho\ (E[|e|]\rho\ (\varnothing, H_i))\ =\ E[|\text{main}|]\rho\ (H_i, H_{i+1})\ =\ (H_i \cup H_{i+1} \cup C_{i+1}, H)$ where $(C_{i+1}, H)\ =\ E[|e\ \underline{AND}\ \text{main}|]\ \rho\ (\varnothing, H_{i+1})$. Hence the collection defined by main is $C\ =\ H_0 \cup H_1 \cup C_1\ =\ H_0 \cup H_1 \cup H_1 \cup H_2 \cup C_2\ =\ ...\ =\ \bigcup_{i=1...\infty} H_i$. From property (*), it follows that $L(gg) \subseteq L_{g_0}(p)$.   ∎

The theorem proves that any graph derived in the execution of a programmed graph rewriting system is a sentential form of an underlying ordinary rewriting system as well. As a consequence, if we have proven that for a rewriting rule a connected enumeration exists bypassing the strong V-structures of an ordinary graph rewriting system, then the applicability of that rule to any graph derived by the programmed graph rewriting system can be decided in constant time. Thus when an underlying graph rewriting system matches in constant time, any programmed graph rewriting system built on top matches in constant time too.

4.2.4   Analysis of Further Control Structures

The basic set of control structures is powerful enough to *simulate* a number of *other programming constructs* given in the literature. We give a definition in the failure semantics for three of them. Furthermore, we extend our programming formalism to support pattern matching for the non-deterministic choice of simple rules.

A control structure widely used is the repeated application of rule expressions. We used the loop ... end construct in the insertion example. It is similar to the WAPP-construct (WAPP = while applicable) introduced by Göttler [Gött88,p.103]. Our framework is designed to use recursion instead of iteration. Hence we define the WAPP as a recursive application.

$$<\text{exp}>\qquad ::= ...\ |\ \underline{WAPP}\ <\text{exp}>$$
$$E[|\ \underline{WAPP}\ e|]\rho\ =\ E[|e\ \underline{AND}\ n|]\rho'$$
$$\text{where } n \text{ is such that } \rho(n)\ =\ \bot_{Exp}$$
$$\text{and } \rho'\ =\ \rho\ [E[|e|]\rho'/n]$$

Its intuitive meaning is to iteratively apply a rule expression to a host graph and the sequence of generated result graphs until the expression becomes not applicable. We show that our definition covers that intuition.

Let $e \in EXP$, $n \in IDENT$ and $\rho \in Env$ with $\rho(n)\ =\ \bot_{Exp}$. Let $(g_1, g_2, \mathbf{v})$, $(g_2, g_3, \mathbf{v})$, $(g_3, g_4, \mathbf{f}) \in E[|e|]\rho'$ be three derivations performed by e in the extended environment $\rho' = \rho\,[E[|e|]\rho'/n]$. That is, e derives g_2 from g_1, and then g_3 from g_2, and lastly g_4 from g_3. Since the last derivation yields a failure, e is not applicable to the graph g_4, i.e. $(g_4, g_4, \mathfrak{f}) \in E[|e|]\rho'$

We evaluate $E[|\ \underline{\text{WAPP}}\ el|]\rho$ to show that $(g_1, g_4, \mathfrak{f}) \in E[|\ \underline{\text{WAPP}}\ el|]\rho$:

$$E[|\ \underline{\text{WAPP}}\ el|]\rho\ =\ E[|e\ \underline{\text{AND}}\ nl|]\rho'$$
$$\subseteq\ \{\ (g, g'', s) \in Exp|\ (g, g', \mathbf{v}) \in E[|el|]\rho'\ \text{and}$$
$$(g', g'', s) \in E[|nl|]\rho'\ \}\,.$$

With $E[|nl|]\rho'\ =\ E[|e\ \underline{\text{AND}}\ nl|]\rho'$ it follows that

$$(g', g'', s) \in\ \{\ (h, h'', s') \in Exp|\ (h, h', \mathbf{v}) \in E[|el|]\rho'$$
$$\text{and}\ (h', h'', s') \in E[|nl|]\rho'\ \}$$

and with the identifications $g = g_1$, $g' = h = g_2$, $h' = g_3$, $h'' = g'' = g_4$, and $s = s' = \mathfrak{f}$ it follows that $(g_1, g_4, \mathfrak{f}) \in E[|\ \underline{\text{WAPP}}\ el|]\rho$.

Another construct has been used by Lewerentz [Lew88, p.139]. It improves the reliability of rewriting systems because it reduces the number of failed applications. Lewerentz defines the $\underline{\text{IF-POSSIBLE}}$ statement. It behaves similarly to the conditional application, with the exception that the selector rule is applied, if possible. Afterwards, the execution proceeds in the appropriate branch.

$$\text{<exp>}\qquad ::= \dots |\ \underline{\text{IF-POSSIBLE}}\ \text{<rule>}\ \underline{\text{THEN}}\ \text{<exp>}\ \underline{\text{ELSE}}\ \text{<exp>}\ \underline{\text{END}}$$

Our semantic reduction of that statement is as follows:

$$E[|\ \underline{\text{IF-POSSIBLE}}\ r\ \underline{\text{THEN}}\ e_1\ \underline{\text{ELSE}}\ e_2\ \underline{\text{END}}\ |]\rho\ =$$
$$E[|\ \underline{\text{IF}}\ r\ \underline{\text{THEN}}\ (r\ \underline{\text{AND}}\ e_1)\ \underline{\text{ELSE}}\ e_2|]\rho$$

Last of all, we analyse a modified version of ordinary rewriting systems. The modification provides means to shorten specifications because they consist of a smaller number of rules.

Often, labels represent different states of a specified component. In this case, a specification contains rewriting rules which perform identical structural transformations whenever a transformation can be executed in several states. To reduce the number of similar rules, the concept of *set-valued vertex labels* is introduced. It embodies the basic principle of vertex types and vertex classes found in PROGRES. Rewriting rules are modified such that their left- and right-hand sides may contain vertices with set-valued vertex labels. We first define rewriting with modified, so-called *sl*-rewriting rules. The resulting *sl*-rewriting formalism has the disadvantage that the results on constant-time matching cannot easily be applied. Hence, second, we give a reduction of *sl*-rewriting to programmed graph rewriting systems.

Definition 4.2.4   *sl*-GRAPH, *sl*-REWRITING STEP

a) Let V and E be sets of vertices and edges. A function $s: V \to \wp(\Sigma_v)\backslash\varnothing$ is a *set-valued labelling* and $sg = (V, E, s)$ is an *sl-graph*. Any ordinary graph (V, E, l) is an *instance* of sg iff $l(v) \in s(v)$ for all $v \in V$.

b) Let g_l and g_r be *sl*-graphs with $l_l(v) = l_r(v)$ for all $v \in V_l \cap V_r$ and M be a set of embedding descriptions. The triple $r = (g_l, g_r, M)$ is an *sl-rewriting rule* is for all $v \in V$, with $|l_l(v)| > 1$ holds $v \in V_l$. Hence all vertices with a set-valued label of size larger than 1 are in the context.
Two instances g'_l and g'_r of g_l and g_r *correspond* iff $l_{l'}(v) = l_{r'}(v)$ for all $v \in V_l \cap V_r$. The ordinary rewriting rule (g'_l, g'_r, M) is an instance of r.

c) Let g be an ordinary graph and $r = (g_l, g_r, M)$ be an *sl*-rewriting rule. A graph g' is the result of *sl-rewriting* g by r iff there is an instance r' of r such that $g \to^r g'$.   ■

At first sight, an *sl*-rewriting step can be stated as an ordinary rewriting step which applies an arbitrary instance. This impression, though, is misleading because the semantics of an <u>OR</u>-expression implies *no priority for successful applications*. Hence the application of an *sl*-rule represented as a non-deterministic choice may fail, although there are applicable instances. To enforce the selection of an applicable instance according to the definition, we must introduce an alternative control structure. The selection of applicable instances can be controlled by the conditional branch. In the case of the <u>IF-POSSIBLE</u> construct, for example, we can avoid the application of failing rules by a previous test. The instances are skipped as long as an applicable one is found which is then selected for application.

The introduction of set-valued edge labels $E \subseteq V \times \wp(\Sigma_E)\backslash\varnothing \times V$ would be an extension to ordinary labelled graphs analogous to *sl*-graphs, but it contradicts the interpretation of set labels, because the existence of multiple edges is not included in the definition of a graph. Thus a graph with set-labelled edges could represent graphs with different underlying unlabelled graphs, as an example will show. Take the graph g of figure 27 with set-valued edge labels. Three instances of this graph have two edges, but the fourth instance just one. Because of this irregular feature, this graph

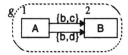

Figure 27   Graph with set-valued edge labels

with set-valued edge labels does not describe graphs with the same structural properties, as expected. Hence they will not be considered further.

In a general view, all instances of an *sl*-rule form a set of rules. From the specification point of view, the rule set is a construct for a pattern-matching-like application of a number of rules. Only the applicable rules of a set can be selected for a rewriting step. Hence, for example, mutually exclusive operations can be represented by one rule set.

We make an overloaded use of the keyword OR to construct rule sets in the sense sketched above. Because rule sets satisfy the application dichotomy, they may show up in the conditional part of a branch expression. Thus a rule set will itself belong to RULE. Because all terminal elements of a rule set must be single rules, the overloading of OR can be syntactically resolved.

The definition of rule sets in the failure semantics is as follows:

<rule>   ::= ... | <rule> OR <rule>

$R[|r_1$ OR $r_2|] = E[|$ IF r_1 THEN r_1 ELSE (IF r_2 THEN r_2 ELSE FAIL)

            OR IF r_2 THEN r_2 ELSE (IF r_1 THEN r_1 ELSE FAIL) |] $\perp$

The nested conditional postpones the application of a rule until an applicable one is found. Otherwise, it returns FAIL. The application of a rule set is still non-deterministic because of the definition of the non-deterministic choice for rule expressions. The choice is consistent in the sense that, whenever one alternative fails, the other fails too. Hence the rule set preserves the application dichotomy.

Rule sets are important from another point of view also. In theorem 4.2.3 we demonstrated that the rewriting program $p = $ "main = $(r_1$ OR ... OR r_k) AND main" can generate the graph language defined by the underlying rewriting system. Hence the repeated application of the rule set $(r_1$ OR ... OR r_k) simulates a derivation in the ordinary rewriting system.

4.3 Summary and Related Works

In this chapter, we extended the basic formalism of graph rewriting by components which are typically used in applications of graph rewriting systems for specification and programming. Both extensions use the structural representation provided by graph rewriting. They add specific capabilities to represent properties which are hard to express purely by graphical structures. Attributes provide a means to denote continuous, *non-graphical information*, whereas programming constructs allow us to write structured specifications. Both extensions have the advantage that they provide means to represent non-graphical properties in an appropriate way.

We did not develop a baroque formalism, but introduced instead the *basic concepts of attribution and programming*. In the presentation of attribution, it was sufficient to state attribute function transformations and application predicates as the additional components of an ordinary rewriting rule. We did not deal with syntactic sugar, but presented the mathematical concepts provided by attribution.

For programming the situation appeared to be different. The adequate definition of programming constructs requires a distinction between syntax and semantics. Therefore, we introduced the abstract syntax of a programming language for graph rewriting systems which provides a small but sufficient number of basic constructs. Using this approach, we gave a precise definition of *two denotational semantics*. In the failure semantics, rule expressions basically denote the relation between a host and a result graph which is derivable by that expression. The failure semantics of a complex rule expression is therefore similar to that of a single rule. This similarity proves to be valuable for the analysis of advanced program properties like associativity of constructs. The definition of the collection semantics sets up the link from programming to the theoretical studies on constant-time matching. Overall we gave the first denotational semantics of programmed graph rewriting systems with mathematical domains.

The extensions by attribution and programming can easily be linked to gain a definition of *attributed programmed graph rewriting systems*. Therefore the concepts of ordinary graph rewriting which occur in the definitions comprising a programmed graph rewriting system must be replaced by the corresponding concepts of attributed graph rewriting, e.g. replace applicability by attribute-applicability and rewriting by attribute-rewriting. The resulting formalism is powerful enough to support a structured and comfortable specification. It will be compiled to code executable on an abstract machine. Both the compilation and the abstract machine are presented in the next chapter.

Our definition of an attributed graph rewriting system embodies the fundamental properties of related definitions in the literature. The concept of an attribute function occurs in the definitions of, for example, [En86], [Lew88], or [FrHa92]. The definitions vary in the domains of attributes which may occur in an attribute computation rule. In [En86] and [Lew88], a computation rule does not contain any references to attributes, but only constant values; whereas Freund and Haberstroh accept references to attributes assigned to left-hand side vertices, as we do. In both cases, the attribute function can be computed in one rewriting step using local information, i.e. either attributes in the image of the left- or right-hand side, or constant values.

More elaborate approaches like those of [Gött88] and [Schü91] maintain *attribute dependencies* which expand over several rewriting steps. As with for synthesized attributes known from attributed string grammars, the value of so-called derived attributes may depend on values which will be set in future rewriting steps. The two authors chose different implementation techniques.

Göttler introduces attribute evaluation programs which take over the role of attribute computation rules. Such a program is assigned to the host graph to define its attribute values. At first, each program statement is a computation rule for the value of an attribute assigned to the image of a right-hand side vertex. The statement takes constant values and references to attributes of the image of the left-hand side and embedding vertices. In contrast to the basic approach to attribution, an instance of the evaluation program is appended to the program of the host graph whenever an attributed rewriting rule is applied. To gain well-defined attributed host graphs, the vertex identifiers occurring in the program are textually replaced by their corresponding images. Furthermore, the potential ambiguity introduced by a multiple application of a rewriting rule to an identical subgraph is dissolved by counting the number of applications. This counter is added to the vertex identifier used in the program instance. As a consequence, the attribute evaluation program represents the attribute dependencies. An update of dependent attributes is initiated whenever an undefined attribute is accessed in a rewriting step. For an update, the current attribute evaluation program of the host graph is executed repeatedly until all attributes are evaluated. A characteristic property for Göttler's technique is that the dependencies of new attributes are determined when they are inserted by a rewriting step. The dependencies between attribute instances remain for the rest of the derivation.

In the specification language PROGRES, the dependencies of derived attributes are set up by path-expressions. For a path of length one, path-expressions are equal to our notion of cut-descriptions. Each derived attribute holds its definition based on path-expressions and whenever the value of the attribute is required but invalid, the definition is evaluated. The references set up by path-expression are interpreted to gain actual values. Similar to cut-descriptions, multiple defining attributes can be determined. Therefore, special constructs are provided for selection of potential definitions. Whenever the value of an attribute is updated, all depending attributes are marked as invalid. Hence this evaluation scheme performs lazy updating and computes new values based on the dynamic interpretation of path-expressions.

We chose the simpler attribution semantics because it is sufficient for most applications. Moreover we did not want to go into the details of the implementation of attribute dependencies. There exists a number of solutions which can be added to our implementation when required.

The use of attribute values as an additional condition for the applicability of a rewriting rule is a natural characteristic of attributed graph rewriting systems. Hence our concept of application predicates defined over attribute and parameter values is also included in the definitions given by the authors mentioned above.

Göttler claims to give a denotational semantics as well, but he defines the semantics of programming constructs as a transformation to a metalanguage based on ordinary rewriting. The metalingual concepts are the conditional application and a no-operation construct NOP, both not formally defined. They are used for the definition of the semantic function EVAL which transforms the programming constructs to meta-lingual sequences. The WAPP-construct will, for example, evaluate to an infinite sequence of NOP's when all component rules are not applicable. A further difference in our definitions lies in the semantic domain for a programmed graph rewriting system. Göttler defines a graph rewriting program as one of all possible derivations. Therefore he assumes the existence of a possibly infinite sequence of graph isomorphisms which map an applied rule into the current host graph. We, on the contrary, chose the relation given by all possible derivations as the semantic object for a graph rewriting program.

More common are operational semantics in terms of *control diagrams*. Their basic components are nodes representing rewriting rules and calls to sub-diagrams as well as entry and exit nodes. The semantics of a programmed graph rewriting system is then given as the set of all paths between the entry and the exit node of a diagram. This set is dependent on the initial host graph. Nagl uses control diagrams directly as programming language [Nag76], whereas Schürr uses them as an intermediate semantic level to which he translates the programming constructs of PROGRES [Schü91]. For that purpose, Schürr gives a formal definition of a control diagram such that his semantic definitions are well-founded. Based on control diagrams, Schürr defines a derivation relation. The semantics of programmed graph rewriting systems can thus be given as a derivation relation which is set up via control diagrams. We, on the contrary, chose the mathematical representation of the derivation relation itself as the semantic domain.

The *transaction semantics* is a special feature of the specification language PROGRES. A sequence of rule application is successful only when all rules could be successfully applied. Otherwise, the intermediate rewriting steps have no effect on the initial host graph. We can easily modify the failure semantics of a rule sequence and gain a transaction semantics.

$$E_t[\![e_1 \text{ AND } e_2]\!]\rho = \{ (g, g, \mathsf{f}) \in E[\![e_1]\!]\rho \}$$
$$\cup \{ (g, g, \mathsf{f}) \mid (g, g', \mathsf{v}) \in E[\![e_1]\!]\rho \text{ and } (g', g', \mathsf{f}) \in E[\![e_2]\!]\rho \}$$
$$\cup \{ (g, g'', \mathsf{v}) \mid (g, g', \mathsf{v}) \in E[\![e_1]\!]\rho \text{ and } (g', g'', \mathsf{v}) \in E[\![e_2]\!]\rho \}$$

The sequential application of two subexpressions is successful only if both subexpressions can be applied successfully. Otherwise, the application fails and all intermediate graph transformations are undone.

Engels and Lewerentz used programming constructs provided by a standard imperative language. They gave no formal definition of the semantics of their chosen constructs, but refer to their intuitive understanding. The reason for that lack of formal treatment may be that their main interest lay in the implementation and application of programmed graph rewriting systems.

The attributed elementary programmed graph grammars introduced by Freund and Haberstroh were not directly intended for application purposes. They provide a set of basic graph productions like deletion or insertion of an edge or a vertex. The elementary programming facility is made up of two sets of productions which are added to each basic production. The first set comprises productions out of which one may be applied when the basic production was successfully applied. The other set resembles productions to be applied in case the application failed. By this simple mechanism of success and failure sets, elementary programmed graph grammars represent a basic control diagram. Freund and Stary have proven that any computable graph transformation can be given as a deterministic elementary programmed graph grammar [FrSt93]. The programming constructs of elementary programmed graph grammars can be simulated by our non-deterministic choice, conditional application, and the binding of expressions to names.

5 The Abstract Machine for Graph Rewriting — Supporting a Fast Implementation

The definition of an abstract machine is a widely used technique to support a structured compiler construction. A compiler which embodies the concept of an abstract machine splits the translation of a program, at least virtually, into two phases. First, the given source program is analysed and compiled to a code executable on the abstract machine. Second, that intermediate code is translated to the target hardware or executed by a separate interpreter. The interface between the two phases may, at one extreme, be a plain text file or, at the other extreme, the abstract machine serves just as a set of compilation principles which determine, for example, memory layout or parameter passing. Hence the abstract machine will occur more or less explicitly in a compiler.

The use of abstract machines in compiler construction has several objectives. The most important are:

- structured code generation
- portability of the compiler
- rapid prototyping of a language and its compiler.

The implementation of block-oriented languages with scopes requires elaborate techniques for code generation and address assignment. In the early Pascal compiler named "P", the abstract machine SC (Stack Computer) was designed to support both tasks [NAJ81]. The machine provides a stack for procedure frames and is capable of determining valid objects according to static scopes. Its instruction set is known as *P-code*.[1]

The designers of SC mention that their approach led to a *portable* Pascal compiler, although this was not primarily intended. They provided an implementation kit consisting mainly of the sources of the Pascal P-compiler, as well as a version already compiled to P-code and an additional P-code interpreter. The interpreter is a hardware-dependent implementation of the stack computer. The P-compiler can be reasonably fast ported to a new platform when reimplementing the P-code interpreter. Then the P-code version of the compiler, as well as the compiled Pascal programs, are executable

---

1. The textbook [Wir86] presents a very restricted version of SC and its use in compiler construction.

on the new platform via the P-code interpreter. Obviously, the resulting Pascal implementation is not efficient, but the code generator of the compiler sources can now be adapted to the new platform.

The third objective, iterative development of compilers by *rapid prototyping*, is adopted by several projects implementing declarative languages. For these types of languages, the gap between the von Neumann architecture and an intuitive execution model is wide, and the generation of low level code is cumbersome. An abstract machine bridges the gap and provide an implementation of the intuitive execution model. It supports the development and testing of various code generation schemes and language features during the experimental stage of a compiler. Furthermore, the front-end of the compiler can be raised in a final version producing efficient code for low-level hardware. This approach led to several designs such as the Warren Abstract Machine [War77], the G-machine [Joh84], the Spineless Tagless G-Machine [PJS89, PeJo91] or the Parallel Abstract Machine [LKI89, Loo89].

We design the Graph Rewriting Abstract Machine (GRAM) as a *rapid prototype* for

(i)   the execution of programmed attributed graph rewriting systems, and

(ii)   the development of optimization techniques.

Our optimization exploits the semantics of rule sets. In general, each set comprises a number of rules. The application of a rule set is realised by rewriting the current host graph with an applicable rule, if one exists in the set. Otherwise, the set itself is not applicable. If there are several rules applicable, the execution component may select one for rewriting. A straightforward compilation of rule sets can be acquired from their semantic reduction to conditional application and non-deterministic choice (see page 117). According to the semantic reduction, the applicability of the elements will be checked sequentially. When an applicable rule is found, it is then applied.

Rule sets provide pattern matching for programmed graph rewriting systems. As in functional languages, there will be overlapping patterns which are, with respect to graphs, common subgraphs. A more sophisticated implementation of rule sets will therefore determine *common subgraphs* in advance. For example, given a rule set with two elements, the refined execution of the matching procedure will first determine the set of handles for the largest common subgraph. If this set is empty, neither rule is applicable. If there are handles for the common subgraph, the applicability of the first rule will be checked by subsequently extending the handles according to the first rule. If it turns out to be applicable, it may be applied. Otherwise, the applicability of the second rule must be determined. This check must not be performed from scratch, but can be initialized with the handles already found for the common subgraph. This optimization scheme can easily be extended to rule sets with more than two elements.

The optimization for rule sets requires the management of partial handles which are determined for common subgraphs. Thus the abstract machine for the labelled subgraph matching is refined by a stack for partial handles. Furthermore, it provides mechanisms to access uniquely labelled vertices. Finally, the machine must provide basic mechanisms to implement attributed programmed graph rewriting systems in general. Overall we must design a new abstract machine which embodies the refined machine for the subgraph machine as well as the components required for the execution of a rewriting step. Hence we will perform another iteration in the implementation cycle.

In the following section, we will develop the proposed optimization scheme for the general case as well as for constant-time matching rewriting systems. Then we present the specification of the abstract machine for graph rewriting, and rules for the generation of code out of an optimized search tree. Last, we present measurements of the prototype implementation.

5.1   Optimization of the Application Test for Rule Sets

In this section we develop the optimization strategy for rule sets and give an algorithm to compute an approximate optimization. A straightforward implementation which deals only with individual rules must check the applicability of all elements of a set in sequence. When an applicable rule is found, no further test is necessary and the rewriting step can be performed. Our optimization strategy exploits the fact that, when a rule set is applied, the applicability of its elements must be checked with respect to the same host graph.

Take, for example, the removal operations of the refined priority queue (see page 93). Their left-hand sides are the graphs

 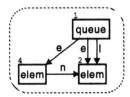

We combine both rules to set "removal" which, when applied, selects the appropriate rule for application.

removal =   remove

OR remove_last

In the straightforward implementation, the application of "removal" on the queue with
at least two elements may proceed as follows. First, the applicability of "remove_last"
is checked, possibly in the following order.

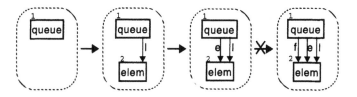

When the existence of the "f"-edge is checked, the matching algorithm notices that
"remove_last" is not applicable. Hence it tries to match the left-hand side of "remove",
perhaps in the same order as for "remove_last".

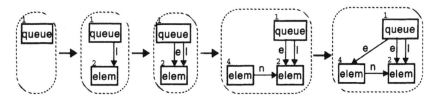

Finally it succeeds and the host graph can be rewritten by "remove".

Obviously the implementation performs redundant matching steps. We know that
both left-hand sides have a common subgraph which must be mapped to the same set
of partial handles. A clever matching algorithm should exploit this redundancy. There
is a major problem to be solved first: which are the common subgraphs? This problem
is already NP-complete when the *largest common subgraph* of two graphs must be
determined [GaJo79, p.202]; and rule sets may be arbitrarily large. Thus the identification of common subgraphs is not feasible.

Hence we must encode the information on common subgraphs in the rules of a set.
We use the same mechanism as for the indication of context vertices: the identification
of vertices. As opposed to context vertices, we now identify vertices of different left-
hand sides. The largest common subgraph of two graphs g and g' is then easily determined assuming that the labelling functions are equal on the intersection of the vertex
sets. Formally it is given as

$$(V \cap V', E \cap E', l|_{V \cap V'}).$$

In our example, we already anticipated that mechanism. The largest common subgraph, the graph

can now be determined without redundancy. So the matching algorithm will, under an optimized control, at first determine the set of partial handles for the common subgraph and then branch to the alternative rules.

The optimization of rule sets with more than two elements is not as trivial as for the two-element case. Moreover, the optimization must solve a packing problem, i.e. find a good combination of subgraphs common to subsets of the rule set.

For the precise definition of the optimization goal, we assume that the elements of a rule set are applicable with the same probability. This assumption meets the fact that the order of elements has no semantic relevance. Consequently no rule can be preferred. Thus we try to reduce the number of search steps in the worst case, which is the inapplicability of all rules in the set.

The optimization strategy is based only on the analysis of *common prefixes* of connected enumerations. It is totally independent of the arbitrary host graph on which the rule set is applied. Thus the optimization can be performed at compile time. For the prefixes of connected enumerations, it holds that equal prefixes determine the same set of partial handles. Hence, whenever the application test fails at a certain prefix, it fails also for all other enumerations with an identical prefix. Conversely, whenever two connected enumerations have a common prefix, they determine the same set of partial handles for that prefix. Thus when an application test fails for one element of the rule set, the matching algorithm can re-use intermediate results for another element. If, for example, there is a further left-hand side with the same prefix, the algorithm matches that prefix also. When the matching algorithm fails later for the first rule, it may enter the application test for the second rule at the state computed for the common prefix.

It is obvious that the matching algorithm presented in chapter 2 does not re-use former matchings. A more sophisticated version must be able to cancel most recent extensions or to undo deletions of partial handles due to checks. By this capability, the matching algorithm backtracks to a former state representing a prefix, now shorter, of a failed rule. Intermediate states, i.e. sets of partial handles, can thus be re-used for other elements of the rule set.

A basic assumption which was briefly mentioned is the consistency of the labelling functions of the left-hand sides of the rule set's elements. The labelling function of all

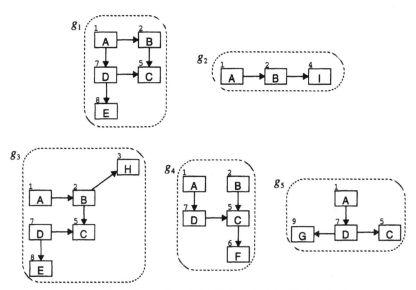

Figure 28   Five consistently labelled graphs (edge labels omitted)

pairs of left-hand sides must be identical on the intersection of the vertex sets. Only under this assumption does it hold that identical prefixes of different left-hand sides are mapped to the same set of partial handles. Formally consistent labelling is defined as follows.

Definition 5.1.1   CONSISTENT LABELLING

A set of graphs $G = \{g_1, ..., g_n\}$ is *consistently labelled* iff for all $i, j \in \{1, ...n\}$ and all vertices $v \in V_i \cap V_j$ it holds that $l_i(v) = l_j(v)$.   ∎

Figure 28 gives an example for five consistently labelled graphs. Edge labels are omitted for the sake of clarity.

The requirement of consistent labelling introduces a strong link between vertices of the left-hand sides of a rule set. Based on this assumption, the optimization goal can formally be stated. We therefore consider the search space traversed by the matching algorithm. It consists of graphs which are represented by a prefix of a connected enumeration of a left-hand side. Since the search space is independent of an actual host graph, we call it *static search space*. The order on the static search space is derived from the "is-prefix-of" relation on the set of prefixes. For two elements g_1 and g_2 of the static search space, it holds that g_1 is smaller than g_2 if there exists a connected enumeration of g_2 with a prefix inducing g_1. Hence when the algorithm evaluates the enumeration of g_2, it will compute a set of partial handles for g_1 also. The static search space models the growth of partial handles by checks and extensions controlled by connected enumerations.

Definition 5.1.2   STATIC SEARCH SPACE

a) Let g be a graph. Let $PR(g)$ be the set of all prefixes of all connected enumerations of g. For all prefixes $p \in PR(g)$, let $G_g(p)$ be the *subgraph* of g *induced by the prefix* p, i.e. $G_g((e_i)_{i=1,...,n}) = (V, E, l|_V)$ where $E = \{e_i | i = 1...n\}$ and $V = inc_g(E)$.

b) Let $R = \{r_1, ..., r_n\}$ be a set of rewriting rules with consistently labelled left-hand sides. The structure $(SS(R), \subseteq)$ is the *static search space* spanned by the rule set R where

$$ SS(R) = \bigcup_{(g_l, g_r, M) \in R} \{G_{g_l}(p) | p \in PR(g_l)\} \cup \{(\{v\}, \varnothing, l_l|_{\{v\}}) | v \in V_l\} \cup \{g_\varnothing\} $$

and $\subseteq$ is the subgraph relation.   ∎

Note that the structure $(SS(R), \subseteq)$ is a partial order with the empty graph as its bottom element. The corresponding Hasse diagram is an alternative representation of the set of potential connected enumerations; any path from the bottom element to a left-hand side is related to a connected enumeration of the considered left-hand side. Conversely, it holds that any connected enumeration of a left-hand side g_l is represented by a path from g_0 to g_l. Common prefixes of enumerations form sub-trees in the Hasse diagram.

The goal of the optimization is now to find a sub-tree of the Hasse diagram rooted in the bottom element and with the left-hand sides as leaves. Each edge of the tree represents a search step. Hence we have an optimal search strategy if the number of edges is minimal. In graph theoretic terms, we have to solve a minimal Steiner tree problem. The resulting minimal Steiner tree becomes a search tree. It defines a set of connected enumerations with *maximum overlap*.

Definition 5.1.3   CONNECTED ENUMERATIONS WITH MAXIMUM OVERLAP

Let $R = \{r_1, ...r_n\}$ be a set of rewriting rules with consistently labelled left-hand sides. Let $H = (V_H, E_H)$ be the Hasse diagram of the static search space $(SS(R), \subseteq)$. Let CE be a set of connected enumerations containing exactly one connected enumeration for each rule $r_i, i = 1...n$. The members of CE have a *maximal overlap* iff the corresponding Steiner tree is minimal.   ∎

As an example for the proposed optimization, we give a minimal Steiner tree for the graphs shown in figure 28. The tree is rooted in the empty graph and has the graphs

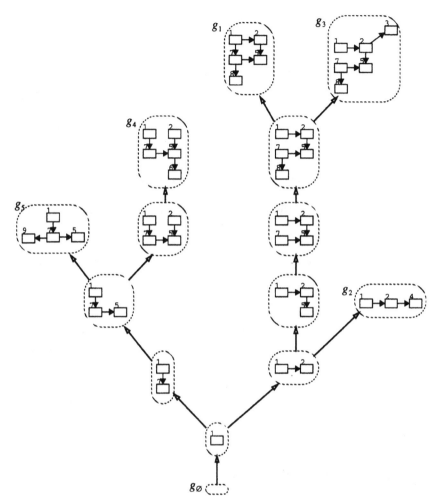

Figure 29   Minimal Steiner tree rooted in $g_\varnothing$ with leaves $g_1, ..., g_5$ (labels omitted)

$g_1,...,g_5$ as terminal nodes. Again we further simplify the picture in figure 29 and omit vertex labels also.

The Steiner tree reads as follows. Enter the search with the root vertex 1. Then try to extend the current match along the edge $(1, 7)$. This extension is taken as a common prefix of enumerations for the graphs g_4 and g_5. After extending with the edge $(7, 5)$ the matching algorithm checks the applicability of a rule with g_5 as its left-hand side. If the edge $(7, 9)$ is not present in the host graph, the matching algorithm backtracks to the inferior node and tries the extension $(2, 5)$ on its way to g_4. When an extension fails during that search, the algorithm backtracks to the root vertex and traverses the right sub-tree.

With this search strategy, the algorithm can determine the applicability of a corresponding rule set in at most 12 steps. This is the minimum number of search steps in the worst case, because it is given by a minimal Steiner tree. The set of connected enumerations induced by the tree has a maximum overlap. An unoptimized implementation which tests the applicability of each individual rule in sequence must, in the worst case, traverse all five graphs individually. This makes 19 steps to detect that the rule set is not applicable.

Now the optimization problem for the application of rule sets is precisely stated. The definition does not, however, lead to an instantaneous solution, because the minimal Steiner tree problem lies in NP [GaJo79,p.208]. Thus no compiler would perform an exact optimization in an acceptable time. Since an approximate solution will be in general sufficient, one might choose, for example, an algorithm with a time complexity of $O(|R|^2|H_E|\log|H_V|)$ to compute an overlap with an error ratio of $2 - 2/|H_V|$ [HRW92,p.173]. Further approximation algorithms are given in [Vos90]. Still the algorithm would not be applicable, because the problem is represented as a partial order and its Hasse diagram. To apply an approximation algorithm, the Hasse diagram must be generated either implicitly or explicitly.

We therefore conjecture that the optimization problem is NP-complete as well, because it has a strong relation to partial orders and the minimal Steiner tree problem. We leave the conjecture open to a formal proof or rejection. Assuming the conjecture is true, an exact optimization is intractable for a compiler. Instead, we will present an approximate solution which is generated by a greedy optimization strategy.

Conjecture 5.1.4 MAXIMUM OVERLAP OF CONNECTED ENUMERATIONS IS NP-COMPLETE.

Instance: Let R be a set of rewriting rules with consistently labelled left-hand sides.

Question: Find a connected enumeration for each left-hand side such that the set of connected enumerations has a maximum overlap.

The complexity of that problem is NP-complete. ∎

Before we introduce the greedy algorithm, we show that the complexity of the optimization problem is not reduced by additional restrictions given by unique vertex labels and bypassing enumerations. The restriction leads to a smaller problem size, but the complexity remains. We map the conditions of constant-time matching to the static search space. The requirement of being rooted in a vertex with a unique label disables all graphs without any uniquely labelled vertex. Additionally, search steps along a strong V-structure must be impossible in the restricted search space. Hence the order relation must be reduced to contain only bypassing search steps.

Definition 5.1.5   RESTRICTED SEARCH SPACE

Let *svs* be a set of strong V-structures and *uv* be a set of unique vertex labels. Let *R* be a set of rewriting rules with consistently labelled left-hand sides.

The *static search space* spanned by *R* and *restricted by svs and uv*, $(RSS_{uv}(R), \leq_{svs})$, is defined as: $RSS_{uv}(R) = \{(V, E, l) \in SS(R) \mid uv \cap l(V) \neq \varnothing\} \cup \{g_{\varnothing}\}$ and the relation $\leq_{svs}$ is the transitive closure of

$$\{ (g, g') \in RSS_{uv}(R)^2 \mid E' \backslash E = \{(s, el, t)\}, \quad \text{if } s \in V: (l'(s), l'(t), el, \text{out}) \notin svs,$$
$$\text{if } t \in V: (l'(t), l'(s), el, \text{out}) \notin svs \}. \quad \blacksquare$$

The deletion of edges in the restricted search space realizes that rewriting rules may have no bypassing enumeration. Their left-hand sides become unreachable from the bottom element. Furthermore, when a left-hand side of a rewriting rule does not contain a unique vertex label, it does not occur in the restricted search space at all. Consequently any path in the Hasse diagram of the restricted search space from the bottom element to a left-hand side represents a bypassing connected enumeration rooted in a uniquely labelled vertex. Thus the optimization problem with the additional restrictions is still stated as a minimal Steiner tree problem and the complexity remains.

We propose a *greedy algorithm* to determine an approximate solution. Instead of generating the restricted search space explicitly, we use the union of the left-hand sides of a consistently labelled rule set as the underlying data structure. The greedy algorithm traverses the union graph recursively. In each step it selects an edge and appends it to the search tree. In the end, the tree represents a set of overlapping connected enumerations, one for each left-hand side.

For the basic idea of the algorithm, recall the interpretation of the search tree. Take the tree shown in figure 30 as an example. Each left-hand side has a corresponding path from the empty graph to the node representing the left-hand side. For each inner node of the tree, there exists a subset of terminal nodes which can be reached from that node.

From the node

the terminals g_4 and g_5 are reachable. Thus every node represents a prefix which is common to at least one connected enumeration for each left-hand side reachable from the node.

Each node represents also a set of vertices for which an image in the host graph is determined. Furthermore there is a set of edges which are not mapped. From this set, an edge may be selected as an extension which must be incident to a vertex occurring in the prefix. For the node

possible selections are the edges $(1, 7)$, $(7, 5)$ and $(2, 3)$. Several extensions at a node may be necessary to cover all reachable left-hand sides. So if we would select at the node above the edge $(1, 7)$, we cannot reach g_3 any more. Thus we must introduce a second sub-tree by selection of either $(7, 5)$ or $(2, 3)$. Both sub-trees then cover the set of reachable nodes. Hence a node will have a number of children, each representing an extension. The sub-trees rooted at the children represent suffixes of the parent's prefix which yield a connected enumeration for each reachable left-hand side from the parent.

The basic idea of the optimization algorithm is that each node selects an edge to extend the parent's prefix. Then the node creates at most two further nodes, one being a first-born child, the other being a younger sibling.

The edge is selected with respect to the left-hand sides, which are reachable from the parent and the elder siblings. The node must try to reach a left-hand side of the parent only if it is not covered already by an elder sibling. Hence it is responsible only for the remaining left-hand sides. According to the greedy strategy, the node selects that edge which is present in the largest number of remaining left-hand sides and assigns it to the global data structure.

After the selection of the edge, two further nodes may be created. If the extension does not cover all remaining left-hand sides, the node creates a sibling which, in accordance with the recursion scheme, determines a further extension. Besides a sibling, the node creates a child to take care of the left-hand sides, which are reachable under the chosen extension. The recursion stops when the selected edge completes a connected enumeration and no further left-hand side can be reached along the extending edge. The first level of recursion determines the root vertex of the connected enumerations in the same greedy manner.

For the following presentation of the algorithm we assume that the nodes of the search tree are labelled with Dewey numbers over non-negative integers as follows: the n

children of a node labelled with d are labelled by $d.1$ up to $d.n$. A node $d.j$ is elder than its sibling $d.i$ iff $j<i$. The root node has the label 0. This labelling scheme identifies the nodes of a tree of arbitrary degree and height.

The optimization algorithm consists of two recursive procedures. The procedure "init-and-build-tree" determines the nodes of the first level of the tree. These nodes contain the root vertices. To create nodes of lower levels, extensions are performed by "extend-and-build-tree".

Algorithm 5.1.6   OVERLAPPING CONNECTED ENUMERATIONS

Let $G = \{g_{l_1}, ..., g_{l_n}\}$ be a set of consistently labelled graphs.
INPUT: G
OUTPUT: *tree*, a set of overlapping connected enumerations

PROCEDURE init-and-build-tree $(G, d.i)$
    IF $G \neq \varnothing$
        THEN   choose a vertex $v \in \bigcup_{g \in G} V$ such that the number of
                reachable graphs, i.e. $|\{g \in G|\, v \in V\}|$ is maximal
              SET $G':= \{g \in G|\, v \in V\}$ and $tree(d.i) := v$
              CALL extend-and-build-tree $(\{v\}, \bigcup_{g' \in G'} E', G', d.i.0)$
              CALL init-and-build-tree $(G\backslash G', d.\,(i+1))$
    ENDIF
END init-and-build-tree;

PROCEDURE extend-and-build-tree $(W, E, G, d.i)$
    IF $G \neq \varnothing$
        THEN   choose an edge $e = (s, el, t) \in E$ which extends the current
                prefix, i.e. $s \in W$ or $t \in W$, such that the number of
                reachable graphs, $|\{g \in G|\, e \in E\}|$ is maximal
              SET $G':= \{g \in G|\, e \in E\}$, $E':= E\backslash \{e\}$, and $W':= W \cup \{s, t\}$
              SET $tree(d.i) := e$
              CALL extend-and-build-tree $(W', E', G', d.i.0)$
              CALL extend-and-build-tree $(W, E, G\backslash G', d.\,(i+1))$
    ENDIF
END extend-and-build-tree;

    1.   **CALL** init-and-build-tree $(G, 0.0)$ ■

The result of the algorithm is non-deterministic, since the chosen edges and vertices may not be uniquely defined. The algorithm terminates, because in each recursive call the number of either available edges or reachable graphs decreases. The number of node-creating recursive calls is bound by $|G| + \sum_{g \in G} |E|$ which is the number of search steps for a set of connected enumerations with no overlap.

When applied to the set of left-hand sides given in figure 28, the algorithm may generate the search tree shown in figure 30. We display at each node the subgraph which is covered by the current prefix, and not only the extending edges. We inspect the algorithm at node 0.0.0. It is created by a call of "extend-and-build-tree ({1,7}, {(1,2), (2,5), (5,6), (7,5), (7,8), (7,9)}, {g_1, g_4, g_5}, 0.0.0)". The set of extending edges is {(1,2), (7,5), (7,8), (7,9)}. The best edge is (7,5). It occurs in all reachable

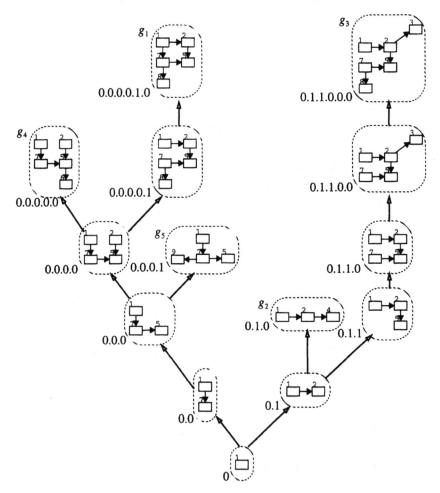

Figure 30   Output of the greedy algorithm for $g_1, \ldots, g_5$ (labels omitted)

graphs. Hence it is uniquely determined. The first recursive call to "extend-and-build-tree" causes the creation of node 0.0.0.0. The second call has no effect because all reachable graphs are covered by the extending edge and the set of remaining graphs is empty. As the first child of the next level, the edge (2,5) is chosen. It represents only graphs g_1 and g_4. Therefore the second call to "extend-and-build-tree" creates a sibling being responsible for the remaining graph g_5.

Following the search strategy represented by the tree, we can determine the applicability of a rule set in at most 13 steps. Hence the algorithm provides an approximation with an error of 15% in our example. Certainly there are pathological cases where the approximation is worse. The basic reason for that behaviour lies in the fact that we look for a global minimum using only local decisions.

The algorithm also generates bypassing connected enumerations which are rooted in a uniquely labelled vertex. Therefore the sets of possible selections must be restricted to uniquely labelled vertices and edges which are not searched along a strong V-structure. The latter condition depends on the set of vertices being part of the current prefix because bypassing is dependent on the direction of an extension. Under this restriction, the algorithm is able to find a bypassing connected enumeration, if there is one.

When there is no bypassing connected enumeration for a left-hand side, the algorithm outputs only a prefix. This prefix is the longest bypassing prefix for all enumerations of the left-hand side. Since any further extension violates the constant-time matching property, the algorithm may release the restrictions enforcing bypassing connected enumerations for the next selection. Hence the optimization is still performed, but the bypassing property is invalid. The modified algorithm computes a set of connected enumerations which, first, have an optimized overlap and, second, bypass strong V-structures as long as possible.

5.2 The Graph Rewriting Environment

The execution of programmed graph rewriting systems is supported by an environment consisting of two major components: a compiler and an abstract machine. The individual components and the data flow are depicted in figure 31. The compiler inputs an attributed programmed graph rewriting system and generates a piece of code for each rule set and the initial graph. Furthermore it extracts the higher levels of the control structure and passes it straight through to the abstract machine. The front end of the compiler performs the analyses and computes the net effect of a rewriting rule. The last task takes the context information and breaks down the graph transformation imposed by a rule to basic operations on edges and vertices. This component also reduces the sets of embedding descriptions based on the approximation of label triples.

The analyses presented in chapter 3 and the optimization from the previous section are executed in three steps. First, the unique labels of the input rewriting system are computed. They are passed to the following analysis component to improve the analysis of strong V-structures. Furthermore the unique vertex labels motivate the selection of root vertices of search trees. Thus the information is passed to the optimization component as well. To implement a fast access to uniquely labelled vertices, they must be handled by separate basic operations. Hence the information is also necessary to compute the net effect. Second, the *ltr*- and *svs*-analyses are performed. To enforce *ltr*- and *svs*-applicability before the effect of a rewriting rule is taken into account, both analyses are done in combination. The results of the strong V-structures and the label triples analyses are passed to the optimizer. This component executes the greedy optimization algorithm developed in the previous subsection for each rule set.

The code generator takes the search tree representation of each rule set and the basic operations for each rule. Each tree is transformed to an instruction sequence controlling the matching algorithm. The basic operations are inserted in place of the appropriate leaf. For each rule set there is an individual segment of code which performs the application test.

The remaining control structure, in which rule sets are replaced by calls to the set, is scanned by an interpreter built into the abstract machine. This simple component selects the next rule set to be applied. The interpreter generates a so-called rewriting sequence, mainly a stream of calls to rule sets. It is input by the core of the abstract machine. It executes the code and therefore performs the application of rule sets. The only feedback from the core to the interpreter is a binary flag indicating the successful

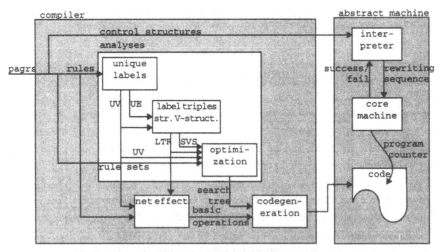

Figure 31   Components of the graph rewriting environment

or failed application of a rule set. This feedback mechanism implements the conditional applications of rule expressions.

5.2.1 The State of the Core Abstract Machine

The state of the core abstract machine for graph rewriting consists of seven components. 1) There is a *directed, labelled, and attributed graph*. This graph is successively rewritten by the application of rule sets. 2) The machine holds a *program counter* determining the instruction to be executed. 3) Direct access to *uniquely labelled vertices* is enabled by a particular function. 4) A *multi-purpose stack* supports the search for handles, the evaluation of attribute function transformations, and the determination of embedding edges. 5) Two pointers to the stack enable the access to handles while the application predicate is evaluated on the stack. 6) The *rewriting sequence* and 7) a *boolean flag* serve for the interaction with the control structure interpreter. The core abstract machine inputs a rewriting sequence and keeps a flag indicating the success or failure of a rule set application.

The host graph is denoted by set-theoretic terms as in the preceding chapters. This level of abstraction is sufficient for a first implementation, especially when the effect of the optimizations is studied. A refined implementation might already use the frame representation of vertices, but our specification will not go into that detail.

The value of the program counter pc is the address of the current instruction. Hence pc is element of the address space *Adr*, a sequence of natural numbers. The program counter accesses the separately stored code sequence via the function *Code: Adr → inst*, which maps an address onto an instruction. The function *Code* is provided by the compiler, and it consists of a sequence of instructions for each rule set. We will fully specify the instruction set *inst* in the next subsection.

The information on the set of unique vertex labels *UV* given by the analysis of the underlying rewriting system is stored as the function $u: UV \to V$. The function accesses uniquely labelled vertices via their label and is defined in the initialization phase of the machine.

One multi purpose stack supports the application of a rule set with respect to three tasks: 1) In the matching or search phase, it holds the sets of vertex maps. They induce the partial morphisms of the set A_i used in the abstract machine for labelled subgraph matching. In each search step, a set of new maps is constructed by either extending a former set of maps, or by reducing the former set according to a check. The new set is pushed onto the stack. If no extension and no check is successful for the current set of maps, the search backtracks to another alternative and pops the latest results. The stacking mechanism supports the backtracking search controlled by a search tree.

Since a vertex map induces a handle we often speak of a set of handles instead of a set of vertex maps.

2) The stack holds information determined in the embedding phase. When the embedding descriptions of an applied rule are evaluated, the embedding vertices and edges determined by a cut-description are pushed on the stack. After the evaluation of all cut-descriptions, the embedding vertices are used by the corresponding paste-descriptions to embed the inserted right-hand side into the rest graph. The edges which connected the image of the left-hand side to the rest graph are removed from the graph. The stack elements for that purpose are pairs of sets of vertices and sets of edges.

3) The stack is used for the evaluation of attribute expressions of application predicates and attribute function transformations. The evaluation of an expression may access the attribute function of the host graph. The result value is stored on the stack because the values of all expressions must be computed for the attribute function of the host graph. When all values are determined, the attributes of the graph are updated to obtain the attribute function of the result graph. The stack holds, for that purpose, values of the domain D. The stack is denoted as a list where $x{:}ST$ indicates that x is the top element and ST the rest of the stack.

After the determination of a set of full handles, the application predicate must be evaluated for each handle before that can be selected for actual rewriting. For that purpose, the core machine provides two pointers referring to the stack. The morphism pointer mp refers to that full handle for which the application predicate is currently evaluated. The lowest handle on the stack which is available for the application predicate is referred by the stack pointer lp. The elements of the stack are referred by natural numbers, and the bottom element is identified by 0.

The core abstract machine provides no features for the execution of control structures. They are interpreted separately and input by the core machine simply as a stream of calls to rule sets. For each call, a number of actual parameters is passed which may be referred by an attribute expression. Hence the rewriting sequence RS consists of pairs of an address and a tuple of parameter values. The set of parameter tuples is $Par = \cup_n D^n$ with $n \in \mathbb{N}_0$. During the application of one rule set, just one element of the stream is visible by the core machine.

The interpreter must determine the applicability of rule sets to select the right branch of a conditional application. Therefore the core machine provides a boolean flag a for applicability. It is set when the application test of a rule set is successful.

Formally, the *state of the machine* is the tuple $(g, u, pc, RS, ST, (mp, lp), a)$ with the following components:

(i) $g = (V, E, l, f)$ is a directed, attributed, and labelled graph,

(ii) $u: UV \rightarrow V$ is an inverse labelling function with domain $UV \subseteq \Sigma_V$,

(iii) $pc \in Adr$ is the program counter,

(iv) $RS \in (Adr \times Par)^*$ is the rewriting sequence, and

(v) $ST \in$ stack_of $(A \cup (\wp(V) \times \wp(E)) \cup D)$ is the stack, where V_R is the set of vertices of all rewriting rules R and A is the set of all sets of partial maps with identical domain from V_R to V, i.e.
$$A = \bigcup_{W \subseteq V_R} \bigcup_{A_W \subseteq \{h\mid h: W \rightarrow V\}} A_W$$

(vi) $(mp, lp) \in \mathbb{N}^2$ is a pair of pointers into the stack, and

(vii) $a \in \{\text{true, false}\}$ is the applicability flag.

The *initial state* of the machine is $((\emptyset, \emptyset, \bot, \bot), \bot, 0, RS, \{\bot\}, (0, 0), \text{true})$. The first element of the rewriting sequence RS must be $(0, \varepsilon)$ where ε is the empty tuple. Thus the execution starts at address 0 and interprets the initialization code. That code sequence builds up the initial graph and returns the control to the interpreter, which then calls the application of the rule set provided by the rewriting required.

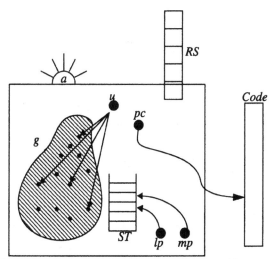

Figure 32   The core of the graph rewriting abstract machine

In the following, the instructions of the core machine are grouped according to the phase in which they are executed. General control instructions are listed in an extra subsection. We use the following notations for the operands of instructions:

- v, w vertex
- s source of an edge
- vl vertex label
- el edge label
- t target of an edge
- ul unique vertex label
- $fail, pred$ return addresses
- p index of a value in the parameter list
- a attribute name
- d constant value

5.2.2   Matching Instructions

Two instructions determine an image for a single vertex. They are mainly provided for the root vertex of a connected enumeration. The instruction "find-unique-vertex" constructs an initial handle via the function u. When there is a vertex with label ul, the vertex map h is extended and pushed on the stack. If there is no vertex with the appropriate label, the search jumps to the address $fail$.

find-unique-vertex ul w $fail$:
[$g, u, pc, RS, A : ST, (mp, lp)$, false]
   if $u(ul) = v \Rightarrow$ [$g, u, pc+1, RS, A' : A : ST, (mp+1, lp)$, false]
   if $u(ul) = \bot \Rightarrow$ [$g, u, fail, RS, A : ST, (mp, lp)$, false]

where $A' = \{ h' | \ h'(w) = v$ and $\exists h \in A$ such that $h'|_{dom(h)} = h \}$.

If the left-hand side of a rule contains no uniquely labelled vertex, the connected enumeration must have an ordinary vertex as its root. The instruction "find-vertex" must scan all vertices of the host graph to find the set of handles. The search branches to another alternative at the address $fail$ if the set of current handles is empty.

find-vertex vl w $fail$:
[$g, u, pc, RS, A : ST, (mp, lp)$, false]
   if $A' \neq \emptyset \quad \Rightarrow$ [$g, u, pc+1, RS, A' : A : ST, (mp+1, lp)$, false]
   otherwise $\quad \Rightarrow$ [$g, u, fail, RS, A : ST, (mp, lp)$, false]

where $\bar{V} = \{ v \in V | \ l(v) = vl \}$ and
   $A' = \{ h' | \exists h \in A , \exists v \in \bar{V} \backslash rg(h)$ such that $h'(w) = v, h'|_{dom(h)} = h \}$.

Extensions of current handles are determined by two instructions, depending on the direction of the extension. By this distinction we implement the modified matching procedure which interprets augmented enumerations (see page 61). When the source vertex of the extending edge is known, the instruction "find-neighbour-forward" is executed. It tries to extend the current vertex maps by the target vertex t. To find a valid extension, there must be an edge in the graph incident to the image of the source vertex, labelled by el, and joining to a vertex labelled with vl. This vertex is then bound to t.

find-neighbour-forward s el vl t *fail* :

[g, u, pc, RS, A : ST, (mp, lp), false]

  if $A' \neq \emptyset$ $\Rightarrow$ [g, u, $pc+1$, RS, A' : A : ST, $(mp+1, lp)$, false]

  otherwise $\Rightarrow$ [g, u, *fail*, RS, A : ST, (mp, lp), false]

where for all current handles $h \in A$ let T_h be the set of vertices labelled with vl, i.e. $l^{-1}(vl)$ which are not already in the range of the morphism and target of an edge with source $h(s)$ and label el,

$$T_h = \{t|\ (s, el, t) \in E \cap (\ \{h(s)\} \times \{el\} \times [l^{-1}(vl) \backslash rg(h)]\ )\ \} .$$

The set of extended morphisms is

$$A' = \bigcup_{h \in A} \{h'|\ \exists t' \in T_h \text{ such that } h'(t) = t' \text{ and } h'|_{dom(h)} = h\ \} .$$

Extensions in the reverse direction are determined by the similar instruction "find-neighbour-backward".

find-neighbour-backward t el vl s *fail* :

[g, u, pc, RS, A : ST, (mp, lp), false]

  if $A' \neq \emptyset$ $\Rightarrow$ [g, u, $pc+1$, RS, A' : A : ST, $(mp+1, lp)$, false]

  otherwise $\Rightarrow$ [g, u, *fail*, RS, A : ST, (mp, lp), false]

where for all $h \in A$ let

$$S_h = \{s|\ (s, el, t) \in E \cap (\ [l^{-1}(vl) \backslash rg(h)] \times \{el\} \times \{h(t)\}\ )\ \} \text{ and}$$

$$A' = \bigcup_{h \in A} \{h'|\ \exists s' \in S_h \text{ such that } h'(s) = s' \text{ and } h'|_{dom(h)} = h\ \} .$$

Checks for the existence of an edge in a current handle are performed by the instruction "exists-edge". It removes those current morphisms which do not map the required edge into the graph. Note that, due to the set-theoretic representation of the graph, the specification cannot express whether the existence of an edge is checked at its source or its target vertex.

exists-edge s el t $fail$:

[g, u, pc, RS, A : ST, (mp, lp), false]

   if $A' \neq \varnothing$ $\Rightarrow$ [(V, E, l, f), u, pc+1, RS, A' : A : ST, (mp+1, lp), false]

   otherwise $\Rightarrow$ [(V, E, l, f), u, $fail$, RS, A : ST, (mp, lp), false]

where $A' = \{ h \in A | \ (h(s), el, h(t)) \in E \}$.

In case a search step is not successful, the current set of partial handles is removed from the stack to realize backtracking. The backtracking mechanism can be explained for a sub-tree of figure 30 (see page 135). The left branch of node 0.0.0 is entered by the instruction "find-neighbour-backward 5 .. .. 2". We assume that can success-fully extend some handles. Thus a new set of handles is pushed on the stack. If, now, the further extensions fail, the matching algorithm backtracks to node 0.0.0 and tries the other branch. Before it can execute "find-neighbour-forward 1 .. .. 9", however, it must pop the set of handles determined for the left child 0.0.0.0. After popping, the set of handles for node 0.0.0 is on top of the stack and the algorithm can correctly try to extend each handle by execution of "find-neighbour-forward 1 .. .. 9".

pop-handles :

[g, u, pc, RS, A : A' : ST, (mp, lp), false]

        $\Rightarrow$ [g, u, pc+1, RS, A' : ST, (mp-1, lp), false].

When the complete left-hand side matches, a non-empty set of current handles is on top of the stack. Before the actual rewriting step may take place, one handle must be selected for which the application predicate evaluates to true. Therefore we unfold the set and push the individual elements on the stack. The morphism pointer is set to the top element $\{ h_n \}$, whereas the low pointer refers to $\{ h_1 \}$.

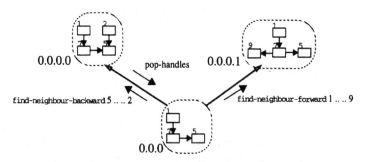

Figure 33   Backtracking in the abstract machine

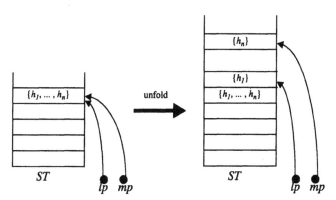

Figure 34   Unfolding the top element of the stack

unfold :

[$g, u, pc, RS, \{h_1, ..., h_n\}$: ST, (mp, lp), false]

$\quad \Rightarrow$ [$g, u, pc+1, RS, \{h_n\}$: ... : $\{h_1\}$: $\{h_1, ..., h_n\}$: ST,

$\qquad\qquad\qquad\qquad\qquad\qquad\qquad (mp+n, mp+1)$, false].

If the application of a rule depends on an application predicate, this must be evaluated for all handles which have been found. The preceding execution of "unfold" has pushed them in individual sets onto the stack. The application predicate is evaluated with respect to the top handle. The value of the application predicate for the top handle is left on top of the stack. If the value is true, the top handle is selected for the rewriting step. The stack is cleared from information gathered in the search phase, i.e. the selected handle is the only stack element and it is referred by lp and mp. If the predicate evaluates to false the evaluation must be performed on the next handle if that is available. Thus the execution jumps back to *pred*, the beginning of the instruction sequence of the application predicate and decrements mp. When no further handle is available, the element of the rule set is not applicable and the search backtracks. The operation of "choose-handle" is shown in figure 35.

choose-handle *pred fail* :

[g, u, pc, RS, res : $\{h\}$: ST, (mp, lp), false]

$\quad$ if res = true $\qquad\qquad\qquad \Rightarrow$ [$g, u, pc+1, RS, \{h\}, (0, 0)$, true]

$\quad$ if res = false and $mp \neq lp$ $\quad \Rightarrow$ [$g, u, pred, RS, ST, (mp-1, lp)$, false]

$\quad$ if res = false and $mp = lp$ $\quad \Rightarrow$ [$g, u, fail, RS, ST, (mp, lp)$, false]

where $A' = \{h \in A|\ (h(s), el, h(t)) \in E\}$

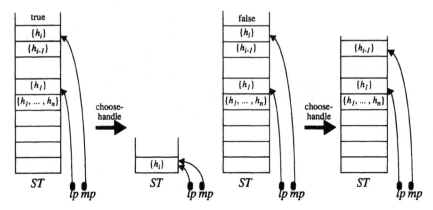

Figure 35   Choosing the appropriate handle

5.2.3   Structural Graph Updates

The abstract machine provides five instructions for the insertion and deletion of vertices and edges. When a vertex is added to the graph, it is assigned a new identifier. Furthermore the current morphism is extended to address the inserted vertex as well.

add-vertex w vl :
$$[(V, E, l, f), u, pc, RS, \{h\}, (mp, lp), \text{true}]$$
$$\Rightarrow [(V \cup \{v\}, E, l', f), u, p+1, RS, \{h'\}, (mp, lp), \text{true}]$$

where v is a new vertex, i.e. $v \notin V$ and the new labelling function equals the old one on V, $l'|_V = l$, $l'(v) = vl$ and $h'|_{dom(h)} = h$, $h'(w) = v'$.

When uniquely labelled vertices are inserted the machine must update the access function also.

add-unique-vertex w vl :
$$[(V, E, l, f), u, pc, RS, \{h\}, (mp, lp), \text{true}]$$
$$\Rightarrow [(V \cup \{v\}, E, l', f), u', pc+1, RS, \{h'\}, (mp, lp), \text{true}]$$

where $v \notin V$, $l'|_V = l$, $l'(v) = vl$, $h'|_{dom(h)} = h$, $h'(w) = v$ and
$u'|_{dom(u)} = u$, $u'(vl) = v$.

The deletion of a vertex is a complex operation because it must ensure the consistency of the graph. All edges incident to a removed vertex are deleted implicitly.

```
delete-vertex w :
```
[$(V, E, l, f), u, pc, RS, \{h\}, (mp, lp)$, true]
$\Rightarrow$ [$(V', E \setminus inc(v), l \mid_{V'}, f \mid_{V' \times A}), u, pc+1, RS, \{h \mid_{V'}\}, (mp, lp)$, true]

where $v = h(w)$ and $V' = V \setminus \{v\}$.

An edge can be inserted into the graph and deleted from it only when the incident vertices are present.

```
add-edge s el t :
```
[$(V, E, l, f), u, pc, RS, \{h\}, (mp, lp)$, true]
$\Rightarrow$ [$(V, E \cup \{(h(s), el, h(t))\}, l, f), u, pc+1, RS, \{h\}, (mp, lp)$, true].

```
delete-edge s el t :
```
[$(V, E, l, f), u, pc, RS, \{h\}, (mp, lp)$, true]
$\Rightarrow$ [$(V, E \setminus \{(h(s), el, h(t))\}, l, f), u, pc+1, RS, \{h\}, (mp, lp)$, true].

5.2.4   Evaluation of Embedding Descriptions

The embedding descriptions of a rewriting rule must not be evaluated in sequence because inserted paste-edges may interfere with the evaluation of cut-descriptions. Therefore the evaluation of an individual embedding description is performed in two phases: 1) The cut-description is evaluated. The computed sets of embedding edges and vertices are pushed on the stack. They stay there until the remaining embedding descriptions are evaluated. 2) New embedding edges are inserted in the graph according to the paste-descriptions and the formerly determined embedding vertices. The definition of the rewriting step requires the deletion of old embedding edges. Throughout the embedding phase, the graph morphism is hidden in the stack because the results of previous evaluations are pushed on top of the stack. Therefore the current morphism is accessed via the morphism pointer, i.e. $ST[mp] = h$.

Again, we distinguish the cut-descriptions by their direction. A cut-description (t, el, vl, in) must determine those edges with target vertex $h(t)$, label el and a source vertex with label vl. All edges with the given characteristics and the incident source vertices are pushed onto the stack. The restriction "$\setminus rg(h)$" ensures that only vertices outside the range of h, i.e. vertices of the rest graph, are taken into consideration.

```
find-embedding-in vl el t :
```
[$g, u, pc, RS, ST, (mp, lp)$, true]
$\Rightarrow$ [$g, u, pc+1, RS, (V_{emb}, E_{emb}) : ST, (mp, lp)$, true]

where $ST[mp] = h, E_{emb} = E \cap ([l^{-1}(vl) \setminus rg(h)] \times \{el\} \times \{h(t)\})$, and $V_{emb} = \{ s | (s, el, t) \in E_{emb} \}$.

The instruction for outgoing cut-descriptions has a similar structure.

```
find-embedding-out s el vl :
```
[$g, u, pc, RS, ST, (mp, lp)$, true]
$\Rightarrow$ [$g, u, pc+1, RS, (V_{emb}, E_{emb}) : ST, (mp, lp)$, true]

where $ST[mp] = h$, $E_{emb} = E \cap (\{h(s)\} \times \{el\} \times [l^{-1}(vl) \backslash rg(h)])$,
and $V_{emb} = \{ t | (s, el, t) \in E_{emb} \}$.

After the evaluation of all cut-descriptions of a rewriting rule, the contribution of the embedding description is applied to the graph. The definition of the rewriting step first requires the deletion of the edges determined by a cut-description.

```
delete-embedding-edges :
```
[$(V, E, l, f), u, pc, RS, (V_{emb}, E_{emb}) : ST, (mp, lp)$, true]
$\Rightarrow$ [$(V, E \backslash E_{emb}, l, f), u, pc+1, RS, (V_{emb}, E_{emb}) : ST, (mp, lp)$, true].

Next, new edges connecting right-hand side vertices to the rest graph are introduced according to given paste-descriptions. Here also, the two possible directions of edges lead to two similar insert instructions.

```
add-embedding-edges-in el t :
```
[$(V, E, l, f), u, pc, RS, (V_{emb}, E_{emb}) : ST, (mp, lp)$, true]
$\Rightarrow$ [$(V, E', l, f), u, pc+1, RS, ST, (mp, lp)$, true]

where $ST[mp] = h$ and $E' = E \cup \{ (v, el, h(t)) | v \in V_{emb} \}$.

```
add-embedding-edges-out s el :
```
[$(V, E, l, f), u, pc, RS, (V_{emb}, E_{emb}) : ST, (mp, lp)$, true]
$\Rightarrow$ [$(V, E', l, f), u, pc+1, RS, ST, (mp, lp)$, true]

where $ST[mp] = h$ and $E' = E \cup \{ (h(s), el, v) | v \in V_{emb} \}$.

5.2.5 Attribute Evaluation

Attribute expressions are evaluated either at the end of the search phase or after evaluating the embedding description. When only the application predicate is computed, no updates are performed. Therefore there is no risk of inconsistent attribute function. When, though, attribute function transformations are processed, the update of an attribute value must take two steps, similar to the evaluation of an embedding description. Each attribute expression is evaluated on the stack and leaves its value on the top. When the last expression is evaluated, the results are popped and stored in the appropriate attributes.

There are various sources for operands. Constant values $d \in D$ are included in the code.

```
push-constant d :
```
$[\, g,\, u,\, pc,\, RS,\, ST,\, (mp,\, lp),\, \text{true} \,]$
$\qquad \Rightarrow [\, g,\, u,\, pc+1,\, RS,\, d : ST,\, (mp,\, lp),\, \text{true} \,].$

Values included in the actual parameter list are addressed by their index.

```
push-param p :
```
$[\, g,\, u,\, pc,\, (n,\, (par_1,\, \dots\, ,\, par_m)) : RS,\, ST,\, (mp,\, lp),\, \text{true} \,]$
$\qquad \Rightarrow [\, g,\, u,\, pc+1,\, (n,\, (par_1,\, ...,\, par_m)) : RS,\, par_p : ST,\, (mp,\, lp),\, \text{true} \,].$

To allow successive computation of attribute values, values of the current attribute function are referenced via a vertex and an attribute name.

```
push-attrib v a :
```
$[\, g,\, u,\, pc,\, RS,\, ST,\, (mp,\, lp),\, \text{true} \,]$
$\qquad \Rightarrow [\, g,\, u,\, pc+1,\, RS,\, f(h(v),\, a) : ST,\, (mp,\, lp),\, \text{true} \,]$

where $ST[mp] = h$.

An arbitrary number of unary and binary operations might be supported by the machine. They also operate on the stack.

```
un-op op :
```
$[\, g,\, u,\, pc,\, RS,\, d : ST,\, (mp,\, lp),\, \text{true} \,]$
$\qquad \Rightarrow [\, g,\, u,\, pc+1,\, RS,\, op(d) : ST,\, (mp,\, lp),\, \text{true} \,].$

```
bin-op op :
```
$[\, g,\, u,\, pc,\, RS,\, d' : d'' : ST,\, (mp,\, lp),\, \text{true} \,]$
$\qquad \Rightarrow [\, g,\, u,\, pc+1,\, RS,\, op(d',\, d'') : ST,\, (mp,\, lp),\, \text{true} \,].$

After evaluating all attribute rules, the new attribute values are stored by redefinition of the attribute function of the graph.

```
update-attribute v a :
```
$[\, (V,\, E,\, l,\, f),\, u,\, pc,\, RS,\, d : ST,\, (mp,\, lp),\, \text{true} \,]$
$\qquad \Rightarrow [\, (V,\, E,\, l,\, f'),\, u,\, pc+1,\, RS,\, ST,\, (mp,\, lp),\, \text{true} \,]$

where $ST[mp] = h, f'(h(v), a) = d$ and $f'\mid_{(V' \forall A) \setminus \{(h(v), a)\}} = f$.

5.2.6   Control Instructions

When the instruction "end-rewriting-step" is reached, the application of a rule set is terminated. The flag a indicates whether the application was successful or not. Thus, on the execution of this instruction, the control structure interpreter is called to provide the next element of the rewriting sequence. Execution proceeds at n_2, the entry point of the new rule set to be applied to the graph. The stack, its pointers, and the applicability flag are initialized.

```
end-rewriting-step :
[ g, u, pc, (n₁, Par₁) : (n₂, Par₂) : RS, ST, (mp, lp), true ]
        ⟹ [ g, u, n₂, (n₂, Par₂) : RS, {⊥}, (0, 0), true ].
```

The instruction "skip" does nothing. It supports the compilation of nested structures.

```
skip :
[ g, u, pc, RS, ST, (mp, lp), a ]
        ⟹ [ g, u, pc+1, RS, ST, (mp, lp), a ].
```

The instruction set is capable of implementing the execution of rule sets of a programmed attributed graph rewriting system. What remains is to provide a number of code generation rules which assemble the instructions in an appropriate order. The code generation rules therefore must obey the implicit dependencies between instructions. So, for example, a "delete-embedding-edges" instruction must not be executed when no set of embedding edges is on top of the stack. We give the code generation rules in the next section.

5.3   Code Generation for the Abstract Machine

The link between an optimized graph rewriting system and the core abstract machine is realized by the code generation rules. They translate the initial graph and a number of rule sets into code executable by the machine. We do not generate code for control structures other than rule sets. The design of the graph rewriting environment provides a separate interpreter for the control part of a programmed graph rewriting system.

For the definition of the code generation rules, we must fix the syntactical notation for the accepted input. Since the compiler is able to perform an optimization of rule sets, we take the optimized search tree as the basic structure of the input. The code generator translates each tree into an instruction sequence which performs a backtracking matching algorithm.

Before we specify the code generation rules, we give the abstract syntax of their input, i.e. the optimized rule sets of a programmed attributed graph rewriting system together with the initial graph.

5.3.1 The Syntax

For the code generation for a given graph grammar with rule sets, we assume that the left-hand sides of a rule set are analysed and transformed to a search tree by the optimizer. Its nodes represent individual search steps which may be an extension, a check, operation or the determination of an initial handle. Each leaf potentially contains the basic operations of more than one rewriting rule. If there are multiple rules present at a leaf, they must have an identical left-hand side, such as, for example, the rules "swap" and "no swap" (see page 103).

The application predicate and the attribute function transformations are input as attribute expressions and attribute assignments respectively. Their syntactical structure complies to the usual abstract syntax of expressions.

We assume that the input complies with the following abstract syntax where $x*$ is a maybe empty sequence of x.

An attributed programmed graph rewriting system consists of an initial graph and a sequence of rule sets. The initial graph is given as the sequences of labelled vertices, edges and attribute assignments. From these sequences, the instructions producing the initial graph will be generated.

> <pagrs>   ::=<graph> <ruleset>*
> <graph>   ::=<lvertex>* <edge>* <attrassign>*

The syntactical structure of a rule set covers optimized and unoptimized sets. In the unoptimized case, a rule set consists of individual connected enumerations which can be viewed as a path. The greedy optimization algorithm outputs a number of search trees. The example in figure 30 is not typical in this respect, because it generates a single tree. This is caused by the fact that there is one vertex present in all graphs. This property does not hold in general. Therefore, according to the algorithm, several trees may be generated rooted in different vertices. The overall structure of a rule set is thus a forest, syntactically represented as a sequence of trees.

The leaf of a tree consists only of a node which carries a number of conditional rules. If the matching enters a leaf, one of the conditional rules may be applied. Therefore the corresponding application predicate must evaluate to true for at least one handle.

```
<ruleset>   ::=<forest>
<forest>    ::=<tree>*
<tree>      ::=<node> <forest> | <node> <condrule>*
```

A node contains the information on an individual search step. This step may either determine the images of a labelled vertex, check the existence of an edge, or try to extend a current handle. The required data for the latter case has the syntactical form of the first alternative. The first vertex is already matched, and the extension proceeds along an edge to a vertex with the given labels. All determined vertices are bound to the vertex given as the fourth component. The orientation of the edge is explicitly given.

A conditional rule represents a rule together with an attribute expression which denotes the application predicate.

The basic operations which are determined by the net effect component of the compiler are syntactically given as six sequences. The first two sequences list the vertices and edges to be inserted. The next two sequences denote the components to be deleted. The lists of embedding descriptions and attribute assignments complete the syntactical representation of a rule.

```
<node>       ::=<vertex> <label> <label> <vertex> <dir> | <edge> | <lvertex>
<condrule>::=<attrexp> <rule>
<rule>       ::=<lvertex>*<edge>*<vertex>*<edge>* <embdesc>*
                                                  <attrassign>*
```

The remaining syntactical rules reflect the definitions of the previous chapters, e.g. the non-terminal <lvertex> denotes a labelled vertex and is a pair <vertex> <label>, where a <vertex> is a natural number and <label> is an element of Σ_V.

```
<attrassign>::=<vertex> <attname> := <attrexp>
<attrexp>   ::=<const> | <param> | <vertex> <attname> | <op> <attrexp> |
               <attrexp> <op> <attrexp>
<embdesc>::=<cut> <paste>
<cut>        ::=<vertex> <label> <label> <dir>
<paste>      ::=<vertex> <label> <dir> | del
<lvertex>    ::=<vertex> <label>
<edge>       ::=<vertex> <label> <vertex>
<dir>        ::=in | out
<op>         ::= ... (*symbols for a unary and binary operations*)
<attname>  ∈ $\Sigma_A$
<label>    ∈ $\Sigma_V \cup \Sigma_E$
```

$$\begin{array}{ll} <\text{vertex}> & \in \mathbb{N} \\ <\text{const}> & \in D \\ <\text{param}> & \in \mathbb{N} \end{array}$$

5.3.2 The Code Generation Rules

The code generation is performed by a number of semantic functions which map syntactic objects to sequences of labelled instructions. Each major syntactic domain has a corresponding code generating function. The approximation of the set of unique vertex labels is passed to the subsequent function calls to provide a separate treatment of uniquely labelled vertices.

The top-level generation rule **PAGRS** takes a graph and a sequence of rule sets together with a set of vertex labels which must be unique. It applies **INIT** to the graph, which generates the instructions for the allocation of the initial graph. According to the initial state of the core abstract machine (see page 138), this code is entered before any rewriting rule can be applied. The initialization instructions are followed by sequences for each rule set. The first call to the generation function **RULESET** is provided with the label 1. It will serve as the entry to the code of the first rule set.

$$\begin{array}{lll} \textbf{PAGRS} \; [\![\, g \; rs^* \,]\!] \; UV & = & \textbf{INIT} \; [\![\, g \,]\!] \; UV \\ & & \textbf{RULESET} \; [\![\, rs^* \,]\!] \; UV \; 1 \end{array}$$

The function **RULESET** initializes the compilation of the head element rs of a sequence of rule sets. The entry into the code generated for the set rs by **FOREST** is at the label i. That label is equal to the position of the set in the sequence. It is incremented in the application of **RULESET** to the rest of the sequence. Two rule sets are separated by the instruction "end-rewriting-step", which causes the interpreter to select the next rule to be applied. For the sake of completeness, we translate the empty sequence to a single "skip".

$$\begin{array}{llll} \textbf{RULESET} \; [\![\, rs \; rs^* \,]\!] \; UV \, i & = & i\text{:} & \texttt{skip} \\ & & & \textbf{FOREST} \; [\![\, rs \,]\!] \; UV \, i.0 \\ & & & \texttt{end-rewriting-step} \\ & & & \textbf{RULESET} \; [\![\, rs^* \,]\!] \; UV \, (i{+}1) \\ \textbf{RULESET} \; [\![\quad \,]\!] \; UV \, i & = & i\text{:} & \texttt{skip} \end{array}$$

FOREST must generate the code for a sequence of trees. Hence it must realize the back-tracking mechanism by an appropriate assignment of labels. The rule **FOREST** has the address of the code for the first tree as a parameter. It places the code generated for that tree at that label. **FOREST**, for the remaining sequence, as well as **TREE**, for the current tree, are called with an incremented label. Hence the translation of the head of the sequence *tr* is provided with the label for its following sibling. Thus, in case the matching fails for that tree, it can jump to an alternative branch, namely its sibling. The labelling mechanism reflects the labels assigned to the nodes of the optimized search tree in figure 30. The head of a label indicates the rule set for which the code is generated. The tail of the labels of matching instructions is equal to the label of the corresponding node in the search tree. The instruction "pop-handles" is preceded by a "skip", which takes the label of a virtual right-most sibling on each sub-tree.

$$\text{FOREST } [\![\, tr\ tr^*\ ]\!]\ UV\ d.i\ =\ d.i\!:\quad \text{TREE } [\![\, tr\ ]\!]\ UV\ d.(i+1)$$
$$\text{FOREST } [\![\, tr^*\ ]\!]\ UV\ d.(i+1)$$
$$\text{FOREST } [\![\qquad\ ]\!]\ UV\ d\ =\ d\!:\quad \text{skip}$$

The root of a tree is a node which contains the information of an actual matching step such as an extension or a check. Hence **TREE** calls **NODE** to generate the corresponding search instruction. **NODE** is provided with the address of the tree's sibling. If the matching fails, the search will jump to the alternative branch. If the matching succeeds, the search either enters the next level or a sequence of conditional rules is applied. In the first case, the label is initialized and passed to the translation of the forest. In the latter case, **CONDR** generates the code for the conditional rules *cr**. Here again we open a new level of labels.

Note that **CONDR** is provided with the address at which the generated code is to be placed. In the definition of **TREE** and **NODE**, to the contrary, the label parameter should enable the jump to a search alternative in case of a failure. In **CONDR**, however, no nested matches are performed. Thus the execution does not need to jump in case of a failure, but can just proceed with the following code. Furthermore, we may have several conditional rules whose application predicates are to be evaluated for each handle until one handle satisfies the predicate. The instruction "choose-handle" realizes the iteration. It requires the address of the application predicate which is provided by the evaluation of **CONDR**. Consequently **CONDR** must know its own address to generate the appropriate labels.

The execution of code generated by **CONDR** is then straightforward. First of all, the set of handles on the stack top is unfolded and then the application predicate is evaluated. Depending on the result and the availability of further handles, "choose-handle" either skips to the next instruction, jumps to the repeated evaluation of the predicate, or jumps to the next conditional rule. In case no condition evaluates to true, the set of current handles is popped. Thus an alternative branch of the search can be entered. Its code follows directly after the final "pop-handles" instruction.

TREE $[\![\, n\, f\,]\!]\, UV\, d$ =   **NODE** $[\![\, n\,]\!]\, UV\, d$

                                                     FOREST $[\![\, f\,]\!]\, UV\, d.0$

                                                     `pop-handles`

TREE $[\![\, n\, cr^*\,]\!]\, UV\, d.i$ =   **NODE** $[\![\, n\,]\!]\, UV\, d.i$

                                                   CONDR $[\![\, cr^*\,]\!]\, UV\, d.(i\text{-}1).0$

CONDR $[\![\, ae\ r\ cr^*\,]\!]\, UV\, d.i = d.i{:}$ `unfold`

                                   $d.(i{+}1){:}$ **ATT** $[\![\, ae\,]\!]$

                                                 `choose-handle` $d.(i{+}1)\ d.(i{+}2)$

                                     RULE $[\![\, r\,]\!]\, UV$

                                     CONDR $[\![\, cr^*\,]\!]\, UV\, d.(i{+}2)$

CONDR $[\![$ $]\!]\, UV\, d$ = $d{:}$ `pop-handles`

For each node of the search tree the appropriate matching instruction is generated. Here, the set of unique vertex labels comes into play. When the images of a vertex are to be determined, one of the two "find-... -vertex" instructions is selected. The explicit information on the direction in which an extension is to be performed is reflected by two rules, one for each direction.

NODE $[\![\, v\, vl\,]\!]\, UV\, d$ =   `find-unique-vertex` $vl\ v\ d$ if $vl \in UV$

                                          =   `find-vertex` $vl\ v\ d$ otherwise

NODE $[\![\, s\, el\, t\,]\!]\, UV\, d$ =   `exists-edge` $s\ el\ t\ d$

NODE $[\![\, s\, el\, vt\, t\ \text{in}\,]\!]\, UV\, d$ =   `find-neighbour-backward` $s\ el\ vl\ t\ d$

NODE $[\![\, s\, el\, vt\, t\ \text{out}\,]\!]\, UV\, d$ =   `find-neighbour-forward` $s\ el\ vl\ t\ d$

The code generation function **RULE** initiates the output of instructions for the actual rewriting. The rewriting effect of a rule is given by lists of inserted and deleted vertices and edges, and embedding rules and attribute function transformations. The instruction sequence terminates with an "`end-rewriting-step`". It passes the control to the interpreter, which in turn may initiate the next rewriting step.

RULE $[\![\, iv^*\ ie^*\ dv^*$

          $de^*\ m^*\ at^*\,]\!]\, UV$ =   **INS** $[\![\, iv^*\,]\!]\, UV$

                                          INS $[\![\, ie^*\,]\!]\, UV$

                                          EMB $[\![\, m^*\,]\!]$

                                          ATT $[\![\, at^*\,]\!]$

                                          DEL $[\![\, dv^*\,]\!]$

                                          DEL $[\![\, de^*\,]\!]$

                                          `end-rewriting-step`

The insertion and deletion instructions are directly translated from the syntactical information.

INS $[\!\![v \; vl \; lv^*]\!\!]\, UV$	=	add-unique-vertex $v \; vl$
		INS $[\!\![lv^*]\!\!]$ if $\in UV$
	=	add-vertex $v \; vl$
		INS $[\!\![lv^*]\!\!]$ otherwise
INS $[\!\![s \; el \; t \; e^*]\!\!]\, UV$	=	add-edge $s \; el \; t$
		INS $[\!\![e^*]\!\!]$
DEL $[\!\![v \; v^*]\!\!]$	=	delete-vertex v
		DEL $[\!\![v^*]\!\!]$
DEL $[\!\![s \; el \; t \; e^*]\!\!]$	=	delete-edge $s \; el \; t$
		DEL $[\!\![e^*]\!\!]$
DEL $[\!\![\;]\!\!]$, **INS** $[\!\![\;]\!\!]\, UV$	=	skip

The code generation functions for both embedding descriptions and attribute function transformations implement the stacking mechanism for the individual results. The instructions generated for the determination of cut-edges and the evaluation of the paste-descriptions of one embedding description frame the code generated for the remaining elements of the list. The same outline of the code is realized for the attribute expression evaluation and updating of the attributes respectively. The evaluation of attribute expressions is straightforwardly performed on a stack. The respective results remain on the stack and are popped by the "update-attribute" instruction.

EMB $[\!\![c \; p \; m^*]\!\!]$	=	**EMB** $[\!\![c]\!\!]$
		EMB $[\!\![m^*]\!\!]$
		delete-embedding-edges
		EMB $[\!\![p]\!\!]$
EMB $[\!\![v \; el \; vl \; \text{in}]\!\!]$	=	find-embedding-in $vl \; el \; v$
EMB $[\!\![v \; el \; vl \; \text{out}]\!\!]$	=	find-embedding-out $v \; el \; vl$
EMB $[\!\![v \; el \; \text{in}]\!\!]$	=	add-embedding-edges-in $el \; v$
EMB $[\!\![v \; el \; \text{out}]\!\!]$	=	add-embedding-edges-out $v \; el$
EMB $[\!\![\text{del}]\!\!]$	=	skip
ATT $[\!\![v \; a \; ae \; attr^*]\!\!]$	=	**ATT** $[\!\![ae]\!\!]$
		ATT $[\!\![attr^*]\!\!]$
		update-attribute $v \; a$
ATT $[\!\![d]\!\!]$	=	push-const d
ATT $[\!\![v \; a]\!\!]$	=	push-attrib $v \; a$
ATT $[\!\![p]\!\!]$	=	push-param p
ATT $[\!\![op \; ae]\!\!]$	=	**ATT** $[\!\![ae]\!\!]$

$$\textbf{ATT } [\![ae \; op \; ae' \;]\!] \quad = \quad \begin{array}{l} op \\ \textbf{ATT } [\![ae \;]\!] \\ \textbf{ATT } [\![ae' \;]\!] \end{array}$$

$$\textbf{ATT } [\![\;]\!], \textbf{EMB } [\![\;]\!] \quad = \quad \begin{array}{l} op \\ \texttt{skip} \end{array}$$

The initial graph is input into the machine by means of insertion instructions.

$$\textbf{INIT } [\![\, lv^* \; e^* \; attr^* \;]\!] \, UV \quad = \quad \begin{array}{l} \textbf{INS } [\![\, lv^* \;]\!] \, UV \\ \textbf{INS } [\![\, e^* \;]\!] \, UV \\ \textbf{ATT } [\![\, attr^* \;]\!] \\ \texttt{end-rewriting-step} \end{array}$$

We present a fragment of code as a code generation example in figure 36. This code is generated from the search tree shown in figure 30. This tree represents a single rule set with graphs g_1 up to g_5 as left-hand sides. The generated code reflects the structure of

```
              INIT [l g l]
     1:   skip
   1.0:   find-vertex A 1    1.1
 1.0.0:       find-neighbour-forward 1 .. D 7   1.0.1
1.0.0.0:          find-neighbour-forward 7 .. C 5   1.0.0.1
                     FOREST [l (2,..,5) ..... l] UV   1.0.0.0.0
                  pop-handles
1.0.0.1:       skip
               pop-handles
 1.0.1:       find-neighbour-forward 1 .. B 2   1.0.2
1.0.1.0:          find-neighbour-forward 2 .. I 4   1.0.1.1
1.0.1.0.0:           unfold
1.0.1.0.1:           ATT [l ae l]
                     choose-handle    1.0.1.0.0   1.0.1.0.2
                     RULE [l ... l]
1.0.1.0.2:        pop-handles
1.0.1.1:          find-neighbour-forward 2 .. C 5   1.0.1.2.
                     FOREST [l (7,..,5) ..... l] UV   1.0.1.1.0
                  pop-handles
1.0.1.2:       skip
               pop-handles
 1.0.2:   skip
          pop-handles
   1.1:   skip
          end-rewriting-step
     2:   skip
```

Figure 36   Fragment of generated code (edge labels omitted)

the tree. Branches in the tree indicate alternative extensions. They show up in the code as chains of failure addresses of equal depth. For example, the find-instruction at 1.0.0 jumps in case of a failure to 1.0.1. If that find-instruction fails also, the execution passes to the failure address 1.0.2. Because at that stage of the matching all extensions have failed, the former extension, determined by "find-vertex" at label 1.0, is therefore removed from the stack.

The repetitive evaluation of an application predicate will be executed at label 1.0.1.0.0. If the search step is successful, the set of handles is unfolded. For each handle, the predicate at label 1.0.1.0.1 is evaluated, and the instruction "choose-handle" branches dependent on the computed value. When the predicate is false for all handles, another conditional rule with identical left-hand side may be applied. At the failure label of "choose-handle" (i.e. 1.0.1.0.2), though, the instruction "pop-handles" indicates that no further conditional rule is available. It moreover pops the handles determined at label 1.0.1.0.

5.4 Improvements by Rule Set Optimization

The base of the following measurements is a prototype implementation of an earlier version of the graph rewriting environment. The compiler performs the analyses and optimization. It generates a Miranda program, which basically consists of the code sequences for each rule set and the initial graph. Each instruction is realized as a

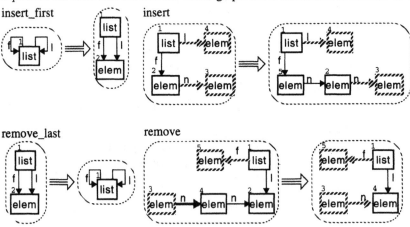

Remove = remove OR remove_last

Insert   = insert OR insert_first

Figure 37   Insertion and deletion operations for FIFO lists

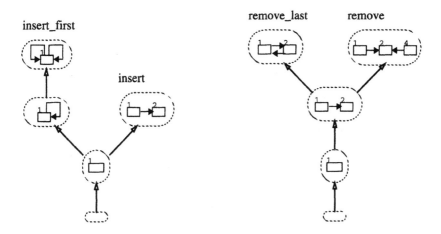

Figure 38   Optimized search trees for "Insert" and "Remove" (labels omitted)

Miranda function. Thus the output of the compiler is compiled again by the Miranda system, which generates an object file executing the core abstract machine.

For the measurements, we have chosen the graph rewriting system specifying operations on FIFO lists (see figure 28). We join the rules for insertion and deletion of elements in two rule sets, "Insert" and "Remove". In a naive implementation, the application test for "Insert" takes at most 5 search steps, whereas "Remove" needs 6. The optimized search trees output by the greedy algorithm are shown in figure 30. Both trees perform at most 4 steps and reduce the number of search steps by 20% and 33% respectively. We do not expect the final speed-up to be of that size because the overall execution time of a rewriting step also depends on the actual graph transformation.

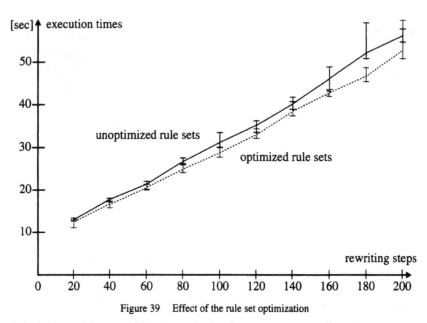

Figure 39   Effect of the rule set optimization

The graphs in figure 39 show the execution time of the abstract machine performing sequences of 20 up to 200 rewriting steps. In each sequence, "Insert" and "Remove" are randomly mixed. For each sequence we did 10 measurements on a SparcStation 10. The graphs connect the average values of the measurements. The vertical lines show the range of values obtained for each number of rewriting steps. We can see from the graphs that the optimization of rule sets effectively reduces the execution time. The percentage improvement does not depend on the number of rewriting steps.

Table 2 lists the speed-ups for the average run time of the different rewriting sequences. From this table, we conclude that the rule set optimization causes an average speed-up of 6.4% for bypassing connected enumerations with uniquely labelled root vertices. The improvement will be even higher for non-bypassing enumerations, because, in that case, one search step can take arbitrary time. Hence, the optimization saves more than just constant time for each search step.

number of rewriting steps	run time unopti-mized [sec]	run time optimized [sec]	speed-up [%]
20	13.0	12.34	5.076
40	17.78	16.62	6.524
60	21.39	20.58	3.786
80	26.66	24.85	6.789
100	31.16	28.75	7.734
120	35.19	33.0	6.223
140	40.2	38.48	4.278
160	46.12	42.78	7.241
180	52.19	46.67	10.576
200	56.09	52.81	5.847
average speed-up			6.407

Table 2 Average speed-up gained by the optimization of rule sets

5.5 Summary and Related Work

In this chapter, we presented an abstract machine which executes programmed attributed graph rewriting systems in general, but which is especially tailored for an optimized application of rule sets. The instruction set of the core machine serves as an intermediate language to which the graph rewriting system is compiled. The intermediate representation is then further compiled to machine code. This approach therefore implements a fast execution of graph rewriting systems in main memory. Moreover, the compilation approach provides space for pre-computation and thus makes time-consuming analyses possible.

The optimization of rule sets aims at a *maximum overlap* of a set of connected enumerations. So the compiler already determines the re-use of partial handles when the application of the set's elements fails. This optimization leads to an average performance improvement of 6.4%. So the novel subject of optimization on the level of control structures promises further improvements.

An optimization goal similar to the maximum overlap of connected enumerations is known from traditional compiler construction and the implementation of functional languages. The common sub-expression elimination in code optimization considers the data flow within and across basic blocks. Aho and Ullman give an algorithm for the elimination of global common sub-expressions [AU77]. The optimization is much easier to perform for pure functional programming languages. Due to the lack of side effects and the referential transparency, any two syntactically equal expressions in the same scope denote the same value. Therefore common sub-expression elimination can be performed either as a syntactic transformation or by sharing common values in the internal representation of the evaluated term [PeJo87]. This representation thus changes from an ordinary abstract syntax tree to a directed acyclic graph. We apply the concept of common subexpressions to graphs.

We defined the optimization goal for rule sets of arbitrary size in terms of a minimal Steiner tree. There is another graph theoretic problem which relates rule set optimization to graph theory. If the rule set has just two elements and their left-hand sides are not consistently labelled, our optimization problem is equal to the largest common subgraph problem. McGregor addressed the maximum common subgraph problem and presented a greedy heuristics to improve the performance of a backtracking algorithm [McG82]. The common subgraph is incrementally constructed, similar to our approach. At each level of the construction, several extensions of the current vertex map are available. The weight of each extension is given as the number of induced edge correspondences. Following the greedy strategy, the extension with highest weight is chosen. Hence this approach is similar to our greedy method, with the exception that we deal with an arbitrary number of graphs for which a number of most common subgraphs is required.

An abstract machine is also used in the implementation of PROGRES. The Progress-GraphCode encapsulates the execution component which supports backtracking across rule applications. The execution is built on top of the non-standard database GRAS (for Graph Storage) [KSW92]. The set of instructions provided by the ProgressGraphCode is therefore much larger; besides access operations, it must also implement the initialization and management of the data base. Additionally, the backtracking requires several book-keeping and selection commands. The level of coding is lower than in our design because multiple partial handles are treated individually during the search phase. Our instruction set, on the other hand, determines a set of full handles which in general is of arbitrary size. Our design is motivated by UBS graph rewriting: if our analyses have determined a bypassing connected enumeration with a unique root, then there is at most one element in the set of partial handles.

The design of our environment supports the traditional edit-compile-run cycle. In this regard it differs substantially from PROGRES, which to a great extent supports incremental programming. Further refinements of the analyses will enable separate analyses and compilation and enhance the compiler's performance. The specification of the ProgressGraphCode is given informally as a set of definition modules [Ano94]. Hence it is not easy to port the implementation to another platform.

The implementation presented by Himsolt is set on top of a graph editor [Him89]. The interpreter can execute context-free graph rewrite rules, but only with support of the user. Thus its functionality is definitely smaller than provided by PROGRES system and our implementation.

Witt proposes an architecture for processing graph grammar applications consisting of six layers [Wit87]. His main interest is to provide a flexible implementation which can execute various graph rewriting frameworks. Thus the intermediate "graph grammar implementation language layer" provides eight primitive commands which are sufficient for the implementation of a graph rewriting system. The commands perform insertion and deletion of sets of vertices and edges. Additionally, marking commands allow the identification of vertices which should be accessed by successive commands, e.g. to realize a rewriting step. The marking commands are not explicitly provided by our machine. We use a stack to keep the information required in a rewriting step.

6 A Graphical Implementation of Functional Languages — A Case Study in UBS-Graph Rewriting Systems

In the previous chapters, we developed a sufficient condition for efficient graph rewriting. Furthermore, we have designed an implementation for the optimized execution of rule sets. Still, we have not demonstrated yet that our results really apply. We therefore present a case study for UBS-rewriting systems in this chapter.

Our example illustrates the use of graph rewriting systems as an integrated formalism for specification as well as for programming. The formalism is integrated in the sense that a number of refinements are applied to the initial specification which yield an efficiently executable program, namely a UBS graph rewriting system. The initial specification is already executable, but has a high computational complexity. We refine the specification step-by-step and modify the rewriting system with respect to the requirements of UBS rewriting. The transformed specification performs constant-time matching. Overall, the example provides an insight into the specification with graph rewriting systems in general, but also introduces the pragmatics of UBS graph rewriting.

The study considers a implementation of functional programming languages by *graphical programming*. A functional program consists of one *expression* and a set of user-defined and built-in *function definitions*. The expression may be just a simple arithmetical term which should be evaluated to its numeric value. The expression however, can also be a complex user-defined function applied to appropriate arguments. The user may have defined a function "compile" which translates a given source program. Thus when this function appears in a correct expression, then the evaluation of the expression will compute its value and thus compile the given source program.

The characteristic difference between functional and imperative languages lies in the concept of variables. In imperative languages, a variable is a container in which several values can be stored throughout a computation. Hence the content of a variable is strongly dependent on the flow of control. In functional languages, on the contrary, variables denote exactly one value, similar to the concept of variables in mathematics. Thus whenever a variable occurs several times in one context, it has the same value. This principle of *referential transparency* is also valid for arbitrary functional expressions; any expression in a given context has exactly one value. Therefore expressions with the same value can be substituted by each other without altering the value of the enclosing expression.

According to the referential transparency, the evaluation is performed as a number of substitutions until the normal form is reached. Such substitution is called a reduction step. So, for example, the expression $2+3$ is reduced to 5; the application of a function to a sufficient number of arguments is replaced by the function's body where the arguments substitute the occurrences of formal parameters.

A sub-expression which may be reduced is called a reducible expression, or *redex* for short. In general, there are several redexes in an expression, such that a specific selection strategy must determine the next redex. The most common strategy of *normal order reduction* selects the leftmost-outermost redex.

Graph reduction is an important implementation technique for functional languages. The usual data structure for the representation of expressions is a tree, but the tree representation does not take the referential transparency into account. For example, if a sub-expression occurs twice, it is represented by two identical sub-trees. Both must be evaluated. Because the sub-expressions denote the same value, they need to be evaluated only once. Therefore the sub-trees may be identified, and the expression tree transforms to a term or directed, acyclic graph. This specific data structure expresses the *sharing* of common values. It leads to the notion of *graph reduction* as an implementation technique for functional languages. The evaluation of a functional expression now consists of a sequence of graph transformation steps, and a graph rewriting system is very well suited to specify valid transformations. Sharing in combination with normal order reduction is called *lazy evaluation*, which is realized in many implementations of functional languages.

The graphical implementation of functional languages has one major advantage compared to low level implementations: at each stage of the reduction, the expression graph is explicitly given. In advanced implementations such as the G-machine by Johnsson, a reduction is performed by a sequence of G-machine instructions [Joh84]. A stack as an auxiliary data structure supports the execution of a reduction step. The stack, for example, stores pointers into the graph. The original graph structure of the reduction is blurred. The explicit representation of the expression graph is therefore an improvement for the analysis of graph reduction. Since the graph in a graphical implementation is directly accessible, the properties and the progress of a graph reduction can be easily studied. This direct access to the expression graph is of great value for debugging and other analysis of functional programs. We do not expect to gain an implementation with competitive run times because we use the execution model of graph rewriting, which is more general than graph reduction.

This chapter develops a graphical implementation of a functional program. First of all we sketch important aspects of functional languages. Then we introduce the representation of functional expressions and definitions as trees and rewriting rules respectively. Expressions are represented as graphs due to sharing. Normal order reduction is realized by a further refinement to the translation. The last part of the translation is the printing mechanism. In the final section we prove that our implementation satisfies the UBS property.

6.1 Aspects of Functional Programming

Functional languages offer a variety of programming constructs, like pattern matching, list comprehensions, guarded and nested definitions, and constructor and functional types. The translation of all constructs to a graph rewriting system will therefore be very tedious. Many constructs can be expressed by simpler ones and are included in the language for the sake of notational convenience. Thus we can restrict our implementation to an appropriate subset without losing the expressive power of the original language.

We give a short introduction in a subset of the functional language Miranda. This subset is selected in such a way that it can easily be translated to graph rewriting systems. For a complete overview on Miranda and functional languages see [Tur86] and [BW88].

A Miranda program, or script as it is called, consists mainly of a set of function definitions. The function identifier and the argument variables occur on the left-hand side of the definition. The value of the function is defined as the expression on the right-hand side. The following script first defines a general polynomial of degree 2, poly2. A specific polynomial f is then defined by the partial application poly2 2 0 5, which binds the first three variables.

```
square x        = x * x
poly2 a b c x   = a * square x + b * x + c
f               = poly2 2 0 5
```

The evaluation of f 3 can be performed as a sequence of reductions.

```
f 3    => poly2 2 0 5 3
       => 2 * square 3 + 0 * 3 + 5
       => 2 * (3 * 3) + 0 * 3 + 5
       => ...
       => 23
```

This example makes use of the most significant type for functional languages, namely the type "function". *Functions are first class objects* that can be bound to identifiers to define other functions. The function poly2, applied to four numeric arguments, represents a simple numeric value. The expression `poly2 2 0 5`, however, cannot be evaluated to a simple value; it is still a function of one argument. Hence the identifier `f` is bound to a function denoted by `poly2 2 0 5`. Since functions are first class objects, they can also appear as arguments of so-called higher-order functions.

The example above shows functions which operate on numerical values only. Further simple data types in Miranda are characters and boolean values. Based on the simple types a user can define so-called *algebraic data types*. The definition of an algebraic data type introduces a number of constructors with a fixed arity, i.e. a fixed number of components. Algebraic data types can implement compound data types known from imperative languages such as enumerations, variable records, and arrays by a single mechanism.

We give four type definitions based on algebraic types. The extension of the data type `day` is the set of constructors on the right-hand side of the type definition.

```
day      ::= Mon | Tue | Wed | Thu | Fri | Sat | Sun
daylist ::= Cons day daylist | Empty
weekend = Cons Sat (Cons Sun Empty)
```

Based on this type, we recursively define the data type `daylist`. An object of `daylist` is a consecutive number of days terminated by `Empty`. The constant `weekend` is an object of type `daylist`. Based on the same principle, complex data types such as tuples or trees can be constructed.

The syntax rules of Miranda require the constructor identifier to start with an upper case letter whereas the first letter of the function and variable identifiers must be lower case. Consequently

```
cons x xs
```

is an application of the list-building function `cons` in contrast to

```
Cons x xs
```

which denotes a list data object. In accordance with our intuition, the function `cons` is defined as

```
cons x xs = Cons x xs
```

The distinction between constructors and functions is necessary to deal with infinite data objects. We can define functions which return infinite data objects, but which are evaluated just as far as the elements of the list are needed. The function `list`, for example, generates an arithmetic sequence with n as the initial element and the constant difference of 3.

```
list n = cons n (list (3 + n))
```

The value of the fully evaluated expression `list 5` cannot be written down, since it is an infinite sequence. We,however, can give the value of `list 5` where the first four elements are evaluated.

```
Cons 5 (Cons 8 (Cons 11 (Cons 14 (list (3 + 14))))).
```

The distinction between the function `cons` and the constructor `Cons` thus also serves to represent explicitly the state of evaluation.

Constructor symbols play an important role for *pattern matching* in functional programming languages. This mechanism provides an elegant means of case analysis in function definitions. Take, for example, the function `length`, which determines the length of a list:

```
length Empty = 0
length (Cons x xs) = 1 + length xs
```

The empty list has length 0. The length of `Cons x xs` is the length of xs incremented by 1.

Uniform function definitions are an important precondition for our translation of functional programs. This special property of function definitions with patterns is defined as follows. For a *uniform function definition* with several cases, none of the left-hand sides may be subsumed by another one. Furthermore, the order of the cases must not influence the result of the evaluation. The translation of uniform definitions has the nice property that the generated rewriting rules are mutually exclusive. They can be put in one set of rewriting rules and only one rule will be applicable, if there is one at all. When we rewrite a certain function definition, we apply the generated set. For each case of the definition, there is one rule in the set and the semantics of the rule set application ensures that the appropriate case is chosen for evaluation.

If a definition would not be uniform, we must somehow map the order of the definitions to the graph rewriting system. Take for example the non-uniform definition

```
length Empty = 0
length xs = 1 + length (tail xs)
```

If both rewriting rules would be equally selected for an application, the reduction may end up in a dead end. The restriction to uniform definitions is an important precondition for the translation of a functional program to a graph rewriting system. In functional languages, the order of the cases of a function definition is exploited to resolve the ambiguities of overlapping patterns. The first case which matches a given expression is chosen for a reduction. The representation of the definitions as a rule set, though, removes the ordering of cases. Therefore our translation can only deal with uniform definitions where the order of the cases is not relevant. We might raise the restriction and therefore implement the order explicitly by programmed graph rewriting, but in that case the translation would become more complicated. Therefore we assume the translated function definitions to be uniform.

The function mappairs is a higher order function. It is applied to a function f and two lists. Furthermore, it contains a multiple occurrence of the variable f. When at least one of the argument lists matches Empty, the result is the empty list as well. Otherwise, f is applied to the head elements of both lists. The resulting value is put in front of the application of mappairs f to the tails of the argument lists.

```
mappairs f Empty xs = Empty
mappairs f (Cons x xs) Empty = Empty
mappairs f (Cons x xs) (Cons y ys)
              = cons (f x y) (mappairs f xs ys)
```

When the function mappairs is applied to infinite lists, it generates an infinite list itself. So the expression

```
mappairs (+) (list 5) (list 7)
```

evaluates to

```
Cons 12 (Cons 18 (...))
```

The components of functional languages presented so far will be the source of the transformation to graph rewriting systems. We assume that the expressions are well-typed.

6.2   Translating Functions to Trees — Graph Reduction approaches Graph Rewriting

6.2.1   A Graphical Notation for Functional Expressions

An implementation of a functional language computes the value of a functional expression given a set of definitions. The common internal representation of an expression is its syntax tree. The application of the function symbol f to its argument 3, i.e. the expression f 3, is represented as where @ denotes the application. The leaves of an expression tree carry constant values, built-in functions, or variable names. A function of several arguments is represented in curried form, i.e. the function is interpreted as the nested application of unary functions. Take poly2 a b c x as an example:

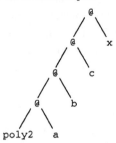

Functional languages, in contrast to other programming languages, are referentially transparent. An expression denotes a value and can be substituted by that value without changing the result of the program. Hence the evaluation of the expression must not have any side-effects. Thus when an expression contains multiple occurrences of one sub-expression, only one instance needs to be evaluated. Thus only one instance appears in the tree which is shared by several nodes. The tree therefore turns into a graph. In the expression x * x, the variable x occurs twice. Because of referential transparency, it needs to be evaluated only once. The expression is therefore represented as the graph

Lazy functional languages deal with infinite data structures, like the sequence of all numbers. To indicate the state of the evaluation of an infinite structure, constructor nodes are included into the internal representation. We will restrict our presentation to the list constructors Cons and Empty in the sequel, but other constructors will be handled similarly. When the application of the function cons to two arguments is evaluated, a constructor node Cons is created which holds pointers to its components. The evaluation of cons e1 e2 is given by

Thus when we inspect the root of the right expression tree, we know that it represents a list with e1 as its head element and the tail list e2. This information is not available at the root of the left tree.

6.2.2 Function Definitions as Rewriting Rules

Based on the graphical notation for expressions, we now approach the representation of function definitions. Basically the semantics of a definition is as follows: replace the expression of the left-hand side by the one of the right-hand side using an appropriate variable substitution. When we consider the graphical representation of expressions, the semantics of a definition is given by a graph rewriting rule: any subgraph which fits to the graphical representation of the left-hand side may be replaced by an image of the right-hand side, supplied with the appropriate pointers to the actual parameters. Since the right-hand side denotes the same value, its root overrides the root node of the left-hand side.

The graphical representations of the definitions of the functions f, poly2, and square are these:

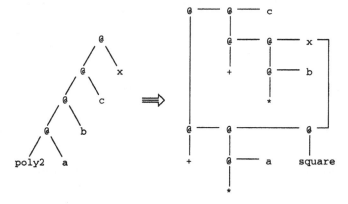

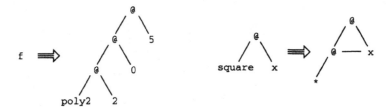

Built-in functions perform value computations. Thus their operation cannot be expressed solely by graphical transformations. When the arguments of the operation have been evaluated to actual values, their sum can be computed.

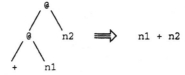

The reduction step then replaces the root by the result. Similar transformations express the reduction by other arithmetic built-in operations.

6.2.3 Translating Expressions

So far, the graphical definition of reductions has been very informal and based on several implicit assumptions. The formal definition of graph rewriting rules requires that a complete specification must, for example, identify vertices and give explicit embedding descriptions. To develop such a formal specification, we will present a translation of functional expressions to attributed, labelled and directed graphs.

We assume the following abstract syntax for expressions

        \<exp\> ::= \<constant\> | \<variable\> | \<exp\> \<exp\>

Constants are basic values like numerals, function identifiers, and constructor symbols. Variables are identifiers occurring as arguments. Hence a variable may not appear as the first symbol of a definition's left-hand side. We distinguish function and variable identifiers because the former serve as a selector of the definition to apply, whereas the latter may represent any expression. The *syntactic domain of constants* comprises the set of values D, and the sets of function identifiers F and constructor symbols C. We assume that simple values which belong to a carrier set of small size are represented as nullary constructor symbols. The boolean values True and False, for example, are members of C, whereas characters and numerals are part of D.

$$CONSTANT = D \cup F \cup C$$

The domain of *variable identifiers VARIABLE* is disjoint from *CONSTANT*. The domain *EXP* contains strings derivable from <exp>.

The translation of expressions to graphs will now be formally defined. Note that the following formal treatment does not cover multiple occurrences of a variable in an expression. Thus sharing of variables and common sub-expressions is not considered, and all expressions are translated to trees. Section 6.3 deals especially with sharing and multiple occurrences of variables.

The translation function **TE** carries two auxiliary parameters. The environment ρ returns the root vertices of expressions. Thus the translated sub-expressions can be connected to the surrounding expression. For instance, the argument and function expressions of an application are attached to the combining apply-vertex via the environment. The second argument of **TE**, the vertex set *W*, collects the vertices already used. Since no vertex can represent more than one sub-expression, new vertices are selected with respect to *W*.

For the formal definition of the translation scheme, we consider the following domains:

G	= set of attributed, labelled, directed graphs
Vert	= set of vertices of all graphs ∈ *G*
Env	= *VARIABLE* ∪ {*root*} → *Vert*

The translation **TE** is of the following type:

$$\textbf{TE} : EXP \rightarrow Env \rightarrow \wp(Vert) \rightarrow (G \times Env \times \wp(Vert))$$

The representation of *simple values*, as stated before, depends on the size of the carrier set. If the carrier is of a large cardinality, the constant values are represented by an attributed vertex labelled with "val". The attribute "Value" takes the value. The constant 3, for example, is translated to the attributed graph $g = (\{1\}, \varnothing, \{1 \rightarrow \text{val}\}, \{1.\text{Value} \rightarrow 3\})$, graphically denoted as

Simple values which belong to a small carrier set and which are therefore members of C are represented like ordinary *nullary constructors*. They are represented by a single vertex graph where the vertex is labelled with the constructor symbol. The list constructor Empty, for example, translates to

For a *nullary constant symbol or simple value* $c \in CONSTANT$, the translation creates a single vertex graph. The vertex v must be a new vertex. In both cases, the root points to v.[1]

TE $[\![c]\!] \rho\, W = (g, \rho\, [root \,/\, v], W \cup \{v\})$

where g is the graph ![v c / val] if c is a value, i.e. $c \in D$. If c is a function identifier

or a constructor symbol, i.e $c \in F \cup C$, then g is ![v / c] .

As mentioned before, we represent *non-nullary constructors* by specific cells which hold pointers to the components of the data object. A `Cons` data object with components $e_1\, e_2$ is represented as follows. The "Cons" vertex points to the subgraphs representing its components by an "c1" and "c2" edge respectively. In general, an *n-ary constructor* object $c\, e_1 \,...\, e_n$ will be represented as

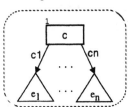

where the edges with label "ci" points to the graph representing the i-th component. An *n-ary constructor* c can be translated only if all components are present.

TE $[\![c\, e_1 ... e_n]\!] \rho_0\, W_0 =$

$((\{v\} \cup \bigcup_{i=1...n} W_i, \{(v, c\,i, \rho_i(root)) \mid i = 1...n\}, l, f)\ , \rho_n\, [root \,/\, v], W_n)$

where the components $e_1,...,e_n$ are translated individually by

$(g_i, \rho_i, W_i) = $ **TE** $[\![e_1]\!]\, \rho_{i-1}\, W_{i-1}$. Each component graph is connected to the new vertex $v \notin W$ by an edge $(v, c\,i, \rho_i(root))$. The resulting labelling function l is defined by the labelling of the component graphs, i.e. for $w \in V_i$

---

1. The update of a function f for a specific argument value x by the result value v is defined as $f\,[x/v]$ where $f\,[x/v]\,(x) = v$ and $f\,[x/v]\,(y) = f\,(y)$ for $.x \neq y$

the labelling is defined as $l(w) = l_i(w)$ and for $w = v$ it holds that $l(w) = c$. Similarly, the attribute function f is defined by the components for all attributes a and $v \in V_i$ as $f(v,a) = f_i(v,a)$, $i = 1...n$.

The translation of a *variable* must take into account that the variable may be bound to any value whether it is evaluated or not. Hence it must match the root of any expression which may be function identifiers, constants, or function applications. Thus we introduce a set-valued vertex label "exp" (for this extension to ordinary graph rewriting see definition 4.2.4) which is defined as

$$\text{exp} = F \cup C \cup \{ \text{@}, \text{val} \}$$

It contains all function identifiers and constructor symbols as well as "val"- and "@"-vertices.

According to the semantics of rewriting with set-valued vertex labels, an "exp"-vertex matches any expression. The graphical representation of a variable is therefore

Because it may be the root of a sub-expression, it may serve as a vertex for which an embedding description may be given. Therefore a reference to v is entered in the environment.

TE $[\![var]\!] \rho\ W = (\ \fbox{exp}\ ,\ \rho\ [root\ /\ v]\ [var\ /\ v],\ W \cup \{v\}\ )$, where $v \notin W$.

The *application* of two expressions, i.e. $e_1\ e_2$, is represented by an apply-vertex pointing to the function expression e_1 and the argument e_2. We follow the convention and call the sequence of function expressions "spine". Hence the left edge is labelled by "sp" for spine.

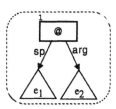

TE $[\![e_1\ e_2]\!] \rho\ W = ((\{v\} \cup W_1 \cup W_2,$

$\qquad \{(v,\ \text{sp},\ \rho_1(root)),\ (v,\ \text{arg},\ \rho_2(root))\ \} \cup E_1 \cup E_2,\ l,f),\ \rho_2\ [root\ /\ v],\ W_2\ )$, where the expression e_1 translates to $(g_1, \rho_1, W_1) = \textbf{TE}\,[\![e_1]\!]\,\rho\,W \cup \{v\}$ with $v \notin W$. The argument e_2 is translated with respect to the environment and set of vertices output by the translation of e_1, i.e. $(g_2, \rho_2, W_2) = \textbf{TE}\,[\![e_2]\!]\,\rho_1\,W_1$. The labelling and the attribute functions of the constructed graph l and f inherit their definition from the subgraphs g_1 and g_2. Their definitions are consistent because the vertex sets of g_1 and g_2 are disjoint. Hence the labelling is $l(v) = $ apply, $l\!\mid_{V_1} = l_1$, and $l\!\mid_{V_2} = l_2$ and the attribute function is defined as $f\!\mid_{V_1} = f_1$ and $f\!\mid_{V_2} = f_2$.

As an example of the definition of **TE**, we apply it to the expression
`length (Cons x xs)`.

$\textbf{TE}\,[\![\texttt{length (Cons x xs)}]\!]\,\bot\,\varnothing =$

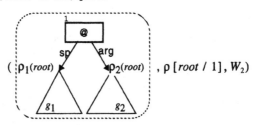

$, \rho\,[root\,/\,1], W_2)$

The sub-expression `length` translates as follows:

$(g_1, \rho_1, W_1) = \textbf{TE}\,[\![\texttt{length}]\!]\,\bot\,\{1\} = ($ 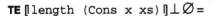 $, \bot\,[root\,/\,2], \{1,2\})$

The graph for `Cons x xs` is generated with $\rho_{10} = \rho_1$, the resulting environment of the left branch.

$(g_2, \rho_2, W_2) = \textbf{TE}\,[\![\texttt{Cons x xs}]\!]\,\rho_{10}\,\{1,2\} =$

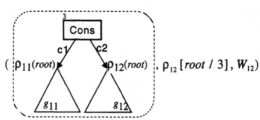

$, \rho_{12}\,[root\,/\,3], W_{12})$

The subgraphs g_{11} and g_{12} result from the translation of `x` and `xs`

$(g_{11}, \rho_{11}, W_{11}) = \textbf{TE}\,[\![\texttt{x}]\!]\,\rho_{10}\,\{1,2,3\} = ($ $\boxed{\texttt{exp}}$ $, \rho_{10}[root/4][x/4], \{1,...,4\})$

$$(g_{12}, \rho_{12}, W_{12}) = \text{TE } [\![\text{xs}]\!] \, \rho_{11} \, \{1,...,4\} = (\;\boxed{\text{exp}}^{\,5}\;, \rho_{11}[root/5][\text{xs}/5], \{1,...,5\})$$

Finally the following graph with $\rho(root) = 1$, $\rho(\text{xs}) = 5$ and $\rho(x) = 4$ is generated:

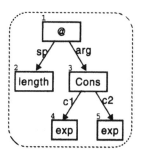

6.2.4 Translating Function Definitions

The translation scheme **TE** computes the graphical representation of an individual expression. The straightforward application of **TE** to function definitions may thus translate both sides of a definition individually. To avoid inconsistent labelling of context vertices, the vertex sets of left- and right-hand sides must be disjoint. The substitution of formal parameters is provided by the set-valued vertex label "exp" and a set of embedding descriptions which retain the reference to eventually connected sub-trees.

The translation scheme **TD** has the task of generating an attributed graph rewriting rule for a function definition. It should translate the definition

```
length (Cons x xs) = 1 + length xs
```

to the rule "length2". The number indicates that the rule implements the second case of the definition of length.

The left- and right-hand sides of the rewriting rule are generated by **TE** [l length (Cons x xs) l] $\perp \varnothing$ and **TE** [l 1 + length xs l] $\perp W$, where W is the set of vertices of the left-hand side.

The embedding descriptions represent two different tasks. The embeddings concerning vertices 15 to 18 connect the result of the reduction to the vertex pointing to the image of the left-hand side. Note that there is at most one vertex pointing to the image of 1 in a rewriting step because we do not represent sharing. Still, we cannot tell how the vertex 1 will be embedded in a rewriting step. Thus we list all possible embeddings and pass them to vertex 6.

length2

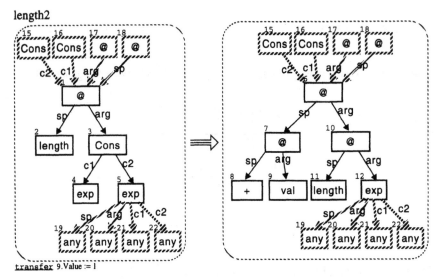

transfer 9.Value := 1

The second type of embedding descriptions realizes the substitution of actual parameters. Whenever a variable appears on both sides of the definition, the corresponding "exp"-vertices must be identically embedded. This requirement ensures that the sub-expression which substitutes the formal parameter is still present in the result graph. When the "exp"-vertex matches a constant or a "val"-vertex, the sub-expression is already represented by that vertex. Only if the "exp"-vertex matches a vertex labelled with "@" or a constructor cell like "Cons", further sub-expressions will be referred. Since we cannot tell from the function definition which sub-expression will appear at a specific rewriting step, we must assume that a vertex with label "any" is referred.

We use a graphical shorthand to denote that set of embedding descriptions.

$$\boxed{\begin{smallmatrix}5\\ \text{exp}\end{smallmatrix}} \overset{\text{sp}}{\dashrightarrow} \begin{smallmatrix}19\\ \text{any}\end{smallmatrix} \qquad \Longrightarrow \qquad \boxed{\begin{smallmatrix}12\\ \text{exp}\end{smallmatrix}} \overset{\text{sp}}{\dashrightarrow} \begin{smallmatrix}19\\ \text{any}\end{smallmatrix}$$

The use of the set-valued vertex label "any" at an embedding vertex denotes the following set of embedding descriptions:

$$\{((7, \text{sp}, vl, \text{out}), (14, \text{sp}, \text{out})) \mid vl \in CONSTANT \cup \{\text{@}, \text{val}\}\}$$

One weakness of the proposed translation scheme is that a huge number of embedding descriptions is generated. Due to their specific purpose, they often transfer the embedding of vertices with the same label without further change. If, in that case, the "exp"-vertices of both sides would be identified, the explicit statement of embedding descriptions is redundant; the default embedding, the identical embedding of context vertices, is completely sufficient. The same refinement can be applied to root vertices, if they are labelled with "@".

We therefore consider context information in the formal translation scheme **TD**. It should generate for the definition

```
length (Cons x xs) = 1 + length xs
```

the simplified rule

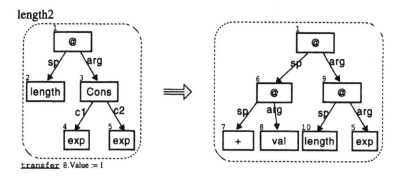

transfer 8.Value := 1

The root of both sides is the context vertex 1; and for the variable xs, the "exp"-vertex 5 is present in the context, hence no explicit embedding descriptions are necessary. Note that the variable x appears only on the left-hand side. Thus no context vertex is generated in the translation of the right-hand side.

We implement a function definition as follows. If both parts of the function definition are applications, the root vertices of the corresponding graphs are both labelled with "@". Hence the left-hand side root need not be removed during a rewriting step but can be reused by the right-hand side. Thus it should be part of the context. The translation scheme, furthermore, must pass information on the left-hand side variables to the translation of the right-hand side expression. Therefore the environment generated by the translation of e_1 is input to the translation of e_2. Together with an appropriate refinement of **TE**, the vertices representing variables of both sides can be located in the rule's context.

The formal translation **TD** distinguishes between two cases. If both sides of a function definition are applications, then no embedding description must be generated. Otherwise the root of the right-hand side expression graph must be embedded explicitly.

If e_1 and e_2 are no application then **TD** is defined as

$$\textbf{TD}\ [\![e_1 = e_2\ ]\!] = (unatt(g_l),\ unatt(g_r),\ \emptyset,\ aft,\ ap)$$

where $(g_l,\ \rho_l,\ W_l) = \textbf{TE}\ [\![e_1\ ]\!] \perp \emptyset$, and the right-hand side expression $e_2 = e_{21}\ e_{22}$ is translated as follows

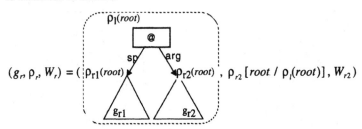

$$(g_r,\ \rho_r,\ W_r) = (\ \rho_{r1}(root)\ \raisebox{1ex}{@}\ \rho_{r2}(root)\ ,\ \rho_{r2}\,[root\ /\ \rho_l(root)]\,,\ W_{r2}\ )$$

The two sub-expressions are translated with the revised translation scheme **TE'**.

$$(g_{r1},\ \rho_{r1},\ W_{r1}) = \textbf{TE'}\ [\![e_{21}\ ]\!]\ \rho_l\ W_l$$

and $(g_{r2},\ \rho_{r2},\ W_{r2}) = \textbf{TE'}\ [\![e_{22}\ ]\!]\ \rho_{r1}\ W_{r1}.$

otherwise

$$\textbf{TD}\ [\![e_1 = e_2\ ]\!] = (unatt(g_l),\ unatt(g_r),\ M,\ aft,\ ap)$$

where the left- and the right-hand sides are the translations of e_1 and e_2:

$$(g_l,\ \rho_l,\ W_l) = \textbf{TE}\ [\![e_1\ ]\!] \perp \emptyset\ \text{and}\ (g_r,\ \rho_r,\ W_r) = \textbf{TE}\ [\![e_2\ ]\!] \perp W_l$$

Embedding descriptions are given for the roots of the expressions and for the variables occurring on both sides of the definition. Note that we assume Cons to be the only non-nullary constructor in the program.

$M = \{\ (\ (\rho_l(root),\ \text{arg},\ \text{@},\ \text{in}),\ (\rho_r(root),\ \text{arg},\ \text{in})\ ),$

$\quad(\ (\rho_l(root),\ \text{sp},\ \text{@},\ \text{in}),\ (\rho_r(root),\ \text{sp},\ \text{in})\ ),$

$\quad(\ (\rho_l(root),\ \text{c1},\ \text{Cons},\ \text{in}),\ (\rho_r(root),\ \text{c1},\ \text{in})\ ),$

$\quad(\ (\rho_l(root),\ \text{c2},\ \text{Cons},\ \text{in}),\ (\rho_r(root),\ \text{c2},\ \text{in})\ )\ \}$

$\cup$

$\displaystyle\bigcup_{var\,\in\,dom(\rho_l)\,\cap\,dom(\rho_r)}\{\ (\ (\rho_l(var),\ \text{arg},\ \text{@},\ \text{in}),\ (\rho_r(var),\ \text{arg},\ \text{in})\ ),$

$\quad(\ (\rho_l(var),\ \text{sp},\ \text{@},\ \text{in}),\ (\rho_r(var),\ \text{sp},\ \text{in})\ ),$

$\quad(\ (\rho_l(var),\ \text{c1},\ \text{Cons},\ \text{in}),\ (\rho_r(var),\ \text{c1},\ \text{in})\ ),$

$\quad(\ (\rho_l(var),\ \text{c2},\ \text{Cons},\ \text{in}),\ (\rho_r(var),\ \text{c2},\ \text{in})\ )$

$\quad vl \in CONSTANT \cup \{\ \text{@},\ \text{val},\ \text{Cons}\ \}\ \}$

For both cases, the application predicate and the attribute function transformation are defined as follows: For all vertices $v \in V_l$ with label "val", we must generate an application predicate. The attribute function f_l returns the required value of attributes of the left-hand side

$$\underline{\text{condition}} \; v.\text{Value} = f_l(v, \text{Value})$$

For all "val"-vertices v of the right-hand side, a transfer statement implements the setting of the attribute

$$\underline{\text{transfer}} \; v.\text{Value} = f_r(v, \text{Value}).$$

The functions *aft* and *ap* follow from the condition and transfer statements according to the standard interpretation (see page 116).

The definition **TD** assumes the updated definition **TE'** to generate context vertices for variables of the right-hand side. Therefore we must alter the definition of **TE** in the case of variables.

Note that for all right-hand side variables there must exist a corresponding occurrence on the left-hand side. Otherwise the variable would occur free, and this is prohibited by our general assumptions. The **TE** scheme, as defined so far, extends the environment by a reference to the "exp"-vertex representing the variable. Recall the original definition:

TE $[\![var]\!] \rho \; W = (\; \boxed{\text{exp}}^{v} \; , \; \rho \; [root \; / \; v] \; [var \; / \; v], \; W \cup \{v\} \;)$, where $v \notin W$.

In the first case of the definition, **TD** passes the environment r_l computed from the left-hand side to the translation of the right-hand side. Thus the references for all variables are accessible in the translation of e_2. Hence whenever a variable appears on the right-hand side, the corresponding vertex can be determined by a look-up in the environment. The **TE'** scheme can tell for a variable whether it appears on the left- or the right-hand side. In the former case, the environment is undefined for the variable, whereas in the latter, it refers to a vertex which was generated in the translation of the left-hand side. This specific property relies heavily on the assumption that multiple occurrences of a variable in a left-hand side expression are forbidden.

The revised translation **TE'** in the case of variables is as follows:

If $\rho(var)$ is defined:

TE' $[\![var]\!] \rho \; W = (\; \boxed{\text{exp}}^{\rho(var)} \; , \; \rho \; [root \; / \; \rho(var)], \; W)$,

otherwise:

$$\text{TE}' \, [\!| \, var \, |\!] \, \rho \, W = (\boxed{\begin{array}{c} v \\ \text{exp} \end{array}}, \rho \, [root \, / \, v] \, [var \, / \, v], W \cup \{v\} \,), \text{with} \, v \notin W.$$

For all other cases **TE'** = **TE**.

The application of the revised schemes to the definition of length generates the simplified rule "length2" shown on page 178.

6.3 Sharing — Graph Reduction Meets Graph Rewriting

The essential property of graph reduction as an implementation method is its operation on graphs. So far, the presentation neglects this property and deals only with trees. In this section, we extend the translation to implement actual graph reduction. For that purpose we must first of all represent *multiple occurrences of a variable as one shared vertex*. Then we must adapt the translation of definitions to the altered representation of an expression.

If we inspect the revised scheme **TE'** with respect to sharing, we notice that it already deals with multiple occurrences of a variable on a definition's right-hand side. If the environment contains an entry for a variable, that entry is not updated any more. Consequently, if there are multiple occurrences of a variable, the **TE'** scheme outputs that vertex which was bound during the translation of the left-hand side. The replicated instances fold onto one vertex. Take, for example, the definition

```
list n = cons n (list (3 + n)).
```

The unfolded representation of the right-hand side is the tree generated by **TE'**

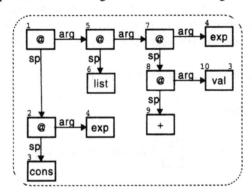

Vertex 4 occurs twice. Hence the tree is actually an alternative view to a graph. The common graphical representation is

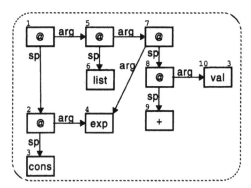

So as a side-effect of the revision to **TE**, we can treat multiple occurrences of variables on the right-hand side.

Allowing multiple variables on the right-hand side causes new insufficiencies. First of all, the shape of the graph is altered due to the integrated representation of multiple occurrences and hence the left-hand sides may not fit any more. Second, we must not remove the image of a left-hand side in a rewriting step. Because of sharing, a sub-expression may be referred to by several other expressions. We will consider these problems now in detail and formulate a solution which overcomes this weakness.

When we translate expressions with **TE'**, we generate trees for the left-hand side and graphs for the right-hand side. For instance the definition

```
doublelem ls = mappairs (+) ls ls
```

translates to

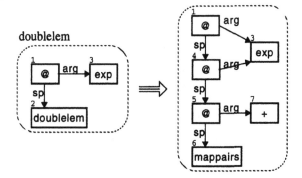

When we now evaluate `doublelem (Cons 1 (Cons 2 Empty))`, the third case of the definition of `mappairs` applies and the expression evaluates as follows:

```
doublelem (Cons 1 (Cons 2 Empty))
      => mappairs (+) (Cons 1(Cons 2 Empty))
                      (Cons 1 (Cons 2 Empty))
      => ... => Cons 2 (Cons 4 Empty)
```

However, the translation scheme **TE'** generates for the definition's left-hand side, i.e.

```
mappairs f (Cons x xs) (Cons y ys)
```

the following graph

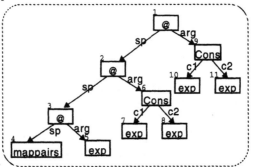

It does not match the graphical result of rewriting `doublelem 1s`, because the rewriting rule generated for `doublelem` represents both occurrences of the parameter `1s` by the shared "exp"-vertex 3.

To rectify this mismatch, we must generate more than one rewriting rule for each definition. The set of rewriting rules must anticipate any possible sharing of arguments. We will not carry out this further refinement formally because this would lead us too far away from our original interest. We will instead sketch the required refinements by examples. First we deal with the left-hand sides, then discuss the consequences of sharing for the translation of right-hand sides.

The example of `mappairs` gives us the first hint for the refinement. Two `Cons`-patterns appear on the left-hand side. In the application to `doublelem 1s`, both should match the single expression referred by `1s`. The general rule drawn from that example is to generate all combinations of sharing for multiple occurrences of a constructor symbol.

Multiple occurrences of "exp"- and "val"-vertices must be processed in the same manner. An "exp"-vertex is generated for a variable, so whenever two variables occur, they eventually match a shared expression. They also may match a "Cons" vertex.

Consequently, to cover all possible sharings, a revised translation scheme must generate a rule for each combination of eventually shared arguments. Hence, for example, the built-in operator * is represented by two rules to express its application to a shared or a non-shared expression. The rule "mult_1_2" covers the sharing of the first and the second argument.

mult_1_2

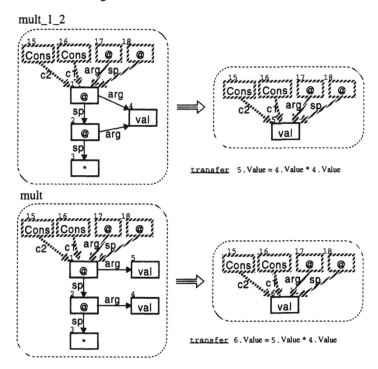

transfer   5.Value = 4.Value * 4.Value

transfer   6.Value = 5.Value * 4.Value

When the translation takes all possible sharings into account, the number of generated rules increases with the number of variables on the left-hand side. The number of rules is reduced when type information is available for the translation. Because any data object has a distinct type, no two variables of different type must share an object. Thus in that case sharing can safely be ruled out and no rule must be generated.

The second implication of sharing requires the modification of the right-hand sides. This is demonstrated by the definition of poly2.

```
poly2 a b c x = a * square x + b * x + c
```

On the right-hand side, the variable x is shared by the sub-expressions square x and b * x. According to the definition, square x evaluates to x * x and the second rewriting rule of * is applicable. The rule, however, is unsatisfactory up to this point,

because its application deletes the argument vertex, although it is still required by b *
x. Since in general the amount of sharing cannot be determined from the definition, we
must keep all components of a left-hand side which are not explicitly re-embedded.

The rewriting rule "mult_1_2" must therefore be transformed to:

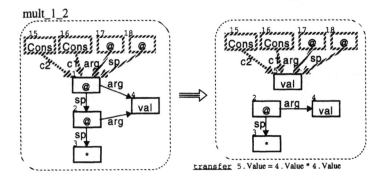

transfer 5.Value = 4.Value * 4.Value

In this modified version, the argument vertex 4 remains in the graph and can be
accessed again in the evaluation of b * x.

The translation scheme can now also deal with shared data and expressions. For a set
of function definitions, it generates a number of graph rewriting rules which
implement the evaluation of a functional expression. To conform to the definitions of
graph rewriting systems, the expression to be evaluated is taken as the initial graph.
The evaluation is then performed as the repeated application of rewriting rules. When
no rule is applicable, the evaluation terminates, and the current host graph contains the
value of the initial expression. Note that, due to sharing, a lot of intermediate partial
results are generated. They remain in the host graph because our rewriting system does
not provide a garbage collection mechanism.

6.4 Normal Order Reduction — Enforcing a Deterministic Evaluation Order

The implementation of functional languages by graph rewriting systems is so far non-
deterministic. Any rewriting rule which is applicable to the current host graph can be
selected for the next rewriting step. Hence any redex of the current expression may be
subject to reduction. Non-determinism has no negative effects if the program deals
only with finite data structures. In the presence of infinite data structures, although, the
evaluation may end up constructing infinite data objects. Therefore the reduction will
not terminate. Lazy evaluation implements a normal order reduction. It chooses

redexes such that the evaluation terminates whenever there is a terminating reduction sequence.

An example expression for which normal order reduction is required for a terminating evaluation

```
mappairs (+) (Cons 1 Empty) (list 3)
```

The value of that expression is the data object

```
Cons 4 Empty.
```

With an arbitrary reduction order the redex list 3 may be repeatedly evaluated to the infinite nesting of applications

```
cons 3 (cons(3+3)
                (cons((3+3)+3)(cons((3+3)+3)+3)...)))
```

and the value of the expression is not determined.

We will explore the importance of normal order reduction by looking at this example in more detail. The definition of mappairs has three cases, but no case applies at once. The third argument must be evaluated first to decide whether the second or third case of the definition must be applied. Hence the definition of list must be applied, reducing the expression to

```
mappairs (+) (Cons 1 Empty) (cons 3(list(3+3)))
```

Still no case of mappairs applies, but at this stage of the reduction we have three redexes to continue with. We may evaluate the applications of cons or list, or compute the sum 3+3. When we choose the second alternative we get

```
mappairs (+) (Cons 1 Empty)
                (cons 3(cons(3+3)list ((3+3)+3))).
```

Hence we still do not know which case of mappairs to apply, but the reduction may proceed towards an infinite nesting of cons applications. If we evaluate instead cons 3 (list(3+3)), we gain a Cons data object, i.e. Cons 3 (list(3+3)).

After this reduction, the appropriate case of mappairs can be selected. The whole expression then evaluates to

```
cons(1+3)(mappairs (+) Empty (list(3+3))).
```

In the latter reduction steps, the innermost expression list (3+3) is not changed. Hence there is no risk of becoming stuck in an infinite evaluation.

If we now reduce the outermost redex a Cons data object is created. The resulting state of reduction is safe, because the current value is definitely a constructor object. The evaluation of any component of the object may initiate a non-terminating evaluation. Therefore expressions of that type make up a specific class of expressions, the so-called weak head normal forms. In general, an expression $c \, e_1 ... e_n$, $n > 0$, is in *weak head normal form* (WHNF) if c is either a variable or an n-ary constructor symbol, or c is a function identifier which requires more than n arguments, i.e. $c \, e_1 ... e_n$ is a partial application.

6.4.1 A Stack of Spine Pointers

The graph rewriting systems generated so far do not enforce any reduction strategy. Furthermore, no mechanism is realized to control the evaluation of infinite data objects. In this section, we therefore extend the generated rewriting systems to, first, realize *normal order reduction* and, second, stop the rewriting process when the evaluation reaches *weak head normal form*.

For the implementation of normal order reduction, we introduce further information in the expression graph. In the mappairs example at the beginning of the section, we saw that the top-level expression could not be evaluated directly. It required the evaluation of its third argument first. Thus the evaluation of the top-level expression is suspended. When the argument has been evaluated, the reduction can return to the top-level expression. Since several suspensions may occur in sequence, they are adequately represented as a stack structure. Each element of the spine stack holds a pointer to the top of the spine of that expression which is to be evaluated or is eventually suspended.

The extended expression graph of

```
mappairs (+) (Cons 1 Empty) (list 3)
```

indicates that the evaluation of the top-level expression is suspended, and that the third argument is required. Therefore the "top"-vertices point to the suspended spines in the graph:

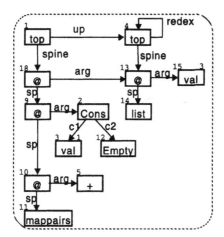

The expression to be evaluated next is indicated by the "redex" edge incident to the corresponding "top"-vertex. If that edge is unique in the graph, there is exactly one expression which is to be evaluated.

To enforce a deterministic rewriting strategy for the whole graph rewriting system we must first add the "top"-vertex and the incident "redex" edge to each left-hand side. Second, we must ensure that the "redex" edge is unique. Thus whenever it appears on the left-hand side, it must appear on the right-hand side also. The reduction step performed on the expression graph above must therefore reduce the list expression. The corresponding rewriting rule transforms the expression graph to a "cons" application and the result graph is :

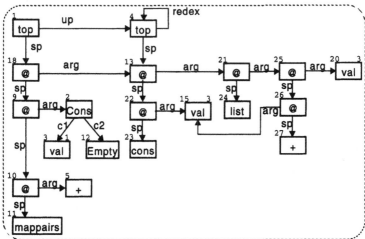

The rewriting rule "list" contains a "redex" edge on the left-hand side. Therefore it is applicable only when the "redex" edge points to the local "top"-vertex.

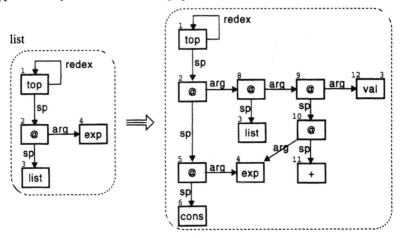

The unique label "redex" also enforces the selection of the applied function definition when the label "redex" appears on the left-hand side of all rewriting rules. Because the label is unique the set of applicable rewriting rules is determined by the function symbol at the bottom of the spine. Only the rules generated for that function definition may be selected for an application.

With the invariant of a unique "redex" edge in mind we can now deal with the suspension of an evaluation when it requires an argument value. We show the rewriting rule which suspends the evaluation of mappairs and invokes the evaluation of the third argument. The evaluation is required when the second argument has been evaluated to a Cons-object but the third argument is not yet in WHNF. In that case it may carry any label except "Cons" and "Empty". Hence we introduce a set-valued vertex label to match the set of possible labels. The label set

$$not\_eval = exp \setminus \{Cons, Empty, val\}$$

expresses that evaluation state. Invocation of the third argument is now performed by the rewriting rule "mappairs_invoke_3".

A new stack element which points to the third argument is pushed. It carries the "redex" pointer to indicate that this argument must be evaluated next. The whole rewriting rule is only applicable when the second argument is already evaluated to a 'Cons'-object.

mappairs_invoke_3

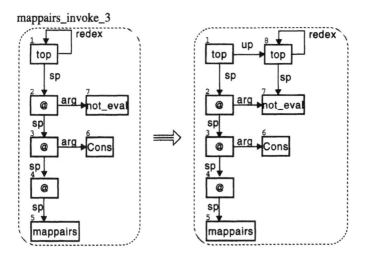

The control need not be returned to the outer expression if the definition generates no weak head normal form. Take, for example, the definition of length

```
length (Cons x xs) = 1 + (length xs).
```

The definition replaces one application with another, and the evaluation may proceed at that sub-expression. Therefore the corresponding stack element should not be popped since it holds the control for the next rewriting step. The rewriting rule "length" for the definition above thus keeps the vertices 1 and 2 in the context. The "redex" edge indicates that the + application is to be evaluated next.

length

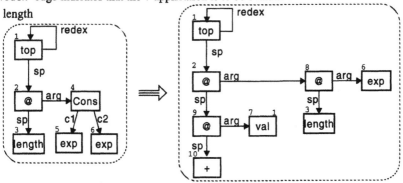

The invocation scheme postpones not only the evaluation of variable arguments, but also of expressions at pattern positions. The evaluation of the third argument of mappairs is not initiated until it is required for the selection of the appropriate case of the mappairs definition. This evaluation strategy concerning patterns is therefore called *lazy pattern matching*.

6.4.2 Deconstruction of the Spine Stack

Up to this point, we have only presented the invocation scheme for the evaluation of an argument, so that the rewriting rules are able to build a stack of spine pointers. Deconstruction is now straightforward: whenever an expression is evaluated to weak head normal form, control is returned to the invoking expression and the stack is popped.

When the rewriting rule for cons has been applied to the mappairs graph on page 189, the third argument of mappairs is reduced to weak head normal form. Thus the evaluation returns to the outer expression, yielding the graph:

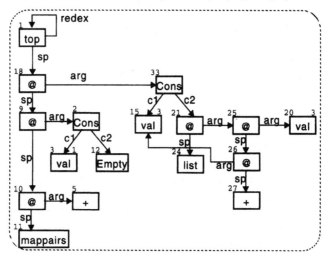

The extended version of the cons rewriting rule which realizes the rewriting step above is:

cons

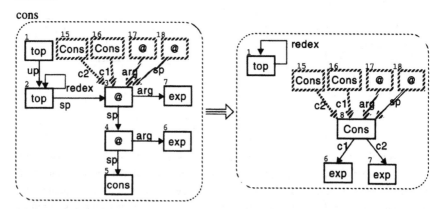

It evaluates the cons application to a Cons object which is in WHNF. Therefore the stack is popped and control returns to the invoking expression.

6.4.3   Unwinding the Spine

The introduction of a stack of spine pointers requires the extension of the left-hand sides. They must contain the stack element pointing to the current spine. The bottom element of the spine denotes the function which is applied. The translation so far assumes that the spine has exactly as many arguments as required by the function. This was motivated by the translations of the last section, where the required number of arguments was visible on the left-hand side. In this section, however, we introduced an explicit upper limit to the spine, the "top"-vertex. Thus the rewriting rules do not match to spines with sufficient length, but the spine must have exactly as many elements as the function's arity. This restriction leads to unintentionally irreducible expressions.

Take, for example, the rewriting rule for f:

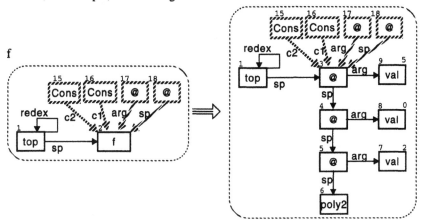

This rewriting rule is never applicable to the graphical representation of f 3, because the spine of the expression is too long.

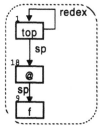

Thus we must modify the translation scheme again. In general we want to cope with spines of arbitrary length l and functions of arity x. For that purpose we might replace any rewriting rule generated so far by a set of rules adapted to each spine length. In this design we again generate a large number of rules. Thus we follow the alternative approach used in the traditional implementation of functional languages. Before a reduction can take place, the root of the redex is especially determined in a separate step. The operation is called *unwinding the spine*. We implement unwinding as a set of rewriting rules for any combination of spine length and function arities. The application of an unwind rule then moves the "redex" pointer to the root of the redex. That expression consists of the function identifier supplied with the required number of arguments.

The reduction of f 3 is now preceded by an unwind step. Note that in accordance with the altered use of the "redex" edge, the rewriting rule for f must also be changed.

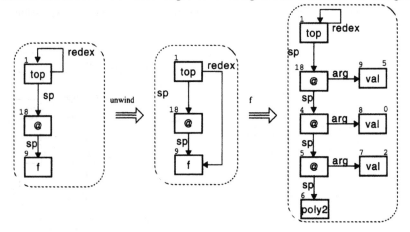

After the execution of a reduction step, the "redex" edge is parked at the "top"-vertex again. With this scheme, we enforce the alternating application of a reduction and an unwinding step.

The adapted rewriting rule for f is:

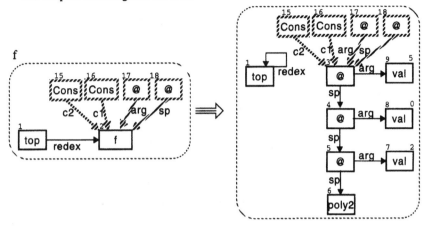

It uses the "redex" edge instead of the "spine" pointer. Hence it is independent of the length of the spine. The spine may have more elements than required. In that case, they remain between the "top"-vertex 1 and the root of the result expression, i.e. vertex 3, by means of the embedding description.

The rewriting rules which set the redex pointer are constructed as follows. Again we use a set-valued vertex label to provide a rewriting rule for each function arity. Thus let the label set "fun_x" contain all identifiers of F with arity x. For each length l of the spine and each occurring arity x, a rewriting rule "unwind_l_x" moves the reduce pointer from the top of the spine to the rule of the reducible expression. If not enough arguments are available, the reduction has reached weak head normal form. In that case, it returns control of the reduction process back to the invoking expression.

The general construction of a rule "unwind_l_x" with $l \geq x$ is as follows:

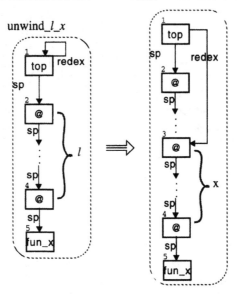

If the expression is a partial application the number of available arguments l is smaller than the function arity x. The expression is in weak head normal form. The control is returned to the invoking expression by the rule "unwind_l_x" with $l < x$.

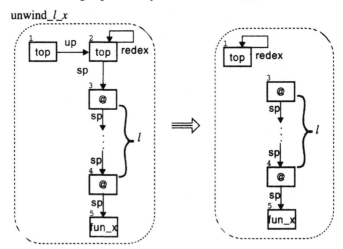

The check for partial applications completes the realization of normal order reduction and lazy pattern matching in terms of graph rewriting rules. We added the following components to the simple rewriting scheme:

- a stack of pointers to expressions for which the evaluation has been suspended;

- unwind rules which 1) determine the root of the redex for a given expression and 2) check whether an expression is a partial application;

- specific rules for each function to invoke the evaluation of required arguments;

- an extension to each rule to keep the control either at the current expression or to return it to the invoking one.

The presentation of this section was limited to non-sharing expressions. Obviously, the extensions must also be applied to the rewriting rules concerned with sharing.

Let us now give an example derivation which exhibits the use of the spine stack. The graph rewriting system which implements a lazy evaluation of length (Cons 1 Empty) performs the following deterministic derivation. The initial graph of the rewriting system represents, first of all, the expression to be evaluated. That element of the stack at which the reduction should start is indicated by the edge with unique label "redex". When the "redex" edge moves to the bottom element, the reduction has successfully terminated.

Whenever the "redex" edge is a loop to a "top" vertex, only unwind rules may apply. Hence the first rewriting step determines the root of the redex.

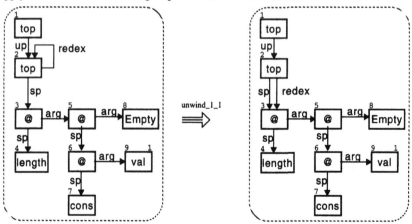

No case of the definition of length is directly applicable. The argument expression must be evaluated to WHNF in order to select the appropriate case. Therefore the reduction of the first argument is performed.

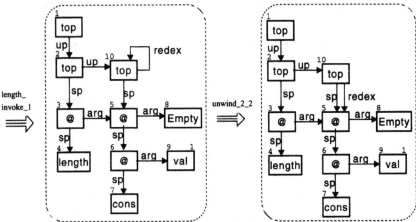

The spine is unwound again and the built-in definition of cons is applicable. Since it evaluates to WHNF, control is returned. A further application of "unwind_1_1" determines the redex again, and so on.

6.5 The Printing Mechanism

The graph rewriting system which is generated at this stage performs normal order reduction to WHNF. With this we are able to evaluate functional expressions which contain infinite data structures. Normal order reduction guarantees termination of the evaluation whenever it is possible; but the evaluation mechanism implemented in the graph rewriting system has one drawback: the evaluation does not proceed further than weak head normal form. The final graph which is derived in the evaluation of mappairs (x) (Cons 1 Empty) (List 3) is thus

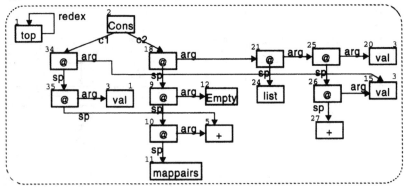

Textually, the graph is equal to the expression

```
Cons (1 + 3) (mappairs (+) Empty (list (3 + 3))).
```

According to our design, the reduction terminates with a "Cons" data object, but we actually expect to see the whole result, i.e. we must further evaluate both components to 4 and Empty respectively. Hence we must realize a further extension.

As with the unwind operation, we also follow the common implementation technique. The runtime environment of an implementation of functional language provides a *printing mechanism* (see [PeJo87,p.196]). This component triggers the evaluation of a current expression to WHNF and outputs the result. Whenever the expression evaluates to a constructor data object, the mechanism outputs the constructor symbol, decomposes the objects, and initiates the evaluation of the component expressions. As a constructor object may consist of several components, the printing mechanism itself must maintain a list of pending expressions: expressions whose value is to be filled into a component of an enclosing data object.

The printing mechanism itself is not a part of the reduction component. Thus it may be interrupted by the user, while the reduction can run to completion without corrupting the internal representation of the evaluated expression.

We sketch the operation of the mechanism for the mappairs example. Remember that the evaluation has reached WHNF when the redex pointer loops at the first top element. We extend the internal representation by a print stack. Its elements hold pointers to expressions whose values should be printed. In the mappairs example, we add a "print"-vertex to the graph pointing to the result of the evaluation. The print vertex is further referred to by the first "top"-vertex. Now, whenever that "top"-vertex carries a "redex" loop the evaluation has reached WHNF. Hence the result can be printed. In our case, a "Cons" is output. Next, both components of the object must be evaluated. Hence there are print-vertices popped onto the print stack which trigger the evaluation of the components. We thus require a rewriting rule which performs the following rewriting step:

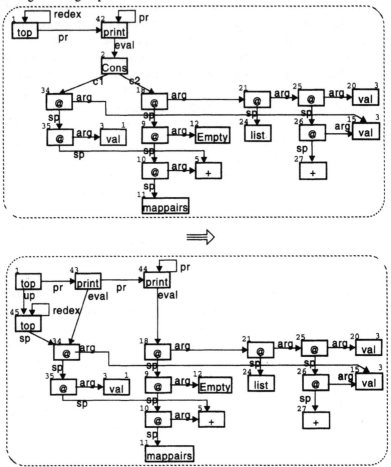

After the decomposition of the "Cons" object, the expression referred to by the first element of the print stack is to be evaluated. The next applicable rule is an unwind rule which sets the "redex" pointer, and the sum expression will be evaluated.

Note that we do not specify the treatment of output results explicitly. Within the rewriting formalism, the output values will best be accumulated in a string located as an argument of the first "top" vertex. For a formal specification we must therefore assume further attributes for all value and constructor vertices which should carry a string representation of the vertex' value. Alternatively, the output of values may be realized as a side effect of the print rules. When applied, they may pass the computed value to an output device. We employ the first approach in our example implementation, but do not go into further detail in the current presentation of the translation.

The printing mechanism is realized by a number of rewriting rules, one for each possible arity of the constructors and for values. If the expression evaluates to a simple value or a nullary constructor, the stack is popped. In case the expression is already referred to by the bottom element, no further expression is to be evaluated. Thus the complete system terminates with the rewriting rule "print_last". Here again we use a set-valued vertex label "con_0" containing the label "val" and all nullary constructor symbols. The bottom element of the stack is indicated by a looping "pr"-edge.

print_last

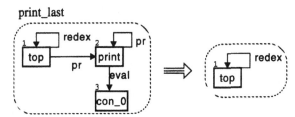

If there are still components of data objects to be evaluated, they are referred to by elements of the print stack. Hence the rule "print_0" pops the current value or nullary constructor, and initiates the evaluation of the next expression.

print_0

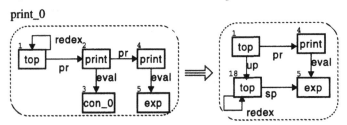

When non-nullary constructors are output, their components are pushed onto the stack for further evaluation. We assume a label set "con_x" containing all constructors of arity $x > 0$. For each arity a print rule is included in the rewriting system.

This set of rewriting rules completes the implementation of auxiliary structures to deal properly with normal order reduction. The example expression at the beginning of this section now evaluates fully to Cons 4 Empty. Again, the print rules are also designed to be mutually exclusive with respect to the rewriting rules already known. They are applicable only when the spine stack is empty, indicated by a looping "redex" pointer attached to the bottom element of the spine stack.

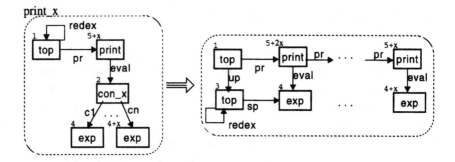

6.6   The Translation of Lazy Evaluation is UBS

In this section, we show that the transformation developed throughout this chapter outputs a UBS graph rewriting system. Obviously, one slight modification must introduce a unique vertex label. Otherwise the first condition for the UBS property, that the connected enumeration must be rooted in a uniquely labelled vertex, could never be satisfied. The proof of the UBS property, then, is split in two parts. First, we inspect the left-hand sides of the generated rules. We determine constraints on the set of possible connected enumerations. The result of the first part of the proof is a critical set of strong V-structures. If none of the structures appears in a generated graph, then for all left-hand sides there is a connected enumeration which bypasses any eventually generated strong V-structure. In the second part of the proof we must ensure that no element of the critical set must be generated by the rewriting system. Putting both parts together, then, it follows that the graph rewriting implementation of functional languages is UBS.

The advantage of this proof strategy is that we must not completely perform the static analysis and compute a superset of the strong V-structures of the rewriting system. Moreover we restrict the analysis to a much smaller set whose elements are required to be absent from the rewriting system to enable bypassing.

A unique vertex label can be introduced into the generated rewriting system by a simple transformation. The system already incorporates "redex" as a unique edge label, but we cannot exploit that property with respect to unique initial handles. The edge is not directly accessible, since initial handles must map vertices. Therefore we globally substitute any occurrence of a "redex" edge by the following structure:

$$\xrightarrow{\quad\text{re}\quad}\boxed{\text{d}}\xrightarrow{\quad\text{ex}\quad}$$

We assume that the labels "re", "d" and "ex" are not used in the rewriting system already. Otherwise we chose some arbitrary new labels instead.

Because the redex edge appeared in all left-hand sides, the "d"-vertex does also. Consequently for all left-hand sides there exist connected enumerations which satisfy the first condition on UBS rewriting systems, namely being rooted in a uniquely labelled vertex. No other label may be unique for arbitrary functional programs. Hence the label "d" is also the only choice for a unique vertex label. The set of connected enumerations which fulfil the UBS requirements is reduced. Any UBS enumeration must be rooted in the "d"-vertex.

6.6.1   A Mandatory Set of Prohibited Strong V-Structures

After the introduction of the unique vertex label "d", we approach the first part of the proof. The basic idea here is to analyse the left-hand sides and determine those extensions which are mandatory for any connected enumeration rooted in the "d"-vertex. If a given left-hand side contains no semi-cycle, then the connected enumeration is fixed up to permutation of its elements. Take for example the following graph which contains no semi-cycle.

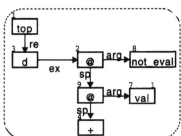

It is obvious that for a connected enumeration rooted in "d", the direction along which it passes the edges of the graph is fixed. The order of elements may vary for different enumerations rooted in "d", but all must traverse the "sp"- "arg"- and "ex"-edges in the original and the "re"-edge in the opposite direction.

From that observation it now follows that whenever, for instance, the strong V-structure (@, @, sp, out) occurs in the graph language, no bypassing connected enumeration rooted in a "d"-vertex exists for that left-hand side. The reverse implication states that when for none of the mandatory elements a strong V-structure exists, and the set of mandatory elements is sufficient to construct an enumeration for all left-hand sides rooted in "d", then the rewriting system satisfies the UBS property.

Before we determine the mandatory elements for the rules of the rewriting system, we recall the three components into which any derived graphs can be separated. 1) There is the expression graph representing the partially evaluated expression. It is constructed by "@"-vertices referring to a functional expression via the "sp"-edge and to the corresponding argument via "arg". 2) The spine stack is realized by "top"-

vertices concatenated with "up"-edges. Each stack element accesses its local sub-expression via a "spine" edge. An element may be incident to the redex structure. 3) There is the print stack consisting of "pr"-edges joining individual "print" vertices, each pointing into the expression graph via an "eval"-edge.

We now scan the set of rewriting rules for a functional program to determine the mandatory elements. We will not consider each individual rule, but group them into sets of rules which have similar mandatory elements. Take, for example, the left-hand sides of the print rules decomposing constructor cells of arity 3 and 4.

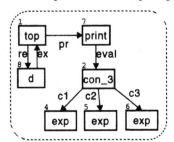 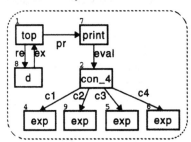

For both rules, the enumeration must determine an image of the "print" vertex by extending the handle containing the images of "d" and "top" along the "pr"-edge. Also, the constructor cells must be found via the "eval"-edge and the components via a "ci" edge. So their set of mandatory edges just differ by the "c4"-edge which does not appear in the third print rule. Due to the set-valued vertex labels "con_3", "con_4" and "exp", we gain a number of mandatory edges for each edge incident to a set labelled vertex. Hence the set of mandatory edges for the right rule requires that the following strong V-structures are prohibited for a host graph.

$\{$(top, print, pr, out), (print, con, eval, out),

$\qquad$ (con, e, c, out) $|$ where $con \in$ con_4, $e \in$ exp and $c \in \{$c1, ...,c4$\}$ $\}$

Otherwise the existence of a bypassing connected enumeration cannot be ensured.

For the printing rules decomposing a constructor cell of arity at least 1 we gain the following set of prohibited strong V-structures:

$\{$(top, print, pr, out), (print, con, eval, out),

$\qquad$ (con, e, c, out) $|$ where $con \in \bigcup_{x>0}$con_x, $e \in$ exp and $c \in \{ci | i > 0\}$ $\}$

Note at this stage of the analysis that we need not explicitly prohibit strong V-structures containing "re", "d", or "ex". These labels are unique and therefore must not be part of a strong V-structure (see lemma 3.3.3). Hence we can traverse a "re"- or "ex"-edge in both directions without any risk of passing along a strong V-structure.

For the set of considered printing rules it now follows that when none of the prohibited strong V-structures is generated by the rewriting system, for all rules there exists a connected bypassing enumeration rooted in "d".

Let us now continue the analysis of the remaining print rules. In case there is a nullary constructor to be output, the print stack is popped. Therefore also the second element of the stack is accessed by the rewriting rule. Its left-hand side is

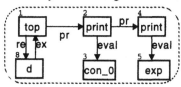

In addition to the connected enumerations of the former print rules, any enumeration of the nullary constructor print rule must contain an extension from "print" vertex 2 to vertex 4. Also it must reach any label of "con_0" via an "eval" edge from the vertex 2. So the set of prohibited strong V-structures is extended by

$$\{(\text{print}, \text{print}, \text{pr}, \text{out}), (\text{print}, con, \text{eval}, \text{out}) \mid \text{where } con \in \text{con\_0} \}$$

Based on this set of prohibited V-structures, a bypassing enumeration exists not only for the nullary constructor rule, but also for the last print rule. Its left-hand side is

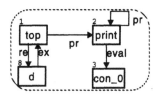

Next we study the left-hand side of the rule realizing the construction of a "Cons" object. This rule may be applied without any specific conditions to the argument vertices. Thus the set of prohibited strong V-structures contains any possible structure in combination with an "arg"-edge. For this left-hand side, the elements of the connected enumerations is fixed:

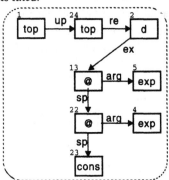

Any edge in the directed spanning tree rooted in "d" is mandatory. The resulting set of prohibited strong V-structures is

$$\{(@, e, \text{arg}, \text{out}), (@, @, \text{sp}, \text{out}), (@, \text{cons}, \text{sp}, \text{out}), (\text{top}, \text{top}, \text{up}, \text{in}) \mid e \in \text{exp}\}$$

This set of prohibited V-structures is also sufficient for the existence of a bypassing connected enumeration. There are no enumerations which are distinct up to permutations of their elements. Hence any element must appear in any enumeration and is therefore mandatory. The set of prohibited V-structures, however, is constructed such that any mandatory edge can safely appear in an enumeration, but because any enumeration consists only of mandatory elements, it is bypassing.

Similar to the cons-identifier, any other function identifier at the bottom of the spine can be accessed only via an "sp"-edge incident to an "@"-vertex. Hence

$$(@, f, \text{sp}, \text{out})$$

must be prohibited for any function identifier f.

The rules for function definitions with pattern matching are already captured by the set of prohibited strong V-structures. Any constructor symbol is a member of the set "exp". Thus whenever a constructor pattern appears at an argument position, the corresponding strong V-structure is prohibited by

$$(@, e, \text{arg}, \text{out}) \text{ with } e \in \text{exp}$$

already. The components of the constructors thus can safely be accessed. The component edges "c1" with arbitrary target vertex and source vertex with label from "con_x", $x>0$, are already covered by the prohibiting set of decomposing print rules. The requirements of invocation rules with respect to a prohibiting set are also met by the given sets. Since "not_eval" is a subset of "exp", no further V-structure must be prohibited.

The unwind rules require a last structure to be prohibited. Any unwind rule accesses the spine via a "spine" edge. To check the applicability of the rule, this edge must be passed. Hence the following V-structure must not appear either

$$(\text{top}, \text{@}, \text{spine}, \text{out}).$$

Finally the analysis of mandatory elements of enumerations gives the following set of prohibited strong V-structures

$\{(\text{top}, \text{print}, \text{pr}, \text{out}), (\text{print}, \text{print}, \text{pr}, \text{out}), (\text{print}, con, \text{eval}, \text{out}),$

$\quad (\text{top}, \text{top}, \text{up}, \text{in}), (\text{top}, \text{@}, \text{spine}, \text{out}),$

$\quad (\text{@}, e, \text{arg}, \text{out}), (\text{@}, \text{@}, \text{sp}, \text{out}), (\text{@}, f, \text{sp}, \text{out}), (con, e, c, \text{out}) \mid$

$\quad \text{where } x > 0, con \in \text{con\_}x, c \in \{ci \mid 0 < i \le x\}, e \in \text{exp}, \text{ and } f \in \bigcup_{y>0} \text{fun\_}y \}$

By inspection of the left-hand sides of the rules, it can be seen that the set of prohibited strong V-structures is sufficient, i.e. given that none of the forbidden structures occurs, for all left-hand sides exists a bypassing connected enumeration. What remains to be proved is that none of the prohibited structures must be generated by the rewriting system.

6.6.2   None of the Prohibited Strong V-Structures Occur

In the second part of the proof, we must ensure that none of the prohibited strong V-structures occurs in the graph language. Therefore we first inspect the initial graph of a rewriting system as it is translated from a functional program. Then we analyse the set of rewriting rules and check the sufficient condition for the introduction of a new strong V-structure. As mentioned before, we do not perform the abstract interpretation for the whole graph rewriting system. So we do not execute the algorithm to compute the approximation of the set of strong V-structures by hand; but we use the information gathered in the first part of the proof and demonstrate the absence of just the prohibited strong V-structures. The complete analysis based on the algorithm for abstract interpretation is performed in the compiler.

The initial graph in our implementation consists mainly of the graphical representation of the expression to be evaluated. The expression graph is attached to the initial spine and print stacks. In general the initial graph looks like this:

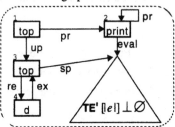

The functional expression must not contain any variables at all. Hence the revised scheme **TE'** introduces no sharing of vertices; and the expression graph is actually a tree. The translation of applications and constructor objects to "@"- and constructor vertices does not create any strong V-structure. The incident outgoing edges have different labels. Consequently, the expression graph contains no instance of a strong V-structure. By inspection of the rest of the initial graph, it follows at last that any initial graph in the implementation is free from strong V-structures.

For the static analysis of the rewriting rules output by the translation, we split the set of prohibited strong V-structures into four disjoint sets. Each set is dedicated to a specific component of any graph which is derived by the translated graph rewriting system. We distinguish the following components

- the print stack,
- constructor vertices,
- the spine stack, and
- the expression graph.

For each component, there will be a specific subsection in the proof.

First we consider those V-structures for which no instance must occur in the *print stack*, i.e. the set

$\{(\text{top, print, pr, out}), (\text{print, print, pr, out}), (\text{print, } con, \text{ eval, out})|\ con \in \bigcup_{x>0}\text{con\_}x\ \}.$

In chapter 3 we observed that an instance of a strong V-structure can be newly introduced only when an edge of the appropriate type is inserted in the host graph. This edge, moreover, must be incident to a context vertex or be the result of an embedding description. Thus when we check, for instance, the contribution of the rule "print_2", only edges incident to vertex 12 may introduce new strong V-structures. Indeed, pred-

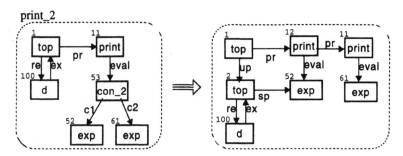

icate $V2$ indicates that the following strong V-structure might be introduced when applying the rule above:

$$\{(top, print, pr, out), (print, e, eval, out),$$
$$(e, print, eval, in), (print, print, pr, in) \mid \text{with } e \in exp \}.$$

The latter two structures do not abolish the UBS property of the rewriting system. They may appear and still there exists a bypassing enumeration for all rules. The first and second structures, however, have severe consequences. If indeed instances of these structures would be apparent in the graph language, any rule which accesses the print stack via the "top"-vertex must pass along a strong V-structure.

For the first structure the refinement of the predicates pays off. The second case of the refined predicate $\overline{V2}$ (see lemma 3.3.15) reflects the transfer of edges between vertices of the same label. The "pr"-edge incident to vertex 1 is moved from one "print" vertex to another. This situation is captured by $\overline{V2}.2$), which says that if for any inserted edge an isomorphic edge incident to a common context vertex is deleted, no strong V-structure is created. Hence also the first V-structure cannot be introduced by application of the studied rule.

The occurrence of the second structure is reasoned by the fact that the "eval"-edge incident to vertex 11 is moved from a vertex with a label of set "con_2" to a vertex with any label of "exp". Hence, in contrast to the former case, no isomorphic edge is replaced. Thus the predicate $\overline{V2}$ must assume that there might already be another "eval"-edge joining the image of vertex 11 with a vertex of appropriate label. This situation can actually appear, so the strong V-structure analysis cannot be further refined. Moreover we must apply the analysis of weak V-structures which runs similar to the strong V-structure analysis. With respect to weak V-structures, the rewriting rule leaves the number of "eval"-edges with source vertex 11 constant. Thus no new weak V-structure

$$(print, eval, out)$$

can be introduced. Consequently no element of the set of strong V-structures

$$\{(print, e, eval, out) \mid \text{with } e \in exp \}$$

is present in the set of derived graphs.

Overall we have now demonstrated that the rewriting rule shown above does not introduce any of the prohibited strong V-structures apparent in the print stack. The same argument holds for all print rules which decompose constructor vertices of arity at least 2. Three further print rules must be analysed with respect to the given subset of prohibited strong V-structures.

The rewriting rule "print_1" removes vertex 51 and connects the "exp"-vertex to

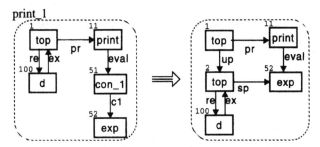

the print stack. This operation is also performed by the print rule for binary constructors considered above. For that rule, we have shown by application of weak V-structure analysis that no strong V-structure can be generated. Thus this rule also does not contribute to the set of strong V-structures concerning the print stack.

The last print rule which may introduce the strong V-structures

$$(\text{top}, \text{print}, \text{pr}, \text{out}) \text{ or } (\text{print}, \text{top}, \text{pr}, \text{in})$$

is "print_0".

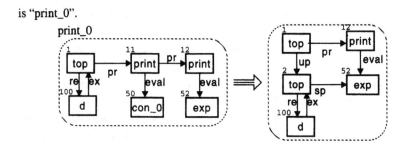

Only the first structure is critical, since the print stack is accessed from the "top"-vertex via the "pr"-edge. The comparison of left- and right-hand sides, however, shows that the "pr"-edge incident to the "top"-vertex is replaced by an isomorphic edge. Hence the second case of predicate $\overline{V2}$ applies and rules out the introduction of the strong V-structure

$$(\text{top}, \text{print}, \text{pr}, \text{out}).$$

Consequently no print rule introduces a prohibited strong V-structure whose instance may appear in the print stack. We complete the analysis with respect to the print stack. We check whether other rewriting rules may cause a strong V-structure which is prohibited to enable the non-branching traversal of the print stack. All that remains, therefore, is to study rules which realize the update of a root of redex by a transfer of the embedding edges.

cons

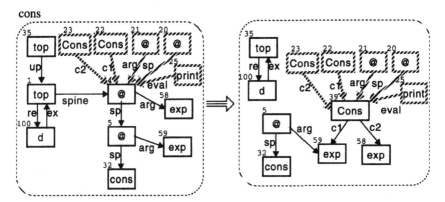

The rule "cons", for instance, moves the eval-edge from vertex 4 to 39. We must show that the structure

(print, Cons, eval, out)

is not created by the application of the rewriting rule. Therefore we must check the validity of predicate $\overline{V4}$. We observe that this predicate evaluates to true because the embedding description moves the "eval"-edge between vertices of different labels. If the embedding edges would be transferred between two "Cons"-vertices, no new strong V-structure would be introduced. Either an instance of it existed before, or the single "eval"-edge incident to the "print"-vertex is re-targeted to another "Cons"-vertex. This situation is captured by the refined predicate $\overline{V4}$; but in the rule above, the label of the target vertex changes, and the analysis based on strong V-structures cannot exclude the introduction of

(print, Cons, eval, out)

Here again the analysis of weak V-structures must support our proof. The analysis is based on the observation that no rewriting rule duplicates an "eval"-edge with a "print"-vertex as its source. Hence there is no instance of the weak V-structure

(print, eval, out)

Especially there must not be two "eval"-edges joining one print-vertex with an "@"- and a "Cons"-vertex respectively. Thus when re-targeting the embedding "eval"-edge from an "@"-vertex to a "Cons"-vertex, no strong V-structure (print, Cons, eval, out) can be created. Hence the embedding description also conforms to the set of prohibited strong V-structures.

For all other occurrences of this type of embedding descriptions, the absence of strong V-structures is proven with the same argument. Hence we have finally demonstrated that none of the prohibited V-structures of the print stack is created by a rewriting rule.

The next sub-goal of the proof is to show that no constructor vertex is the centre of an outgoing strong V-structure, i.e. we demonstrate that the rewriting system does not generate an instance of an element of

$$\{ (con, e, c, \text{out}) \mid \text{where } x > 0, con \in con\_x, c \in \{ci \mid 0 < i \leq x\}, \text{and } e \in \text{exp} \}$$

We prove this property by inspection of the single occurrence of a non-nullary constructor in the mappairs example. A vertex labelled with the binary constructor "Cons" is introduced by the evaluation of a cons application. Whenever a "Cons"-vertex is created, it refers to its two components by a "c1"- and "c2"-edge. Hence the insertion of a "Cons"-vertex introduces neither a strong V-structure nor a weak V-structure with edge label "c1" or "c2". The analysis of weak V-structures again is applied to those embedding descriptions which retarget "c1"- or "c2"-edges. With the same argument as for (print, eval, out) above, it follows that also no weak V-structure containing "c1" or "c2" can be created by any of the embedding descriptions. Hence none of the potential strong V-structures including "c1" or "c2" can be created. Consequently non of prohibited structures

$$\{ (con, e, c, \text{out}) \mid \text{where } x > 0, con \in con\_x, c \in \{ci \mid 0 < i \leq x\}, \text{and } e \in \text{exp} \}$$

is created by the translated functional program.

In the next subsection of the proof, we consider those two strong V-structures which are prohibited to enable the bypassing traversal of the spine stack and the access of the spine itself. Edges which might create an instance of the V-structures

$$(\text{top, top, up, in}), \text{or } (\text{top, @, spine, out})$$

are introduced whenever a new stack element is pushed. The stack is extended in print rules and in rules invoking the evaluation of an argument expression. A typical rewriting rule again is "print_2". This rule inserts a new "top"-vertex and connects it to the preceding stack element and its own "@"-vertex. Both vertices are in the context. Thus the refined predicate $\overline{V2}$ applies. It determines

$$(\text{@, top, spine, in}), \text{and } (\text{top, top, up, out})$$

as potentially created strong V-structures. They are harmless because they need not be passed by an enumeration.

This rewriting rule is a good example for the creation of strong V-structures by edges incident to a context vertex. The vertices 1 and 52 are in the context. Thus they might keep incident edges of the host graph. If any of those edges becomes adjacent to an inserted edge, both may represent an instance of a new strong V-structure. New vertices on the right-hand side, on the contrary, are incident to exactly those edges determined by the rewriting rule. Thus whenever a vertex of a right-hand side must not be the center of a strong V-structure, it should not appear in the context. When it appears in the context, however, the refined predicates must be taken into account. They sharpen the analysis of the introduction of new strong V-structures.

What remains to show in the second part of the overall proof is the absence of strong V-structures concerning the expression graph. These structures are

$$\{ (@, e, \text{arg}, \text{out}), (@, @, \text{sp}, \text{out}), (@, f, \text{sp}, \text{out}), \text{ | where } f \in \bigcup_{y>0} \text{fun\_y} \}$$

We first inspect the insertion of corresponding edges by the right-hand side of a rewriting rule. Only rules which replace an application by another application introduce new sp- and arg-edges and connect them to an "@"-vertex. Take for instance the rewriting rule "list".

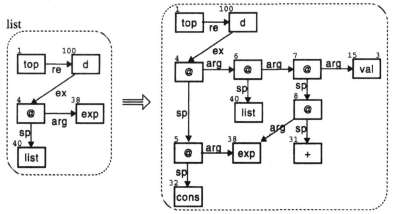

The vertices 4 and 38 are in the context, hence they are potentially the centre of a strong V-structure. With respect to the prohibited V-structures, the potential structures centred in vertex 38 are of no interest. Incident to this vertex, any strong V-structure out of the following set may be created

$$\{ (e, @, \text{arg}, \text{in}) \text{ | } e \in \text{exp} \}.$$

They have the opposite direction and hence pose no risk. According to predicate $\overline{V2}$, vertex 4 may be the center of two strong V-structures, namely

$$(@, @, \text{arg, out}), \text{ and } (@, @, \text{sp, out}).$$

Both structures are prohibited. Since we do not gain any further refinement of $\overline{V2}$, we again must apply the analysis of weak V-structures. When we consider just the number of "sp"- and "arg"-edges which are rooted in an "@"-vertex, we observe that at any time there is exactly one edge of each kind. The rewriting rule above further introduces no additional "sp"- or "arg"-edge with source vertex 4. Hence neither of the two strong V-structures can be generated.

With the same argument on the degree of outgoing "sp"-edges it follows that no strong V-structure of

$$\{ \, (@, f, \textbf{sp}, \text{out}), \mid \text{where } f \in \bigcup_{y>0} \text{fun\_y} \, \}$$

is created.

The embedding descriptions concerning the "@"-vertex are also not harmful. With the same argument as for the embedding descriptions attached to a "Cons"-vertex, it follows that no weak V-structure containing the edge label "sp" or "arg" appears. Hence no strong V-structure

$$(@, @, \text{arg, out}), \text{ and } (@, @, \text{sp, out})$$

is generated.

This argument concludes the last subsection of the proof's second part. Overall we have shown that the translation of a functional program outputs a graph rewriting system which has the UBS property. Especially the second part of the proof has demonstrated the power, but also the limits, of strong V-structure analysis. It was able to recognise several situations which do not create strong V-structures. In some instances, however, the analysis of weak V-structures must enhance the capabilities of the original analysis.

6.7 Summary and Related Work

In the beginning of this chapter, we developed an implementation of a lazy functional programming language step-by-step. First of all we gave transformation schemes to represent functional expressions and definitions as graphs and graph rewriting rules respectively. The translation was enhanced to capture sharing of sub-expressions. Furthermore we realized normal order reduction to deal with infinite data structures. For that purpose, we introduced a stack of spine pointers into the rewriting rules. This stack holds references to those expressions which wait for the evaluation of one of its arguments. The stack is manipulated by extensions of the original rewriting rules and by additional rules triggering the evaluation of required arguments. Finally we extended the implementation by a print stack which manages the evaluation of algebraic data objects.

In the last section we proved that our translation of a functional program outputs a UBS graph rewriting system. Thus we really generate an implementation rather than a specification of lazy evaluation by graph reduction. In the proof we experienced the limits of the static analysis based on strong V-structures alone. Some situations where no strong V-structures could be created were not captured by our analysis. The extension to weak V-structures will improve the automated UBS check.

Our example also demonstrates a method for programming with graph rewriting systems. Starting from an initial, general model of graph reduction, we incrementally refined the rewriting system. For instance, we introduced the redex structure to restrict the applicability of rewriting rules. This refinement enforces the altered application of unwind and reduction rules. The printing mechanism is also realized in a deterministic manner. The result of an evaluation is printed only when the redex structure is looping at the bottom element of the spine stack. The mutual exclusion of rewriting rules is enforced by the unique redex structure. The design of the rewriting rules also guarantees that any rule can be applied to only one subgraph. Otherwise, no deterministic reduction strategy would be implemented. As a side-effect, it follows from these refinements that the initial rewriting system finally satisfies the UBS requirements. Generally speaking, we gained a program out of a specification by successive transformation.

The primary goal of our implementation is to show that there are significant applications for UBS graph rewriting systems. Thus we intend not to compete with highly specialized implementations. Nevertheless, our rewriting systems can successfully be applied to study the runtime behaviour of our implementations. We can inspect the intermediate host graphs derived by successive application of rewriting rules. The internal data structure is available as an explicit graph. Other implementations which aim at a highly efficient evaluation of a functional program use a lower-level internal representation. Thus it is very tedious to reconstruct the expression graph. Our implementation by graphical programming, on the contrary, enables the study of graph reduction on the most appropriate level, namely graphs. Supported with a graph editor a programmer can navigate through expression graphs to analyse the progress of the evaluation. Thus the specific behaviour of lazy evaluation, which is determined by the graphical structure, can be directly explored.

Several implementations of functional languages claim to apply graph rewriting techniques. Due to the specific purpose, however, they do not use the general, rule-based graph rewriting formalism, but exploit the application context. We demonstrate the relation between our general and the problem-dependent formalism with the graph rewriting language Dactl developped by Kennaway [Ken90]. In Dactl the function definition

```
fac 0 = 1
fac n = n * (n-1)
```

is implemented by two rewriting rules

```
Fac[0] => *1
Fac[n:(INT-0)] => #IMul[n ^#Fac[^*ISub[n 1]]]
```

Each side of the rule relates to a term graph. The right-hand side of the second rule is graphically denoted as

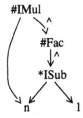

As in our representation, multiple occurrences of a variable are shared. Thus the syntax tree turns into a graph. The vertices and edges are decorated by marks which control the applicability of rewriting rules. Any occurrence of an # indicates that the vertex must await the evaluation of an argument. The specific argument is referred by an edge marked with ^. Only those vertices with * are active. They might be rewritten in the next step. In the example graph above, only the subtraction can be performed.

The marks are an integral part of the rewriting language. Thus it is obvious that Dactl is devoted to the implementation of functional languages. Furthermore it is clear that our general formalism can implement Dactl rewriting rules also. Take, for example, the redex structure in our implementation. It serves the same purpose as the mark * does. In the same manner, the other control information can be expressed by our formalism. On the contrary, Dactl rules can only contain term graphs, i.e. graphs with a one-to-one correspondence to terms. In general graphs have several term representations. Thus our general rewriting rules cannot be simulated by Dactl because it is an application-specific graph rewriting language.

7 Conclusions

Efficient graph rewriting is *no contradiction in terms*. For any UBS graph rewriting system, it holds that the applicability of a rewriting rule can be decided in constant time. Each rule is transformed to a connected enumeration which controls the algorithm for labelled subgraph matching. The algorithm iteratively extends partial graph isomorphisms until they totally map the left-hand side of the rule into the host graph. To gain a constant-time complexity, the enumeration must ensure that the initialization of the algorithm is performed for a vertex with unique label. In the following iterations, the morphisms extensions must bypass any strong V-structure of the graph. If the enumeration satisfies these two conditions, the applicability of the corresponding rewriting rule can be checked in constant time.

To ensure that a rule matches in constant time to any host graph, the connected enumeration must be selected with respect to all derivable graphs. We applied abstract interpretation to gain the necessary information on unique vertex labels and strong V-structures of a graph language.

The abstract interpretation of the rewriting systems, plus the determination of an appropriate connected enumeration for each rule, can be performed by a procedure. It decides whether a rewriting system is UBS. The procedure is constructive and simultaneously generates a bypassing enumeration rooted in a uniquely labelled vertex. Thus we have defined a class of graph rewriting systems similar to LL(1) in the case of string grammars. Again, similar to LL(1), UBS rewriting systems can be executed efficiently. Thus the UBS property will be as important for graph rewriting as LL(1) is for parsing.

We have also designed the *core abstract machine* which executes *programmed attributed graph rewriting systems*. The machine especially supports the optimization of rule sets, a particular control structure. The goal of the optimization is to find a maximal overlapping set of connected enumerations for a set of rules. Because the optimization problem seems to be NP-complete, we designed a simple greedy algorithm. In our implementation, the optimization yielded an average speed-up of 6.4%.

The abstract machine and the code generation rules were formally specified. Thus the implementation could easily be realized. We now have available the basic tool for graph rewriting systems: an execution component for programmed attributed graph rewriting systems.

The third abstract interpretation applies directly to the implementation. It computes a superset of the set of label triples of a graph rewriting system. Thus, static analysis can rule out the occurrence of edges of distinct type. Consequently, an implementation need not allocate storage for these edges.

The application of *advanced compiler construction methods* significantly improved the performance of a graph rewriting system. Abstract interpretation determines properties of the graph language. Thus the compiler can properly predict characteristics of the derived graphs and, for instance, can select bypassing enumerations.

The use of abstract machines allowed the iterative design of an implementation of graph rewriting systems. The abstract machine for the labelled subgraph matching was redesigned and included in the final machine for programmed attributed graph rewriting systems. The next iteration will explicitly use the frame representation of vertices.

Because UBS graph rewriting systems can be executed efficiently, they should no longer be looked upon as being a specification formalism. Moreover, they serve as a *graphical programming language*. If the UBS property is satisfied and the code is optimized, then the execution of a graph rewriting program will be as fast as an imperative program.

The graphical program for the insertion in a priority queue is shown in figure 40. The insertion is realized by prepending the new element to the queue. That element is propagated to the right position by iterative application of the rule set "swap OR noswap OR endswap". For each rule, there exists a bypassing connected enumeration. Thus they can be efficiently applied. Furthermore the propagation of an element is expressed as a rule set. It therefore can be optimized such that the number of basic pointer operations in an implementation comes very close to that required by an imperative program. Hence UBS graph rewriting systems are indeed a graphical programming language.

The efficient and fast implementation can be exploited by hybrid programming combining the graphical with, for instance, an imperative programming language. In this application, a graph rewriting system is a graphical implementation of an abstract data type like a priority queue. A distinct set of rule expressions may be exported. They provide the access to objects of that data type, as, for example, the rule expression "insertion (n)". We realize the hybrid programming language as follows. First, we analyse the graphical program. Then we compile it and generate an efficient implementation based on the abstract machine. That implementation will be realized as an individual module of the chosen imperative language. The module now provides an interface to the graphical program.

Graphical programming is not only suited to the implementation of small data structures like queues or lists, but also to the implementation of problems with higher

insertion (n) =   insert (n)

                     AND WAPP swap OR noswap OR endswap

insert (n)

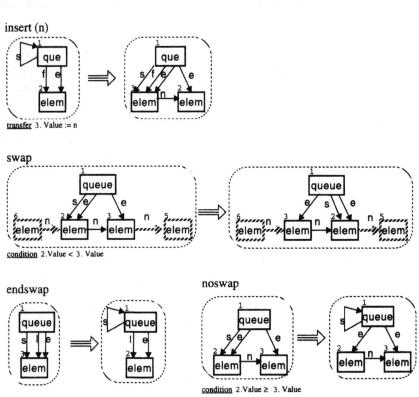

Figure 40   UBS rewriting rules for the insertion in a priority queue

complexity, like the execution of functional programs. Code optimization is another example. The latter is based on data dependency graphs. The optimization is realized as a number of graph transformations. Despite the graphical nature of the problem, most implementations stick to attributed string grammars. They represent the graphical dependencies by several ad hoc extensions, e.g. door attribute grammars by Hedin [He94]. UBS graph rewriting is the appropriate technique to program a code optimization. The hybrid programming approach then generates an efficient optimizer out of the graphical program.

Last but not least, graphical programming with rewriting systems serves as a natural animation formalism. The fast execution of graph rewriting steps allows the animation of technical systems represented as a graphical program. Take for example a UBS graph rewriting system describing the operation of an elevator. Since the number of states of an elevator (and, hence, the size of the graph language) is limited, appropriate

layout information for the host graphs can be provided. Consequently on the execution
of each operation, the result graph can instantaneously be displayed.

Open problems remain in several areas. Firs, the abstract interpretation of graph
rewriting systems must be extended to weak V-structures. The case study has revealed
their importance in detail. Strong V-structures reflect the frame representation of
vertices. Hence they are important for the selection of a bypassing enumeration. Often,
though, edges are redirected between vertices of different labels without being dupli-
cated. Hence they keep their direction, label, and one endpoint. This situation cannot
be discovered by the analysis of strong but only of weak V-structures.

We briefly mentioned that further iterations in the design of the abstract machine will
definitely improve its performance. The refinements will address two subjects. The
optimization of rule sets has led to a significant speed-up. Thus the optimization of
other control structures like sequences is promising. Here also, common subgraphs are
present. They are mapped to the same set of partial handles if they are in the context of
the rules. If a unique vertex label is in the context, then only a certain area is affected
by the rewriting steps. In addition, the information on strong V-structures ensures that
there is only one partial handle for the context. In that case, the sequence of rewriting
rules will not alter the image of the context graph.

   The second improvement is directed to memory consumption. The frame representation up to now consumes a large amount of memory for each vertex. For each type
of edge, a slot is allocated in the frame. Furthermore, each edge is represented twice,
namely in both endpoints. The abstract interpretations provide information on the
derivable graphs which can be exploited for a reduced allocation scheme. The label
triple analysis shows which edges will never appear in a derivable graph. Thus no slot
needs to be reserved for these edges. Furthermore it holds for UBS rewriting systems
that multiple entry slots are not used by the matching procedure. Again, they can be
dropped by the allocation scheme if the corresponding edges are stored in at least one
of its endpoints. Lastly, in the proof that the implementation of functional languages is
UBS, we have operated with mandatory edges. They are essential for the determination of the isomorphic subgraph. Hence they are required for the execution of graph
rewriting. Thus they form a minimal set of edges for which a slot must be provided.
All refinements of the frame allocation scheme must be realized by a refinement of
both the code generator and the abstract machine.

The animation of graph rewriting systems should be supported by an automated
layout. The usual graph layout algorithms are not sufficient, because they are tailored
to specific graph classes like trees or planar graphs. The graphs generated by a
rewriting system are rarely such regular structures; but rewriting systems provide
another approach to layout algorithms. Since each rewriting rule is drawn as basically

two graphs, it already contains layout information. By analysis of the rules, therefore, it must be possible to infer a layout scheme. Two alternatives show up: the layout is based either on the position of a vertex relative to its neighbours, or on the average graphical orientation of edges. Both approaches require only information obtained by analysis of the rewriting rule.

The question whether and how a graph rewriting system can be transformed to an equivalent UBS system is an outstanding challenge. The design of UBS graph rewriting systems has shown that a limited number of design principles are sufficient to satisfy the UBS property. First, unique vertex labels are required. Furthermore the design must ensure that either no instances of strong V-structures must occur, or there must be a bypassing connected enumeration of a rule. The redesign of the insertion example (see figure 40) has applied these techniques. Originally the "swap" operation accessed the queue elements via an instance of a strong V-structure. The redesign introduces a uniquely labelled edge which resolves the ambigous access. Hence the propagation of the inserted element can be performed as the iterated application of three mutually exclusive swapping rules. The auxiliary, uniquely labelled edge and a straightforward redesign of the rewriting rules yielded a UBS graph rewriting system. The generalization of the transformation will not be so easy. UBS graph rewriting systems must be studied extensively to detect general strategies which will enforce compliance to the UBS property. The efficient execution of graph rewriting systems, however, is a reasonable reward for a successful transformation.

Appendix A   List of Figures and Tables

Figures:

Tables:

Appendix B   Implementation of a Functional Program

The appendix applies the translation scheme developed inchapter 6 to the following functional program

```
mappairs f Empty xs = Empty
mappairs f (Cons x xs) Empty = Empty
mappairs f (Cons x xs) (Cons y ys)
                = cons (f x y) (mappairs f xs ys)

mappairs (+) (Cons 4 (Cons 5 Empty)) (Cons 4 Empty)
```

The programmed attributed graph rewriting system complies to the syntactical form required by PROGRES. It is executable in the PROGRES system as well as in our graph rewriting environment. The specification is split into several sections. The section containing the label declarations is required by PROGRES. We use it in our implementation to define the set-valued vertex labels. The following sections provide the definitions of the rewriting rules. First, the user-defined functions are listed, hence the section contains the translation of rules for mappairs. The following section covers the printing mechanism. The third section provides rewriting rules for built-in functions like add and cons. Last, a selected number of rules for unwinding the spine are shown.

```
specification graphreduction

section label_declarations

 section admin_labels
    node type print: org end;
    node type top: org end;
    node type d: org end;
    node class fun_0 is a function_id end;
    node class fun_1 is a function_id end;
    node class fun_2 is a function_id end;
    node class fun_3 is a function_id end;
    node class fun_4 is a function_id end;
    node class fun_5 is a function_id end;
    node class con_0 is a constructor_symbol end;
    node class con_1 is a constructor_symbol end;
    node class con_2 is a constructor_symbol end;
    node class con_3 is a constructor_symbol end;
    node class con_4 is a constructor_symbol end;
    node class con_5 is a constructor_symbol end;
    node class any
      intrinsic
        erg: string := "";
        Value: integer:= 0;
      end;
    node class exp is a any end;
    node class org is a any end;
    node class val_0 is a exp end;
    node class constructor_symbol is a exp end;
```

```
node class not_eval is a exp end;
node class function_id is a not_eval end;
node class apply_node is a not_eval end;
node type apply: apply_node end;
edge type redex: org -> any;
edge type re: org -> org;
edge type ex: org -> any;
edge type spine: org -> exp;
edge type pr: org -> org;
edge type up: org -> org;
edge type sp: apply_node -> exp;
edge type eval: org -> exp;
edge type arg: apply_node -> exp;
edge type c1: constructor_symbol -> exp;
edge type c2: constructor_symbol -> exp;
edge type c3: constructor_symbol -> exp;
edge type c4: constructor_symbol -> exp;
edge type c5: constructor_symbol -> exp;
end;

section built_in_constructors_and_functions
node type val: val_0 end;
node type Empty: con_0 end;
node type Cons: con_2 end;
node type add: fun_2 end;
node type cons: fun_2 end;
end;

section user_defined_symbols_and_identifiers
node type mappairs: fun_3 end;
end;
(*user_defined_symbols_and_identifiers*)
end;


section programs
  transaction MAIN =
    init_graph
    reduce
  end;

  transaction reduce =
     ( predefined_rules
       or user_defined_functions )
     and reduce
  end;
  (* Simulates Graphreduction *)

  transaction predefined_rules =
       print_rules
     or unwind_rules
     or built_in_rules
  end;
end;
(* end of transactions *)
```

<u>production</u> init_graph
=

```
:-------------------:
'-------------------'
```

::=

```
transfer 1'.erg:= "";
   17'.Value:= 4;
   12'.Value:= 5;
    9'.Value:= 4;
end;


section user_defined_function_section
   transaction user_defined_functions =
       mappairs_rules
end;

section mappairs
   transaction mappairs_rules =
       mappairs1
    or mappairs2
    or mappairs3
    or mappairs_invoke_2
    or mappairs_invoke_3
    or mappairs3_2_3
    or mappairs3_21_31
    or mappairs3_22_32
   end;
```

<u>production</u> mappairs1 =

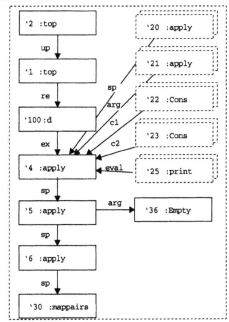

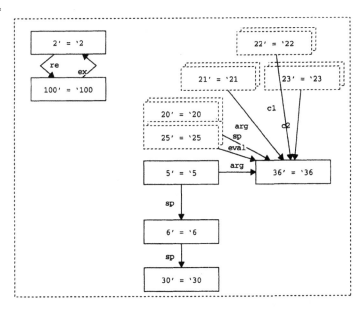

::=

<u>end</u>;

production mappairs2 =

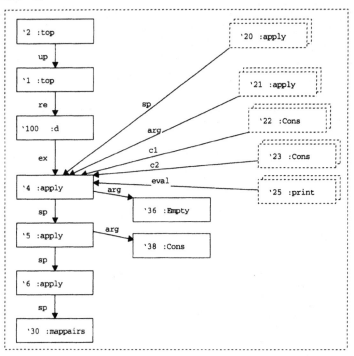

::=

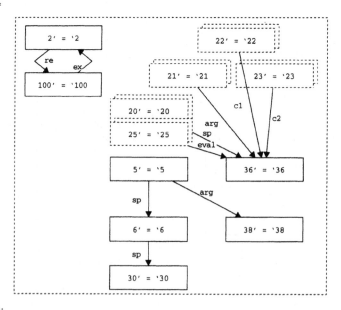

end;

<u>production</u> mappairs3 =

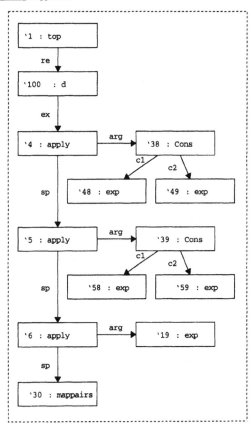

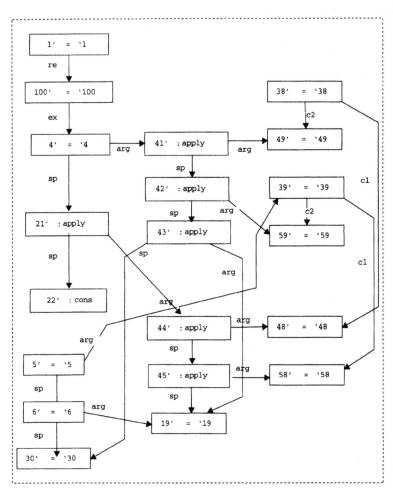

end;

<u>production</u> mappairs_invoke_2 =

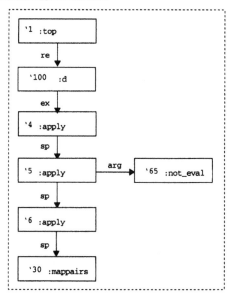

: :=

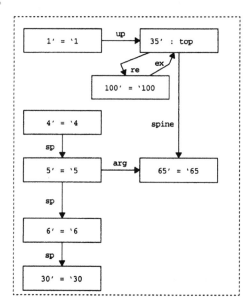

<u>end</u>;

production mappairs_invoke_3 =

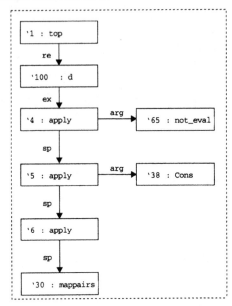

::=

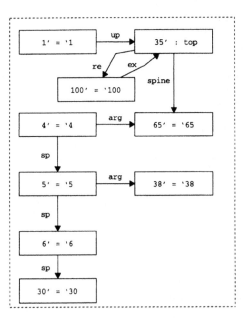

end;

<u>production</u> mappairs3_2_3 =

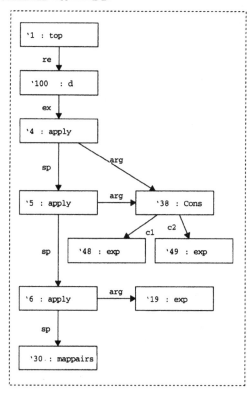

::=

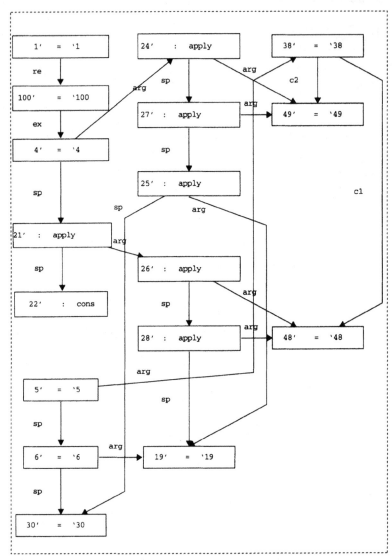

end;

<u>production</u> mappairs3_21_31 =

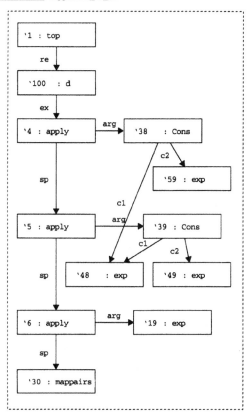

::=

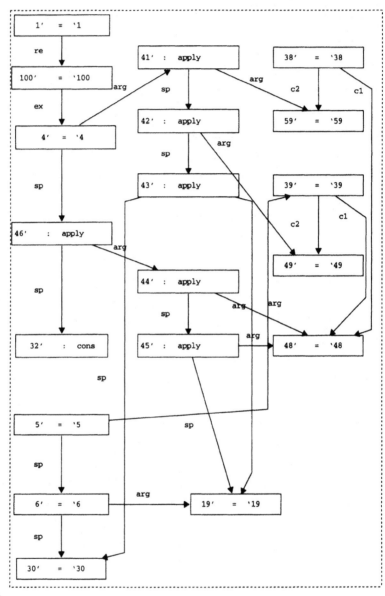

end;

production mappairs3_22_32 =

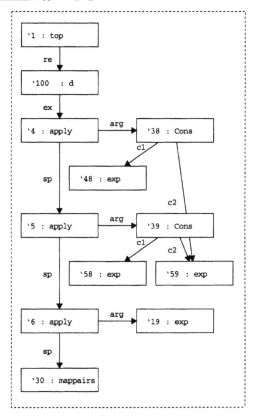

`::=`

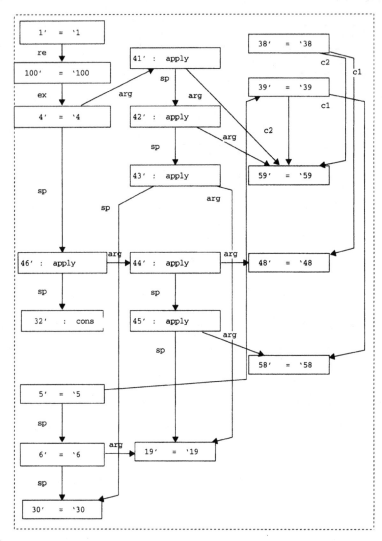

end;
end;
end;

```
section basic_rewrite_rules_of_print
  transaction print_rules =
      print_last_val
  or print_last
  or print_val
  or print_0
  or print_1
  or print_2
  or print_3
  or print_4
  or print_5
  end;
production print_last_val =
```

```
  transfer 1'.erg:= '1.erg & char ( '150.Value );
end;
production print_last =
```

```
  transfer 1'.erg:= '1.erg & char ( '50.Value );
end;
production print_val =
```

`::=`

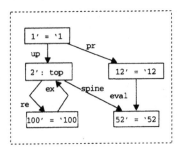

```
transfer 1'.erg:= '1.erg & char ( '150.Value );
end;
production print_0 =
```

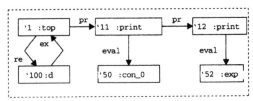

`::=`

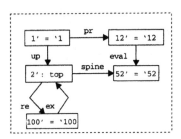

```
transfer 1'.erg:= '1.erg & char ( '50.Value );
end;
production print_1 =
```

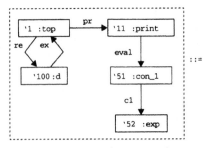

`::=`

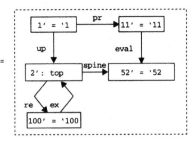

```
transfer 1'.erg:= '1.erg & char ( '51.Value );
end;
```

`::=`

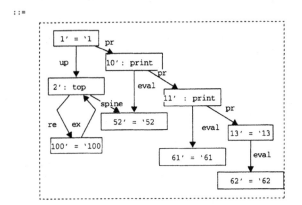

```
transfer 1'.erg:= '1.erg & char ( '54.Value );
end;
end;

section built_in_functions
   transaction built_in_rules =
        add_rules
     or cons_rules
   end;

section add_rules
   transaction add_rules =
        add1
     or add_1_2
     or add_invoke_1
     or add_invoke_2
   end;
```

<u>production</u> add1 =

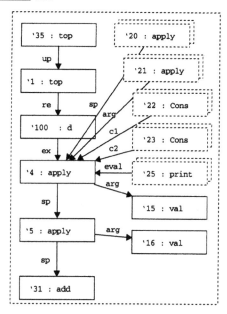

::=

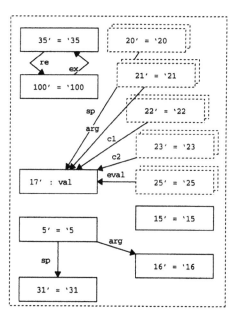

<u>transfer</u> 17'.Value:= '15.Value + '16.Value;
<u>end</u>;

production add_1_2 =

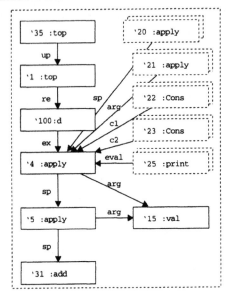

::=

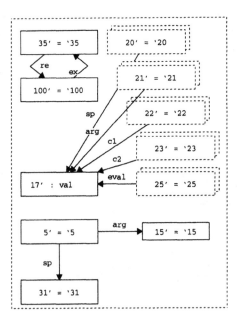

transfer 17'.Value:= '15.Value + '15.Value;
end;

production add_invoke_1 =

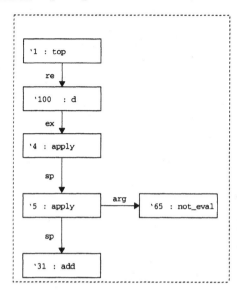

::=

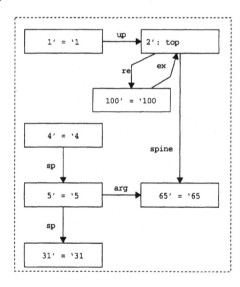

end;

production add_invoke_2 =

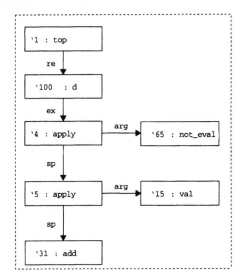

::=

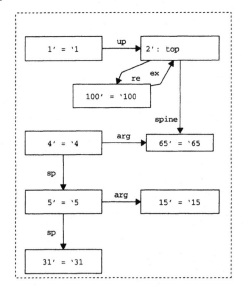

end;
end;

section cons_rules
  transaction cons_rules =
        cons1
    or cons_1_2
  end;

production cons1 =

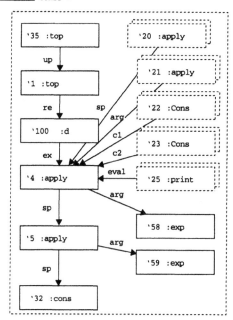

::=

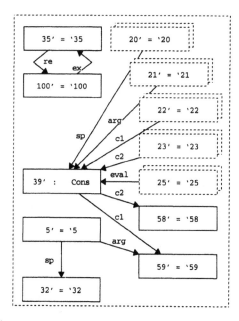

end;

production cons_1_2 =

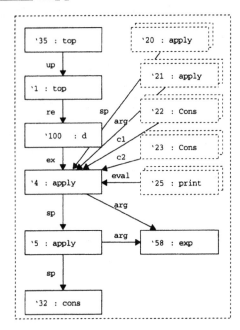

::=

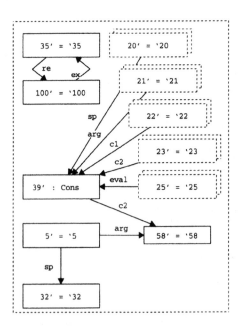

end;

```
end;
end;

section unwind_rules

  transaction unwind_rules =
      unwind_0_rules
    or unwind_1_rules
    or unwind_2_rules
    or unwind_3_rules
    or unwind_4_rules
    or unwind_5_rules
  end;

section unwind_0_x

  transaction unwind_0_rules =
      unwind_0_0
    or unwind_0_1
    or unwind_0_2
    or unwind_0_3
    or unwind_0_4
    or unwind_0_5
  end;
production unwind_0_0 =
```

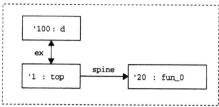

```
::=
```

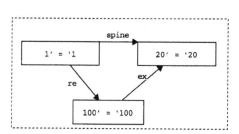

```
end;
production unwind_0_1 =
```

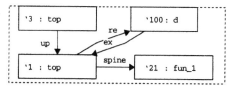

::=

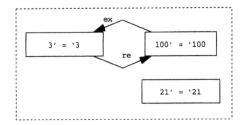

end;

<u>production</u> unwind_0_2 =

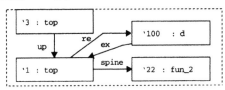

::=

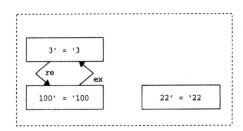

end;

[...] (* rules unwind_0_3,4,5*)

end;

[...] (* unwind_1_rules *)

<u>section</u> unwind_2_x

  <u>transaction</u> unwind_2_rules =
      unwind_2_0
    <u>or</u> unwind_2_1
    <u>or</u> unwind_2_2
    <u>or</u> unwind_2_3
    <u>or</u> unwind_2_4
    <u>or</u> unwind_2_5
  <u>end</u>;

production unwind_2_0 =

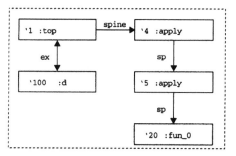

::=

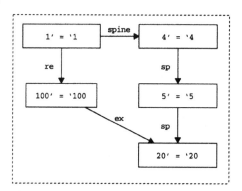

end;
production unwind_2_1 =

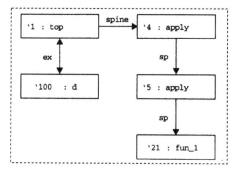

::=

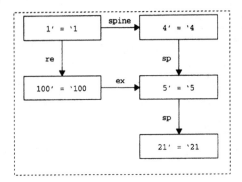

end;

production unwind_2_2 =

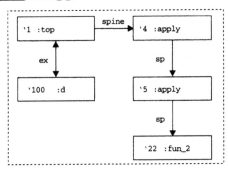

::=

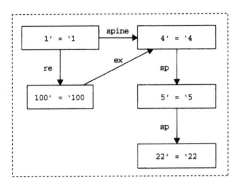

end;

[...] (* rules unwind_2_3,4,5*)

end;

[...] (* unwind_3,4,5_rules *)
end;

end.

Appendix C   References

[AbHa87]   Abramsky, Samson; Hankin, Chris: '*Abstract Interpretation of Declarative Languages*', Ellis Horwood Ltd., Chichester, UK, 1987.

[Alb87]   Albert, Barbara: '*Mikroarchitekturbeschreibung zur effizienten Programmierung anwendungsorientierter Systeme*', *Reihe Informatik Bd. 55*, Bibliographisches Institut & F.A. Brockhaus, Mannheim, 1987.

[Ano94]   Anonymous: 'Description of the ProgressGraphCode' (in german), internal paper of the PROGRES development group, RWTH Aachen, 1994.

[AU77]   Aho, Alfred V.; Ullman, Jeffrey D.: '*Principles of Compiler Design*'; Addison-Wesley, Reading, MA, 1977.

[BGT91]   Bunke, H.; Glauser, T.; Tran, T.-H.: 'An efficient implementation of graph grammars based on the RETE matching algorithm', [EKR91], pp.174-189.

[Bun82]   Bunke, H.: 'On the Generative Power of Sequential and Parallel Programmed Graph Grammars' *Computing*, (**29**) 89-112 (1982).

[Bur87]   Burn, Geoffrey: 'Evaluation Transformers - A Model for the Parallel Evaluation of Functional Languages', *Conference on Functional Programming and Computer Architecture*, Nancy, 1987, *LNCS 274*, Springer, Berlin, 1987

[BW88]   Bird, Richard; Wadler, Philip: '*Introduction to functional programming*', Prentice-Hall, New York 1988.

[CoGo70]   Corneil, D.G.; Gotlieb, C.C.: 'An Efficient Algorithm for Graph Isomorphism', *Journal of the Association for Computing Machinery*, 17 (**1**) 51-64 (1970).

[Cou91]   Courcelle, Bruno: 'The Logical Expression of Graph Properties', [EKR91], pp.38-40.

[DrKr91]   Drewes, Frank; Kreowski, Hans-Jörg: 'A Note on Hyperedge Replacement', [EKR91], pp.1-11.

[EbFr94]   Ebert, Jürgen; Franzke, Angelika: 'A declarative approach to graph based modeling', Mayr, Ernst; Schmidt, Gunther; Tinhofer, Gottfried (eds.) *Twentieth International Workshop WG '94, Graph-Theoretic Concepts in Computer Science*, Herrsching, Juni 1994, Springer, Berlin, (to appear),

[EhKr80]   Ehrig, Hartmut; Kreoswski, Hans-Jörg: 'Applications of Graph Grammar Theory to Consistency, Synchronization and Scheduling in Data Base Sytems', *Information Systems*, (**12**), 225-238 (1980).

[EKL91]   Ehrig, Hartmut; Korff, Martin; Löwe, Michael: 'Tutorial Introduction to
            the Algebraic Approach of Graph Grammars Based on Double and Single
            Pushouts', [EKR91], pp.24-37.

[EKR91]   Ehrig, Hartmut; Kreowski, Hans-Jörg; Rozenberg, Grzegorz (ed.): *Graph-
            Grammars and Their Application to Computer Science, 4th Int. Workshop,
            Bremen, March 5-9, 1990, LNCS 532*, Springer, Berlin, 1991.

[En86]   Engels, Gregor: *'Graphen als zentrale Datenstrukturen in einer Software-
            Entwicklungsumgebung'*; VDI-Verlag, Düsseldorf, 1986.

[En91]   Engelfriet, Joost: 'A characterization of context-free NCE graph languages
            by monadic second-order logic on trees', [EKR91], pp.311-327.

[EnHe91]   Engelfriet, Joost; Heyker, Linda: 'The term generating power of context-
            free hypergraph grammars', [EKR91], pp.328-343.

[ENRR86]   Ehrig, Hartmut; Nagl, Manfred; Rozenberg, Grzegorz; Rosenfeld, A.(ed.):
            *Graph-Grammars and Their Application to Computer Science, 3rd Int.
            Workshop on Graph-Grammars*, Warrenton VA, USA, December 2-6,
            1986, *LNCS 291*, Springer, Berlin, 1987.

[EnSch89]   Engels, Gregor; Schäfer, Wilhelm: *'Programmentwicklungsumgebungen.
            Konzepte u. Realisierung'*; Teubner, Stuttgart, 1989.

[Epp90]   Epp, Susanna: *'Discrete mathematics with applications'*; Wadsworth, Bel-
            mont CA, 1990.

[ER91]   Engelfriet, Jost; Rozenberg, Grzegorz: 'Graph Grammars Based on Node
            Rewriting: An Introduction to NLC Graph Grammars', [EKR91], pp.12-23.

[Fe89]   Fehr, Elfriede: *'Semantik von Programmiersprachen'*, Springer, Berlin,
            1989.

[FeSch90]   Feldmann, Detlef; Alois Schütte: 'Spezifikation einfacher, kontextsensi-
            tiver Syntaxkonstrukte von Occam2 durch eine Graphgrammatik', *Fach-
            berichte Informatik 1/90*, Universität Koblenz-Landau, Koblenz, 1990.

[FrHa92]   Freund, Rudolf; Haberstroh, Brigitte: 'Attributed Elementary Programmed
            Graph Grammars', in Schmidt, Gunther; Berghammer, Rudolf (eds.) *Seven-
            teenth International Workshop WG '91, Graph-Theoretic Concepts in Com-
            puter Science*, Fischbachau, Juni 1991, *LNCS 570*, Springer, Berlin, 1992,
            pp. 75-84.

[FrSt93]   Freund, Rudolf; Stary, Christian: 'Formal Software Specification Using
            Graph Rewriting Systems', unpublished manuscript, 1993.

[GaJo79]   Garey, Michael R.; Johnson, David S.: *'Computers and Intractability'*,
            W.H. Freeman and Co., New York, 1979.

[Gou88]   Gould, Ronald: *'Graph Theory'*; The Benjamin/Cummings Publishing
            Company, Menlo Park, CA, 1988.

[Gött88]   Göttler, Herbert: 'Graphgrammatiken in der Softwaretechnik', *Informatik-Fachberichte 178*, Springer, Berlin, 1988.

[HaKr91]   Habel, Annegret; Kreowski, Hans-Jörg: 'Collage Grammars', [EKR91], pp.411-429.

[Har71]   Harary, Frank: *'Graph Theory'*; Addison Wesley, Reading, MA, 1971[2].

[He94]   Hedin, Görel: 'An Overview of Door Attribute Grammars', Fritzson, Peter A. (ed.) *5th Intern. Conference CC '94, Compiler Construction*, Edinburgh, UK, April 7-9, 1994, *LNCS 786*, Springer, Berlin, 1994.

[Him89]   Himsolt, Michael: 'Graphed: An interactive Graph Editor', in *STACS 89*, *LNCS 349*, Springer Verlag, Berlin, 1989.

[HRW92]   Hwang, Frank K.; Richards, Dana S.; Winter, Pawel: *'The Steiner Tree Problem'*; North-Holland, Amsterdam, 1992.

[Joh84]   Johnsson, Thomas: 'Efficient Compilation of Lazy Evaluation', in *ACM SIGPLAN '84 Symposium on Compiler Construction*, SIGPLAN Notices, **19**, (6) 58-69, (1984)

[Kau86]   Kaul, Manfred: 'Practical Applications of Precedence Graph Grammars', [ENRR86], pp. 326-342.

[KBL91]   Klauck, Christoph; Bernardi, Ansgar; Legleitner, Ralf: 'FEAT-REP: Representing Features in CAD/CAM', *Research Report*, Deutsches Forschungszentrum für Künstliche Intelligenz, Kaiserslautern/Saarbrücken, **DFKI-RR-91-20**, 1991.

[Ken90]   Kennaway, Richard: 'Implementing Term Rewrite Languages in Dactl', *Theoretical Computer Science*, (**72**), 225-249 (1990).

[KlMa92]   Klauck, Christoph; Mauss, Jakob: 'A Heuristic Driven Chart-Parser for Attributed Node Labelled Graph Grammars and its Application to Feature Recognition in CIM', *Research Report*, Deutsches Forschungszentrum für Künstliche Intelligenz, Kaiserslautern/Saarbrücken, **DFKI-RR-92-43**, 1992.

[KSW92]   Kiesel, N.; Schürr, Andreas; Westfechtel, Bernhard: 'Design and Evaluation of GRAS, a Graph-Oriented Database System for Engineering Applications', *Aachener Informatik-Berichte Nr. 92-44*, RWTH Fachgruppe Informatik, Aachen, 1992.

[Lew88]   Lewerentz, Claus: 'Interaktives Entwerfen großer Programmsysteme', *Informatik-Fachberichte 194*, Springer, Berlin, 1988.

[LKI89]   Loogen, Rita; Kuchen, Herbert; Indermark, K.; Damm, W.: 'Distributed Implementation of Programmed Graph Reduction' in Eddy Odijke et al. (ed.) *Conference on Parallel Architectures and Languages Europe*, Eindhoven, The Netherlands, June 12-16, 1989, *Vol. 1, LNCS 365*, Springer, Berlin, 1898, pp.136-157.

[LöBe93]   Löwe, Michael: Beyer, Martin: 'AGG — An Implementation of Algebraic Graph Rewriting', Kirchner, Claude (ed.) *Rewriting Techniques and Applications*, Montreal, Canada, *LNCS 690*, Springer, Berlin, 1993, pp.451-456.

[Loo90]   Loogen, Rita: 'Parallele Implementierung funktionaler Programmiersprachen', *Informatik-Fachberichte 232*, Springer, Berlin, 1990.

[LRS76]   Lewis II, Philip M.; Rosenkrantz, Daniel J.; Stearns, Richard E.: '*Compiler Design Theory*', Addison-Wesley, Reading MA, 1976^2.

[McG82]   McGregor, James J.: 'Backtrack Search Algorithms and the Maximal Common Subgraph Problem', *Software – Practice and Experience,* 12, 23-34 (1982).

[Mil78]   Milner, R.: 'A Theory of Type Polymorphism in Programming', *Journal of Computer and System Sciences*, 17, (3) 349 ff. (1978).

[Nag79]   Nagl, Manfred: '*Graph-Grammatiken, Theorie, Implementierung, Anwendungen*'; Vieweg, Braunschweig, 1979.

[Nag81]   Nagl, Manfred: 'Application of Graph Rewriting to Optimization and Parallelization of Programs'; *Computing*, (**Suppl. 3**) 105-124 (1981).

[Nag86a]   Nagl, Manfred: 'Set Theoretic Approaches to Graph Grammars', [ENRR86], pp.41-54.

[Nag86b]   Nagl, Manfred: 'A Software Development Environment based on Graph Technology', [ENRR86], pp.458-478.

[NAJ81]   Nori, K.V.; Ammann, U.; Jensen, K.; Nageli, H.H.; Jacobi, Ch.: 'Pascal-P Implementation Notes', in Barron, D.W. (ed.) *Pascal - The Language and its Implementation*, Wiley, Chichester, 1981, pp.125-170.

[NaSch90]   Nagl, Manfred; Schürr, Andreas: 'A Specification Environment for Graph Grammars', *Aachener Informatik-Berichte Nr. 90-15*, RWTH Fachgruppe Informatik, Aachen, 1990.

[Pau93]   Paulisch, Frances Newbery: '*The design of an extendible graph editor*', *LNCS 704*, Springer, Berlin, 1993.

[PeJo87]   Peyton Jones, Simon: '*The implementation of functional programming languages*', Prentice Hall, Hemel Hempstead, 1987.

[PeJo91]   Peyton Jones, Simon: 'The Spineless Tagless G-machine: second attempt', in Glaser, Hugh; Hartel, Pieter (eds.) *Workshop of the Parallel Implementation of Functional Languages*, Southampton, UK, June 1991, CSTR 91-07, Dept of Electronics and Computer Science, University of Southampton, 1991, pp. 147-191.

[PJS89]   Peyton Jones, Simon; Salkild, Jon: 'The Spineless Tagless G-machine', in MacQueen (ed.) *Functional Programming and Computer Architecture*, Addison Wesley, Reading, MA, 1989.

[Schü90]   Schürr, Andreas: 'Introduction to PROGRESS, an Attribute Graph Grammar Based Specification Language', in Manfred Nagl (ed.) *Fifthteenth International Workshop WG '89, Graph-Theoretic Concepts in Computer Science*, Castle Rolduc, The Netherlands, June 1989, *LNCS 411*, Springer, Berlin, 1990, pp. 151-166.

[Schü91]   Schürr, Andreas: *'Operationales Spezifizieren mit programmierten Graphersetzungssystemen'*, Deutscher Universitäts-Verlag, Wiesbaden, 1991.

[Schü94]   Schürr, Andreas: 'PROGRES, A Visual Language and Environment for PROgramming with Graph REwriting Systems', *Aachener Informatik-Berichte Nr. 94-11*, RWTH Fachgruppe Informatik, Aachen, 1994.

[Tur86]   Turner, David: 'An Overview of Miranda', *SIGPLAN Notices*, Dec. 1986.

[Vos90]   Voss, S.; 'Steiner-Probleme in Graphen'; *Mathematical Systems in Economics 120*, Anton Hein, Frankfurt/M, 1990.

[War77]   Warren, D.H.D.: 'Implementing PROLOG - Compiling Logic Programs. 1 and 2.' *Departement of Artificial Intelligence, Research Report No.39 and 40*, University of Edinburgh, 1977.

[Wir76]   Wirth, Niklaus: *'Algorithms + data structures = programs'*, Prentice-Hall, Englewood Cliffs, N.J., 1976[17].

[Wir86]   Wirth, Niklaus: *'Compilerbau'*, Teubner, Stuttgart, 1984[3].

[Wit87]   Witt, Kurt-Ulrich: 'An Architecture for processing Graph-Grammar Applications' *Information Systems*, **12**, (7), 353-361 (1987).

[Zün92]   Zündorf, Albert: 'Implementation of the imperative/rule based language PROGRES', *Aachener Informatik-Berichte Nr. 92-38*, RWTH Fachgruppe Informatik, Aachen, 1992.

Appendix D   Index

Springer-Verlag
and the Environment

We at Springer-Verlag firmly believe that an international science publisher has a special obligation to the environment, and our corporate policies consistently reflect this conviction.

We also expect our business partners – paper mills, printers, packaging manufacturers, etc. – to commit themselves to using environmentally friendly materials and production processes.

The paper in this book is made from low- or no-chlorine pulp and is acid free, in conformance with international standards for paper permanency.

Lecture Notes in Computer Science

For information about Vols. 1–865
please contact your bookseller or Springer-Verlag

Vol. 901: R. Kumar, T. Kropf (Eds.), Theorem Provers in Circuit Design. Proceedings, 1994. VIII, 303 pages. 1995.

Vol. 902: M. Dezani-Ciancaglini, G. Plotkin (eds.), Typed Lambda Calculi and Applications. Proceedings, 1995. VIII, 443 pages. 1995

Vol. 903: E. W. Mayr, G. Schmidt, G. Tinhofer (Eds.), Graph-Theoretic Concepts in Computer Science. Proceedings, 1994. IX, 414 pages. 1995.

Vol. 904: P. Vitányi (Ed.), Computational Learning Theory. EuroCOLT'95. Proceedings, 1995. XVII, 415 pages. 1995. (Subseries LNAI).

Vol. 905: N. Ayache (Ed.), Computer Vision, Virtual Reality and Robotics in Medicine. Proceedings, 1995. XIV, 567 pages. 1995.

Vol. 906: E. Astesiano, G. Reggio, A. Tarlecki (Eds.), Recent Trends in Data Type Specification. Proceedings, 1995. VIII, 523 pages. 1995.

Vol. 907: T. Ito, A. Yonezawa (Eds.), Theory and Practice of Parallel Programming. Proceedings, 1995. VIII, 485 pages. 1995.

Vol. 908: J. R. Rao Extensions of the UNITY Methodology: Compositionality, Fairness and Probability in Parallelism. XI, 178 pages. 1995.

Vol. 909: H. Comon, J.-P. Jouannaud (Eds.), Term Rewriting. Proceedings, 1993. VIII, 221 pages. 1995.

Vol. 910: A. Podelski (Ed.), Constraint Programming: Basics and Trends. Proceedings, 1995. XI, 315 pages. 1995.

Vol. 911: R. Baeza-Yates, E. Goles, P. V. Poblete (Eds.), LATIN '95: Theoretical Informatics. Proceedings, 1995. IX, 525 pages. 1995.

Vol. 912: N. Lavrac, S. Wrobel (Eds.), Machine Learning: ECML – 95. Proceedings, 1995. XI, 370 pages. 1995. (Subseries LNAI).

Vol. 913: W. Schäfer (Ed.), Software Process Technology. Proceedings, 1995. IX, 261 pages. 1995.

Vol. 914: J. Hsiang (Ed.), Rewriting Techniques and Applications. Proceedings, 1995. XII, 473 pages. 1995.

Vol. 915: P. D. Mosses, M. Nielsen, M. I. Schwartzbach (Eds.), TAPSOFT '95: Theory and Practice of Software Development. Proceedings, 1995. XV, 810 pages. 1995.

Vol. 916: N. R. Adam, B. K. Bhargava, Y. Yesha (Eds.), Digital Libraries. Proceedings, 1994. XIII, 321 pages. 1995.

Vol. 917: J. Pieprzyk, R. Safavi-Naini (Eds.), Advances in Cryptology - ASIACRYPT '94. Proceedings, 1994. XII, 431 pages. 1995.

Vol. 918: P. Baumgartner, R. Hähnle, J. Posegga (Eds.), Theorem Proving with Analytic Tableaux and Related Methods. Proceedings, 1995. X, 352 pages. 1995. (Subseries LNAI).

Vol. 919: B. Hertzberger, G. Serazzi (Eds.), High-Performance Computing and Networking. Proceedings, 1995. XXIV, 957 pages. 1995.

Vol. 920: E. Balas, J. Clausen (Eds.), Integer Programming and Combinatorial Optimization. Proceedings, 1995. IX, 436 pages. 1995.

Vol. 921: L. C. Guillou, J.-J. Quisquater (Eds.), Advances in Cryptology – EUROCRYPT '95. Proceedings, 1995. XIV, 417 pages. 1995.

Vol. 922: H. Dörr, Efficient Graph Rewriting and Its Implementation. IX, 266 pages. 1995.

Vol. 923: M. Meyer (Ed.), Constraint Processing. IV, 289 pages. 1995.

Vol. 924: P. Ciancarini, O. Nierstrasz, A. Yonezawa (Eds.), Object-Based Models and Languages for Concurrent Systems. Proceedings, 1994. VII, 193 pages. 1995.

Vol. 925: J. Jeuring, E. Meijer (Eds.), Advanced Functional Programming. Proceedings, 1995. VII, 331 pages. 1995.

Vol. 926: P. Nesi (Ed.), Objective Software Quality. Proceedings, 1995. VIII, 249 pages. 1995.

Vol. 927: J. Dix, L. Moniz Pereira, T. C. Przymusinski (Eds.), Non-Monotonic Extensions of Logic Programming. Proceedings, 1994. IX, 229 pages. 1995. (Subseries LNAI).

Vol. 928: V.W. Marek, A. Nerode, M. Truszczynski (Eds.), Logic Programming and Nonmonotonic Reasoning. Proceedings, 1995. VIII, 417 pages. 1995. (Subseries LNAI).

Vol. 929: F. Morán, A. Moreno, J.J. Merelo, P. Chacón (Eds.), Advances in Artificial Life. Proceedings, 1995. XIII, 960 pages. 1995 (Subseries LNAI).

Vol. 930: J. Mira, F. Sandoval (Eds.), From Natural to Artificial Neural Computation. Proceedings, 1995. XVIII, 1150 pages. 1995.

Vol. 931: P.J. Braspenning, F. Thuijsman, A.J.M.M. Weijters (Eds.), Artificial Neural Networks. IX, 295 pages. 1995.

Vol. 932: J. Iivari, K. Lyytinen, M. Rossi (Eds.), Advanced Information Systems Engineering. Proceedings, 1995. XI, 388 pages. 1995.

Vol. 933: L. Pacholski, J. Tiuryn (Eds.), Computer Science Logic. Proceedings, 1994. IX, 543 pages. 1995.

Vol. 934: P. Barahona, M. Stefanelli, J. Wyatt (Eds.), Artificial Intelligence in Medicine. Proceedings, 1995. XI, 449 pages. 1995. (Subseries LNAI).

Vol. 935: G. De Michelis, M. Diaz (Eds.), Application and Theory of Petri Nets 1995. Proceedings, 1995. VIII, 511 pages. 1995.

Vol. 936: V.S. Alagar, M. Nivat (Eds.), Algebraic Methodology and Software Technology. Proceedings, 1995. XIV, 591 pages. 1995.

Vol. 937: Z. Galil, E. Ukkonen (Eds.), Combinatorial Pattern Matching. Proceedings, 1995. VIII, 409 pages. 1995.

Vol. 938: K.P. Birman, F. Mattern, A. Schiper (Eds.), Theory and Practice in Distributed Systems. Proceedings,1994. X, 263 pages. 1995.

Vol. 939: P. Wolper (Ed.), Computer Aided Verification. Proceedings, 1995. X, 451 pages. 1995.

Vol. 941: M. Cadoli, Tractable Reasoning in Artificial Intelligence. XVII, 247 pages. 1995. (Subseries LNAI).

Vol. 942: G. Böckle, Exploitation of Fine-Grain Parallelism. IX, 188 pages. 1995.

Vol. 943: W. Klas, M. Schrefl, Metaclasses and Their Application. IX, 201 pages. 1995.